THE UNITED STATES OF TOYOTA

The United States of
TOYOTA

How Detroit squandered its legacy
and enabled Toyota to become
America's car company

Peter M. De Lorenzo
Edited by Janice J. Putman

AUTOEXTREMIST AGENCY INC

ISBN 978-1-0879-3234-7

Publisher: Autoextremist Agency Inc

In memory of my parents, Tony and Jo De Lorenzo

TABLE OF CONTENTS

Whatever we may think, we move for no better reason than for the plain unvarnished hell of it. And there is no better reason. So God made the American restive. The American in turn and in due time got into the automobile and found it good. The automobile became a hypnosis, the opium of the American people. – James Agee

PREFACE

The auto business is part of the very fabric of Detroit. It's our one true identifier to the nation and the world, and it made the moniker "The Motor City" synonymous with this town. There really is no other place quite like it on earth. There are other automotive centers, of course – in Japan, Europe and other points around the world, including the now-emerging Korea and China connections – but the Motor City remains a unique place, or more accurately, a unique state of mind.

Detroit's version of the automobile business is an acquired taste, but it has a way of getting into your blood. You can live here and pretend you have nothing to do with the business or that it doesn't affect you, but you'd be lying – and you'd be wrong.

It's not a business (or a city) for the faint of heart, but then again, it never was. There's a gritty, gutty atmosphere here in the Motor City, and as if to coincide with the hard-scrabble nature of the car biz, it's the details that make it so special – like the so-called "sky" that acts like a giant drop cloth, while churning through different shades of gray from December through March. Or the snowstorms that brew up at a moment's notice slinging snow sideways, as if to scoff at any protective clothing you may don to gird yourself for the day's battle. Or the grayish brown sludge that freezes at the side of the road and lingers in piles all the way to April. Or the road salt "storm clouds" that materialize and hang in the sub-zero air, coating everything in sight (including your lungs), while adding a touch of perverse symmetry to the proceedings.

All of this is only exceeded by the brutal, pothole-infested roads that provide the wonderful transition to spring and then summer – when the endless construction season creates a maze of chaos that almost saps every last ounce of enjoyment out of the physical act of driving.

And "almost" is the operative word to use, because as daunting as it is to survive and occasionally even thrive around here, there's something addictive in the air that grabs hold of you and won't let go…

INTRODUCTION

A HIGH-OCTANE LIFE

To say that I come from a car family is an understatement. My father, Anthony G. (Tony) De Lorenzo was named Vice President of Public Relations for General Motors in 1957, at the time the youngest VP in the company's history. A talented and proud ex-newspaperman who brought all of his skills to bear on behalf of GM, my dad stocked his staff with some of the savviest newspaper veterans in the business, and to this day his PR staff is considered the model of modern corporate public relations. Because of his role at GM and the fact that I have an older brother (Tony) who often took me along on his car adventures, I've been able to live more mind-blowing car lives than most people can even imagine. And I've been a living witness to some of the most memorable chapters of modern American automotive history…

Riding on Woodward Avenue in the first (and only) pre-production "409" Chevy on the street in '61 (the only other "409" that existed was in "Dyno Don" Nicholson's factory-backed drag racer), or riding in the only pre-production fuel-injected '63 Corvette Stingray in existence (a good month before its official introduction) – both Ed Cole's personal "drivers." Cole was one of the designers of the famed "small-block" Chevrolet V-8 and GM's last great Chief Engineer – and he sent us cars to try out all the time.

Watching Art Malone in his "Golden Rod" rail break the 180mph barrier at The Detroit Dragway in '62.

Grinning as the latest and hottest Pontiac was dropped off for my mom to drive, courtesy of Bunkie Knudsen, another GM legend who contributed greatly to Detroit's "golden" era. The Pontiacs were always red Bonneville convertibles with the biggest "tri-power" engines Pontiac had, or was about to offer.

Working one summer in the Pontiac Motor Division mailroom and delivering mail to John Z. DeLorean (the star-crossed former GM "Golden Boy" and eventual father of the DeLorean sports car).

Spending countless speed-filled weekends shocking the hell out of unsuspecting Corvette drivers in a very early production Black/Black '62 Cobra that belonged to Pontiac engineering at the time. I can still remember the smell of the burning rubber of my sneakers from riding around in the Cobra – which, as Cobra owners will attest, would literally melt while resting on the thinly carpeted aluminum floorboards. My brother and I went on to enjoy many more weekends in Cobras, thanks to orchestrated "swaps" between Ford PR and GM PR (we'd get a 289 Cobra to drive for the weekend; they'd get a Stingray).

Living down the street from wild Bill Mitchell, the famous Chief of GM Design (it was called "Styling" back then) and a hell of a guy, and making sure I rode my bike and parked by his driveway every Friday afternoon, so I could watch as he'd have at least four of his prized concept cars delivered – so he could have them at his disposal over the weekend. He saw to it that I got to ride in some of the most memorable GM Design statements of all time (usually in runs up to the grocery store), like the original Stingray, the Corvair Sebring Spyder, Monza GT and Monza SS, the original Mako Shark, the XP700 "bubble-top" Corvette, the infamous XP400 Pontiac Bonneville convertible (with a blown Mickey Thompson-prepared 421-cu. in. drag motor, no less), and on and on and on.

I watched as the Shelby American factory team of Ken Miles and Bob Johnson decimated the unofficial Corvette semi-factory team led by Dr. Dick Thompson and Co. at Meadowdale Raceway in '63 (a track in Illinois that is long gone now, which had an honest-to-god-replica of the famed "Monza Wall" as part of its design).

We enjoyed many memorable interludes with the famed "father" of the Corvette, Zora Arkus Duntov, as he helped my brother Tony get his early Corvette racing career off the ground. Highlights included watching Zora running the living shit out of my brother's '64 Stingray Coupe on the test track inside the Tech Center, in a final check before we left for Tony's first SCCA driver's school at Watkins Glen. I then watched as Tony put Corvette back on top in SCCA "A" production racing (after years of Cobra dominance) with his famed Owens-Corning Fiberglas Team – barnstorming the country and achieving milestone wins at the Daytona, Sebring and Watkins Glen endurance races, and an incredible streak of 22-straight SCCA victories.

And in the post-Owens-Corning days, when we had bought two ex-factory Bud Moore Ford Mustangs for the '71 Trans-Am season, I remember standing in the pit lane at Lime Rock in a torrential rain-storm, giving Tony his pit signals as he sloshed his way to a second-place finish behind Mark Donohue in the factory AMC Javelin in the season opener. I was soaked to the bone with only a T-shirt and jeans on, and I remember seeing Roger Penske standing there at the opposite end of the pit lane in a perfectly tailored rain suit – cool, calm, collected – and dry. Roger was *always* better prepared than everyone else.

After dropping out of college and pumping gas at all-night gas stations and doing a stint in a steel warehouse, I dabbled in For-mula Ford racing in England in 1971. Wisely determining that I had no chance to be the next Formula 1 World Driving Champion, I returned to finish college at Michigan State University. After gradu-ating, I attempted to sell cars at University Olds-GMC-Datsun in Lansing, which lasted exactly eight weeks, whereupon the general manager called me in and said, "You march to a different drummer," – before firing me. He was right, of course, or as my editor, Janice Putman, says, "Truer words were never spoken."

I then joined a local sales training firm in Detroit as a junior copywriter, spending three years doing Cadillac sales meeting guides, AMC dealer tedium, GMC magazine articles and other stuff before ending up at McManus John & Adams (which soon became D'Arcy McManus & Masius) as a copywriter working primarily on the Pontiac account (with pitch-in stints on Cadillac and General Tire – including orchestrating a three-week orgy of speed at the original

Nürburgring to shoot footage for the introduction of a new performance tire – still the best time I've ever had shooting a commercial). I moved up in the organization; then I left for New York to join The William Esty Company and work on Nissan. Esty recruited me after seeing an ad campaign I had written for Pontiac. I lived in New York City and commuted to our client's offices in L.A. every week. Then I got the call to be Executive Creative Director at BBDO-Detroit, on Dodge car, truck and dealer advertising.

By then, it was the summer of '86, and for two-and-a-half years I slogged away on Dodge when it was still the old Chrysler. Long before Lido Iacocca was "asked off" – and out. Those were some of my best times in the business, but ultimately, it turned out to be the worst. I was off for a year after that and ended up at Campbell-Ewald, on Chevrolet. All I can say about my nine-and-a-half-year stint at C-E was that there were some fleeting moments of fun – and great work – but I was glad to get out of there.

My total time in advertising added up to twenty-two-and-one-half years.

In 1999, I walked away from the car advertising business for good because it had become chock-full of weasels and twerps, no-talent demigods, and more spineless and gutless hangers-on, sycophants and delusional one-hit wonders than your average record company convention. And that was just on the client side. As one ex-boss of mine (a monumental asshole who shall remain nameless) told me a long time ago, "It's not about your creative ability Peter – it's about how you play the game." Well, I've never played the game by "conventional" rules, and I've *always* gone against the grain, and at times I've paid for it dearly. But I had no regrets throughout my ad career, and I can assure you that I have no regrets now. I've never told people what they wanted to hear. Not clients, not colleagues, not anyone. Not now. Not ever.

While I bided my time over the years in advertising, I was able to observe the car business close-up, and I was forming definitive opinions and insights every step of the way. And that's how Autoextremist.com came about – whether people were ready for it or not.

Autoextremist became my crusade. It combined my living, breathing childhood experience, which gave me a historical perspective unmatched in the business, with more than two decades of in-the-trenches battles with the marketing, advertising and product troops who made the decisions that inexorably affected Detroit's course – and led to the predicament in which the Motor City finds itself today.

Autoextremist.com was the "Bare-Knuckled, Unvarnished, High-Octane Truth" about all things to do with the auto business, but, even more to the point, it was my high-octane life brought to life every week.

From Day One, the real essence of Autoextremist.com was the fact that I said what others were merely thinking, or would only discuss in "deep background" and in "off-the-record" conversations. It was never a "touchy-feely" publication that coddled its readers and genuflected at the feet of the car companies. There's plenty of pabulum in this world. And if becoming a lifetime member of the "Milquetoast & Crumpets Afternoon Tea & Automobile Society," while sitting around the fire chatting about Renault Dauphines floats your boat, there are plenty of other automobile publications out there to satisfy your primordial need for blandness. But that was not Autoextremist.

Born out of a defiance and frustration with the status quo that I believed was stifling creativity and squeezing the very life out of the automobile business, particularly as practiced here in the Motor City, and then fueled by my passion and vision for how great the business could become again and what was necessary in order for it to get there, Autoextremist.com was not only a labor of love for me personally – it became an influential force to be reckoned with in this industry with an impact far beyond my most vivid imagination.

I set out to cut through the pap and the puffery proffered by the car company PR departments and to break through the KGB-like control that the car companies love to place on anything and everything uttered or written about them. I refused to drink the Kool-Aid and regurgitate the "prepared" statements and the carefully worded press releases that the car companies dole out as if they were addenda to the Ten Commandments. And I wanted to bring a different perspective to the whole damn business – from the products and the personalities, all the way to the marketing, advertising and motorsports – that no one else was willing to give.

People don't like to be held accountable – especially people who are used to operating under the built-in shield provided by the sheer inertia and bulk of the auto companies. And people don't like to be called on the carpet for at best being mediocre and at worst being just plain stupid. But Autoextremist did just that. And I offer no apologies for doing it, either.

Taking this town and this business by the scruff of its neck and trying to shake some sense into it proved to be, at times, exceedingly difficult, always enlightening, terribly frustrating, wildly exhilarating and every conceivable emotion in between. I never thought it would be easy, not by a long shot. How could it be? After all, this is the most heavily guarded, painfully conservative, religiously self-important, myopically reasoned, carefully orchestrated and minutely calculated business in the world. But I never thought it would be quite like it was, either. I never thought "The High-Octane Truth" would elicit such wildly divergent responses from everybody, but it sure did. And I certainly never thought that simply telling it like it is would be such a controversial and explosive venture. Over the past eight years, I've learned one irrefutable truth: It's far easier to criticize the U.S. Government than it is to criticize the insulated sacred cows of the auto business.

The streets are mean, and the stakes are high in this business. The auto business is *still* such an inexorable part of the basic economy of this country that the decisions made, good or bad, affect each and every one of us every day. It's also the one business that has its own built-in scorecard, one that's larger than life for all to see, sitting in driveways and garages all over the country. If you're a top-notch car executive in Tokyo and you screw-up a last-second product decision in December, you could be disgraced the following fall. Or, if you're an up-and-coming marketing "genius" in Detroit and the toast of the

North American International Auto Show in January, you could be peddling catalog kiosks to Chevy dealers in Dubuque by the end of summer for a "little" mistake you made back before Christmas that ruined a product launch.

When I decided to expose everyone from the fakes to the scammers, the bright lights to the schemers, the ones with the brains to the ones still in search of one, I knew I was venturing into hostile waters, but I was bound and determined to say what everyone else was thinking (but would only talk about in the bar or in double-secret late-night phone conversations). *Nobody* speaks "on the record" in this business, and if they do, it is, of course, "not for publication." But Autoextremist changed all that.

From the very first issue of Autoextremist.com, I began documenting how the Detroit automakers had lost their way and how they were clueless about their true place in the automotive world. I zeroed in on the countless missteps and the mind-numbing culture of bureaucratic mediocrity that was the cancer eating Detroit car companies from within in minute detail. To say the automobile business has changed dramatically in these past eight years is a supreme understatement. Not only has it changed, the industry has been literally turned upside down, with previous auto giants like Ford and General Motors being replaced by Toyota at the top, while a future giant from Korea (Hyundai) – and giants we haven't even heard about yet from China – wait in the wings. The continued erosion of the Detroit-based automakers' market share – and the corresponding ascendancy of Toyota – is clearly the single most significant development in this business during these early years of the twenty-first century.

And that's where *The United States of Toyota* comes in.

PART ONE

WHEN GIANTS
ROAMED THE EARTH

FULL-THROTTLE NATION

I grew up in a different country. America in the 1950s wasn't the America we know today. Finally emerging from the cloud of two major wars, Americans were hell-bent on standing on the gas and making the most of what life had to offer. Americans had a sky's-the-limit attitude that was perfectly timed for the jet age and the dawn of the rocket age – and America was the best place to be – a land of wide-open dreams and unbridled enthusiasm that knew no bounds. Everything was "new" and "improved" – from toaster ovens and washing machines to automobiles – and America was hard on the accelerator and not looking back, even with the new specter of nuclear confrontation looming over everything.

The engine that propelled America at full-throttle was Detroit and the Detroit-based car companies – General Motors, Ford and Chrysler. The biggest of the big-time dreamers were alive and thriving in the Motor City. The designers and engineering innovators working in Detroit helped shape America's dreams by creating visionary rolling sculptures that set the cadence for an entire nation. There was no idea too far-fetched, no dream car too outrageous, no boundaries, no timidity and no apologies, ever. America was a full-throttle nation with a fuel-injected soul and a hot-rod heart.

The executives working at the Detroit car companies mirrored the national attitude perfectly. Flying by the seat of their pants and making gut-level decisions that turned sheet metal into gold, these executives were unfettered by "touchy-feely" workplaces or the con-temporary bureaucratic nonsense that later would bury much of corporate America. Good ideas triumphed over the "cover-your-ass" culture of non-decision so emblematic of American corporate culture today. Detroit auto executives weren't worried about corporate culture, and they didn't have to deal with the anti-productivity mindset that would later paralyze corporate America. Instead, the rules were simple: Make it beautiful, make it faster, build it better (and faster) and then sell the living shit out of 'em. Nothing else mattered.

As hard as it is to believe now, Detroit back then was all about spirit, passion and creativity. There were no limits, because new ones were achieved and then broken the following model year. There was no foreign competition, because other than the VW Beetle and some English and Italian sports cars, foreign competitors weren't even a blip on the radar screen. Detroit ruled the highways and byways of America, and "new car announcement day" in late September was the equivalent of an unannounced national holiday in cities and towns all across the country.

So what happened? How could Detroit get it so wrong after so many years of getting it so right? The short answer? Detroit mirrors American culture, corporate and otherwise, more than anyone realizes. Detroit became smug and complacent just as America became smug and complacent. Detroit ignored the threat of foreign competition and the global economy just as America did. Detroit became saddled with a "touchy-feely," counterproductive corporate culture that avoided risk, reduced everything to the lowest common denominator and rewarded mediocrity over brilliance – just as the rest of corporate America did.

In short, Detroit became the perfect microcosm for what ails America. And now that Detroit is on the ropes, it doesn't take much to see how America has lost its way too. We have gone from being a swashbuckling go-go nation to a nation paralyzed by polarizing factions more interested in perpetuating their particular dogmas than in propelling this country forward. The American educational system has become the land of the "it's okay to fail" attitude – where academic mediocrity has become the currency of a nation rapidly falling behind a world that still places the emphasis on winning and losing. America is stuck in neutral, mired in our rationalized, delusional "pass/fail" synthetic nirvana – while the rest of the world is blowing right past us. As a result of this almost total breakdown of our educational system, America's workplace has become a cesspool of mediocrity – a grim, day-in, day-out slog where entire careers are carved out around a "cover-your-ass" mentality and where more time is spent keeping track of "feelings" and interpersonal issues than productivity.

America the bold, creative, technological force of a nation is being swallowed up by a sniveling, mewling, whining defeatist culture that aspires to mediocrity while carefully monitoring everyone's feelings. Meanwhile, the world is shifting into a higher gear and leaving us in the dust.

It's easy for the media intelligentsia on both coasts of this nation to ignore the plight of Detroit. After all, how is another rust-belt industry going down the drain in the "flyover" states really going to matter in the scheme of things, right? But if they adopt that attitude, they do so at their peril, for the dismantling of Detroit is a precursor to the dismantling of the manufacturing base of this country. And just one more step in the slow, excruciatingly painful slide of a nation.

But it wasn't always this way in Detroit...

DETROIT'S GLORY DAYS

In the red-hot '60s, when the Detroit manufacturers were churning out hit after hit, if you were a divisional General Manager at General Motors, you had the power akin to the potentate of a small country. You controlled your products, manufacturing, sales, marketing, budget and anything and everything that went into getting your division's vehicles to the street. You were the absolute King of your domain, and life was very, very good. The "Glory Days" of Detroit were filled with larger-than-life characters bristling with outsized egos, "golden guts" and blessed with the talent to back it all up. It was a high-octane, pedal-to-the-metal atmosphere powered by unbridled dreams and fueled by unlimited imagination. It didn't last forever, of course, but for one brilliant, fleeting moment in time, Detroit and the giants that ruled the kingdoms of Chrysler, Ford and GM had the automotive world in their hands.

Detroit reigned by churning out massively large road burners that bristled with style, visionary creativity at times and wildly exuberant, fin-flashy excess. Detroit's design prowess set the tone for the entire industry, too, with such automotive luminaries as Mercedes-Benz and Ferrari succumbing to the fin-tastic influence of Detroit's legendary designers.

More so than any other Design House among the domestic car companies, GM Design ruled supreme, tracing its lineage directly to the very beginnings of the "idea" of design in the automobile business.

When the legendary Harley J. Earl was discovered/scouted out in Los Angeles by Fred Fisher (patriarch of *the* Fisher brothers), he was making customized auto bodies for Hollywood types at his family's auto body shop. Earl was the one first credited with using modeling clay to "style" car bodies – that's how far back to the roots of the design business he goes. He was asked in January 1926 to come to Detroit and do a design for an alternative Cadillac, the La Salle, which he did and which everyone raved about. It didn't take long for the powers that be at GM (especially Alfred Sloan) to realize what they had, and Earl was invited back to head up the famed "Art and Colour" section for General Motors in May 1927 (it then became GM Styling and ultimately, GM Design). Earl basically created the entire discipline of design within the automobile business, and General Motors differentiated itself from every other automaker with its visionary designs and set the tone of design "point of view" in the industry for decades.

His successor, Bill Mitchell, carried on the GM tradition of design leadership and became a living legend in his own right. Many famous names in automotive design history at one time or another worked at GM design during Mitchell's era – people like Tony Lapine (who became Porsche's Chief Designer), Peter Brock (who worked on the original Stingray and went on to design the famed Cobra Daytona Coupe) and of course, Larry Shinoda (who for years was Bill Mitchell's "personal" designer and who was one of the most talented individuals ever to pick up a pen). There were many, many more unsung heroes who toiled away in the famed Design Staff in Warren, Michigan, too – people like Jerry Palmer for one, who is the surviving direct link to all of the great GM designers before him.

The point of all of this historical background?

The point is that over a period of about 30 years or so, General Motors slowly but surely neutered its Design Staff. There was an intensely calculated overreaction after Bill Mitchell retired to "rein-in" the Design Staff. And because of the tone set by the bean counters who were bound and determined to bring it in line with "proper" business practices (Mitchell was a notorious big spender), a noticeable shift occurred. GM Design was no longer allowed to be the "star" of the corporation, and a gradual tightening of the noose around its neck started a long, slow and painful slide into mediocrity, sapping the very life out of it all together. The wrong people were promoted, which didn't help. The design "process" became bogged down in the process itself – where meeting after meeting drained the life out of designs and impeded future creativity. And then, once the dreaded Brand Management "Reign of Terror" began at GM (in the early '90s), it was the icing on the cake. Woefully unqualified people were now impacting crucial design decisions. Good designs were "lost" in favor of bland or just plain bad designs, and they made their way into production, leaving their uninspired mark on America's streets and highways – and leaving a very negative impression on consumers everywhere.

The once-proud GM Design Staff had become nothing but a neutered creative force that, though still incredibly deep in talent, had given up and was just going through the motions. It was a sad sight to see considering its once-proud legacy.

Which reminds me...

BILL MITCHELL – THE PASSIONATE DESIGN MAESTRO

To say that the '50s and '60s were a different era in automotive history is not painting a proper picture of just *how* different it was. Detroit was much more of a freewheeling mindset back then. Car executives were bold, decisive, conniving, creative and power-hungry personalities who inevitably went with their gut instincts – which could end up being either a recipe for disaster or a huge runaway sales hit on the streets. The only committees you'd find back then were the finance committees – and they never got near the design, engineering, marketing or even the advertising unless there was some sort of a problem. These Car Kings worked flat-out, and they partied flat-out, too, ruling their fiefdoms with iron fists while wielding their power ruthlessly at times to get what they wanted – and rightly so in their minds, as they were some of the most powerful business executives on earth. In short, it was a world that was 180 degrees different from what goes on in today's rigid, namby-pamby, never-have-a-point-of-view-and-never-take-a-stand automotive environment.

No one represented the spirit of the business back then more than Bill Mitchell. He was bold, powerful, flamboyant, recalcitrant, maniacal, brilliant, frustrating and probably every other adjective you can think of for someone who was one of a kind. He was smart enough to know and he had the innate sense to understand that he had inherited the legacy of the great Harley Earl, and he never for a second forgot that fact – or let anyone else forget it, either. And he played it for all it was worth, with a swagger and strut that haven't been seen since. He often bumped heads with the "suits" down at the corporation when they didn't "get" one of his design recommendations – but he usually won the battles and got his way.

Mitchell was, in fact, his own potentate within the GM monolith, and he did outrageous things and spoke his mind and generally didn't give a rat's ass about any of the other bullshit that was part of corporate life at GM at the time. Mitchell *was* a larger-than-life personality, and it just didn't sit well with a lot of the sober financial suits down on the "14th floor" of the old GM building. He swaggered and strutted his way around the Design Staff like it was his own personal kingdom – and make no mistake about it – it *was*.

To give you just a small glimpse into how Mitchell held sway over things at Design Staff, the Corvette was the one car that meant more to him than any other. And whenever a young designer did a version and started to gloat even just a little bit, Bill would always set things straight with the following famous Mitchell-ism: "Don't flatter yourself, kid – *I'm* the one who does Corvettes here." (As a brief aside, one of the most hilarious things I ever witnessed as a kid was watching the mercurial Mitchell attempt to play golf at the Bloomfield Hills Country Club. He was horrible at it, and his frustration level would grow exponentially with each hole – and you could see his complexion glow even more beet-red than it already was almost by the minute. He had absolutely no patience for the game whatsoever, and finally he'd inevitably storm off the course without finishing his round and jump into one of his concept cars – the original Sting Ray, the Mako Shark, the Monza SS – you name it, and then he'd peel out of the parking lot spinning the tires and grabbing gears all the way down Long Lake Road.)

I've heard countless firsthand stories about the man and his ballistic fits in studios while cajoling his troops to go further and reach higher – but I saw a slightly different side to him too.

Because, after all, he lived just a block away from our house...

And I'll never forget the day I discovered that fact. I was still in my bike-riding days back then, but I remember resting with my buddies one blistering Friday afternoon on a corner in our neighborhood after a long, hot day of riding around aimlessly – we did that often back then – when we heard a rumble and roar coming from off in the distance. I knew right away that it wasn't motorcycles and that it was more than one of whatever it was – and just then a pack of the most stunning cars we'd ever seen burst around the corner and came rumbling right past us – the sun glinting off the barking pipes and the canopy of trees shimmering off the perfect mirror finishes of the paint jobs. This "horsepower train" was led by the "original" Corvette Stingray in Silver, followed by the XP700 Corvette (a "bubble-top" show car with side pipes also in Silver – it was Mitchell's favorite color), the first Mako Shark Corvette and a concept called the Corvair Sebring Spyder (also in Silver), a wild racing-inspired show car with dual cut-down racing windscreens and three pipes curling out and around each side in the back. They were so loud we couldn't even hear ourselves screaming whatever it was we were screaming, but after a split second to think about it, we took off, pedaling our guts out after them. It was apparent that these machines were heading for our part of the neighborhood – and as we tried to keep them in sight I realized they were turning on to my cross street!

We came around the corner and saw them pull into a driveway, exactly one block from my house. We stopped right at the end of the driveway with our mouths gaping down to the asphalt, as the drivers of the other cars handed the keys to the driver of the Stingray and he took them up to the front door where a woman collected them. Then, an Impala pulled up and the four men got in it and were gone, leaving the cars sitting in the driveway all lined up ticking and spitting as their pipes started to cool.

This became the Friday Afternoon Ritual of the summer – at least when Bill Mitchell was in town.

He liked having his "toys" at his disposal on the weekends. And every weekend the collection was different, depending on the mood he was in when he made the call to the Styling garage. I would watch what cars would be delivered on Friday, and then I would ride over there on Saturdays and just linger out in the driveway studying every square inch of every car hoping to get an audience with The Man himself – and maybe, just maybe – a ride in one of the machines. One thing about Bill Mitchell is he never got tired of the cars, and he never got tired of seeing people's reaction to them or answering questions about them. After about the third weekend of this, I finally got the nerve to introduce myself to him one Saturday morning as he was getting ready to go somewhere in the Sebring Spyder. From that moment on I was okay in his book because I was "one of Tony's boys" and he said, "Hop in – I'm just running up to the drugstore, but come on..."

I jumped in the passenger seat (the interior was done in Silver Metallic leather), and he made sure I fastened my seatbelt, even though he didn't bother with his – and we were off. The Sebring Spyder was a revelation to me (although I had to look through the cut-down windscreen or off to the side to see) because it was the first time I had been in anything other than a production automobile. Thanks to my brother, I had ridden shotgun in plenty of fast cars, but this was different – this one was exotic to me. The ride literally lasted five minutes up to the store and five minutes back, but from then on I was a fixture in the Mitchell's driveway for the rest of the summer.

I ended up riding in every one of GM's Concept Cars of that era. All but one of them being chauffeured by none other than Bill Mitchell himself. Just for the record, my favorites were the original Stingray, the Monza GT Coupe in Silver and the Monza SS Spyder in Red (look them up – they were the stunning Corvair-based show cars with the front ends eerily similar to the racing Chaparrals).

Oh, and the one *not* chauffeured by Bill Mitchell? That was an unbelievably wild Pontiac show car called the XP400. It started out as a 1964 Nassau Blue Pontiac Bonneville convertible that had more of a '50s custom look to it (complete with a stowable hard tonneau cover that was way ahead of its time). Big deal, you say? Well, stuffed in the engine bay was a 421-cubic-inch, Mickey Thompson-prepared drag race motor with a 6-71 GMC blower producing, as Ken Eschebach (the gifted technician at "Styling" who basically kept everything running for Mitchell) said, "All Mickey said was that it had almost 700hp." Oh, and one more thing – it had a lever that you could engage that would open up un-muffled side-pipes any time you felt the urge to.

Bill Mitchell had the XP400 dropped off one summer day in 1964 for my older brother to play with for the weekend. I have two memories of that weekend: 1. Sitting in the back seat with two other guys (a total of five in the car), rolling down a two-lane road headed for Woodward Avenue – in first gear. My brother punched it, and that beast shrieked and howled as it charged down the road, spinning its rear tires in the first three gears, our necks snapping in unison with every shift. The acceleration almost took the wind out of me. He backed out of it at 125 only because we had to stop for a light. The thing was brutally fast – a truly nasty-beautiful machine in every sense of the word. And 2. Pulling into gas stations and getting out to check the oil just so we could see the expression on the attendant's face as we unlatched the hood. And we did that often because Mickey had set the motor up with "drag race piston rings" as Ken told us, so it used *21 quarts* of oil in one weekend. Incredible...

Things weren't all blissful in those years. I heard rumblings of things being "different" in the Mitchell household, and the next thing I knew he had gotten divorced – and then he got remarried to a woman who lived around the corner from us, *one block away in the opposite direction*! I guess he liked the neighborhood.

At any rate, Bill Mitchell's new wife had a stepson (though several years younger than our crowd) who became part of our bike-riding gang. It was during this time that I really got to know Bill Mitchell beyond the occasional car rides. I used to hang out in his basement for hours with his stepson, and I'll never forget what a shrine to the automobile it was – a virtual museum of automotive art and automobilia. The man had his favorite drawings plastered all over the place – beautiful illustrations from the time he first started drawing cars as a young boy that were lit with little spotlights. He had personally signed photos of most of the all-time great Grand Prix drivers from the '30s, '40s, '50s and early '60s. He had a Plexiglas case containing the helmet, goggles and gloves that the great Rudolph Caracciola wore in one of his last drives for the Mercedes-Benz factory racing team (I finally understood why Mitchell's favorite color was Silver – he had Silver Mercedes-Benz and Auto Union stuff everywhere).

He had other personal effects from famous drivers all over the place – a Stirling Moss helmet, gloves from the great Juan Manuel Fangio – you name the driver, and he had something personally signed by them and given to him. And there were countless models, original paintings, pictures, plaques and badges – a cornucopia of car stuff that is just staggering to think about now.

There were a few times when he would come down and spend time with us, and since I thought I wanted to be a car designer I'd pepper him with questions about anything and everything. I remember one particular day when he was in an expansive mood, and he took me on a personal guided tour of his collection of stuff – and it was one of the most fascinating experiences of my life. Here was a living automotive legend in every sense of the word, taking the time to convey to a kid what all of this stuff really meant to him. What struck me right away was how he was as much of a pure fan and in awe of his favorite drivers as anyone. He expounded on every single piece of memorabilia – where it came from, how it came about, his personal experiences with the driver, etc. But the best part was when I'd ask him about a particular drawing he had done, and he'd go off for several minutes explaining every nuance, every line and every shape down to the last detail.

In that brief moment of time, I finally understood the passion, the intensity and the love for everything automotive that was Bill Mitchell. And I realized right then and there that my love for everything automotive had some sort of place in life – and maybe even a future – all because Bill Mitchell took the time to give a kid a tour of his personal automotive museum.

For all that has been said and written about Bill Mitchell – the tough-guy persona, the bluster, and all the stories and anecdotes of his temper tantrums in the studio – I think people forget what a truly gifted and talented man he was. And I also think people have forgotten how his relentless, unwavering passion for the automobile and automotive design inspired countless young designers and helped propel General Motors to the top of the automotive design world in his day. Something that was truly lost on this company for the longest time.

Right now, there are car guys and gals from many disciplines slogging away at every car company on the planet – and maybe even some will read this book. An elite few of them may have even managed to rise to the top in their car companies with their spirit and passion intact, which is no mean feat in this day and age.

But in the face of a business that grows more rigid, regulated and non-risk-taking by the day, there are still lessons to be learned from the legacy of Bill Mitchell. If anything, we *must* remember what really matters in this business above all else – something he instinctively knew in his gut – and that is to never forget the *essence* of the machine, and what makes it a living, breathing mechanical conduit of our hopes and dreams. And that in the course of designing, engineering and building these machines everyone needs to aim higher and push harder – with a relentless, unwavering passion and love for the automobile that is so powerful and unyielding that it can't be beaten down by committee-think or buried in bureaucratic mediocrity.

Bill Mitchell had an uncanny knack for getting the best out of the talented people around him. And he led the only way he knew how – and that was by fueling creativity with his passion and by the sheer force of his will. What he believed in is as true and vibrant today as it was in his era – and hopefully, at least in some quarters of a few car companies, that will always be the case.

CARROLL SHELBY – THE FLIM-FLAM MAN WHO MADE RACING HISTORY

In February 2002, a judge entered a final ruling in favor of Carroll Shelby, Carroll Shelby Licensing, Inc. and the Ford Motor Company against Factory Five Racing, Inc., a very high-profile maker of Cobra "kit cars." This was described as a "significant" victory for the Shelby interests, although subsequent clarification of the decision basically said only that Factory Five couldn't put any of Shelby's original logos and badging on the cars they make. The decision did not affect the "shape" of the Cobra, however, which Shelby has been trying to trademark as his own and which he will continue trying to do – even though everyone and his brother readily admits that the Cobra was originally an AC design for the Bristol, which was basically "lifted" from the original design for the Ferrari 166 "Barchetta" etc., etc., etc. Shelby had been on a personal "jihad" for years to put these "Cobra" kit carmakers out of business, acting like a self-righteous, Bible-thumping preacher out to protect the integrity of "his" baby – the Shelby Cobra. Which was amusing in and of itself – since he seemed to have changed his mind about the Cobra over the years according to whichever way the proverbial winds were blowing – or more accurately, where the money was flowing.

I consider the story of the Cobra and how it came about to be one of the greatest chapters in the history of American racing. And the iconic Shelby Cobra remains one of my all-time favorite cars. But from the moment Carroll Shelby first approached Chevrolet (yes, that's true, folks) about supplying him engines for his "little ol' sports car," as he called it, to the time he completely turned his back on Ford and conveniently transformed his act into becoming a huckster for Chrysler, to now, when he's reconciled with Ford and officially back in the fold, giving his blessing on new Shelby-badged factory high-performance Fords while marketing his own "continuation" Cobras – he has always been first and foremost about making a buck.

Despite all the victories and the championships, Shelby always knew he stumbled into his good fortune through blind luck. It was like the planets aligned with the Cosmic Pecos as if to say to Shelby, "Here's your ticket to ride, now don't screw it up." And for the most part, he didn't. He was surrounded by some of the most brilliant minds and some of the most naturally gifted designers, engineers and drivers of the day. And the fact that they all came together, at that particular moment in time, was nothing short of a miracle.

But let's not forget a few key things about the whole odyssey of Mr. Shelby and his Cobra.

By the end of the Cobra heyday in late 1967, Shelby had basically "sold out" – both literally and figuratively – his rights to the Cobra name to the Ford Motor Company. He had stopped making his snarling 427 Cobra in order to watch over Ford's GT40 racing effort, and he sat back and watched as his wonderfully raucous GT350 Mustang became a neutered, bloated, ill-handling parody of itself that was being marketed by Ford in "GT350" and "GT500" versions (1968-1970) to capitalize on the Shelby name – which happened to be an extremely profitable move for him personally but one that did nothing positive for the Shelby reputation.

Shelby had, in fact, moved on. The Cobra was history as far as he was concerned. Nobody cared, least of all Shelby himself. And he gave little thought to the remnants of the glory days of the Cobra legend. Little did he know that by the late '70s people would start seeking out Cobras, rightfully placing them in the pantheon of some of the most famous and sought-after cars ever built. Or that, even stranger, a whole cottage industry of making Cobra reproductions would crop up – on both sides of the Atlantic.

Shelby eventually went on to greener pastures, which took him to Chrysler, where one Lee Iacocca was looking for a way to juice up his dismal Chrysler product line. So, Shelby performed his so-called "magic" with a bunch of lame, turbocharged Dodge "Daytonas" and "Shadows" – which made the Shelby faithful ill for a number of reasons. Probably the thing most disappointing to the Shelby faithful was that Shelby's actions confirmed all the "dark side" stories about their godfather – that he was nothing but a glorified mercenary who would stop at absolutely nothing to enhance his personal cash position.

On a personal note, I remember being summoned (along with a few of my colleagues from BBDO Detroit – the Dodge advertising agency) to a meeting at a condo Shelby owned in the Detroit area where he conducted "bidness" when he was in town, so that we could have an audience with "The Man" himself. In that meeting, he expounded on all the stuff we weren't doing and could be doing to pump up his signature product line for Dodge. That was a real eye-opener for me. Here was this automotive living legend going through the motions and pretending how "excited" he was about this lackluster bunch of nickel-rocket, four-cylinder sporty cars that he was hanging his name on. It was one of the most depressing days in my entire ad career.

Fortunately for everyone concerned, that dismal chapter in the Shelby story eventually faded away, and he moved on just before the Viper appeared on the scene – which was, lo and behold, a modern rendition of the 427 Shelby Cobra.

But there was one thing still gnawing at Ol' Shel, and that was the fact that a whole bunch of people were making boatloads of money off of selling and reselling original and kit car Cobras. How was he going to get back what was once "rightfully" his – even though he gave his "rights" away years before? Shelby had been mildly amused when he first heard of some of the prices that his Cobras were bringing on the open market; he just thought that the world had gone crazy. He even went to some of these Cobra "conventions" and readily autographed originals *and* replicas. But after attending one too many meetings of the Shelby American Automobile Club and seeing the blind fervor that people attached to his "little ol' sports car," a light went on – and he decided that *there was gold in them thar Cobras*, and by god he was going to get his "rightful" piece of it.

But first was the ugly little matter of taking The Ford Motor Company to court to get the rights to the "Cobra" name back. A deal was hammered out – more like a joint-custody arrangement – and Shelby was off to try and capitalize on his previous brilliance. As the market prices soared on Cobras, Shelby's ardor for making some cash off this phenomenon grew exponentially.

It was then that the infamous "lost" Cobras appeared (were there 40? 100?). Real Cobras, Shelby said, made up of genuine pieces piled up in some secret warehouse all of these years – and he was going to finish them and make them available as a "public service" so that enthusiasts wouldn't have to keep buying all of these cheap replica Cobras from these low-life "kit car" manufacturers – even though some of these companies (Kirkham if you wanted an aluminum bodied one and ERA if you'd settle for fiberglass) were responsible for building better-engineered and finished Cobras than the originals. Now, remember, this was the same man who didn't hesitate to sell or give away anything and everything to do with the Cobra at the end of its era. So the likelihood of "lost" Cobras piled up in unassembled pieces in some warehouse all of these years was nothing but pure Texas fiction. And everyone from openly skeptical journalists to bemused enthusiasts knew it was nothing but a tall Texan's tale indeed, expertly spun by the Old Master himself. And the neat trick was that Shelby convinced the U.S. Government that these "lost" Cobras should, in fact, be labeled as "continuation" production vehicles – from 1967, with authentic Shelby American serial numbers attached. And oh yes, by the way, Shelby would be asking well over $100,000 for these continuation Cobras, which would be assembled by Nevada state prison inmates in a very "unique" work-training program.

Not content to keep himself occupied with building replicas of his originals, Shelby then decided that what the world needed most was yet another modern rendition of the Cobra. Only this one would be by The Legend himself, immediately distinguishing it from all the rest. So he began the infamous "Series 1" project, which would see him approach GM yet again – this time the now-defunct Oldsmobile

Division – to supply him with Aurora V8s for his new car. Of course, this project, with all the modern day safety and legal requirements involved – not to mention the finicky expectations of an enthusiast driving public that had little tolerance for poor quality or basic reliability problems – turned into one of your basic nightmares. Cars were excruciatingly late, initial "locked-in" delivery prices were trashed in favor of much higher numbers, convertible tops were engineered after the fact and then delivered and fitted "later," and so on...

And while Shelby was unleashing the Series 1 fiasco on the enthusiast driving public, he was going after kit car manufacturers in court to protect what was "rightfully" his – especially now that it had become such a consistently lucrative endeavor, but one that he had so capriciously given away when it suited him in the past.

Since then, Shelby has made several licensing deals with various Cobra manufacturers, delineating the ones that have Shelby's personal blessing – and the ones that don't. And the Shelby Series 1? It went down in flames in less than three years, a total and highly embarrassing failure.

I know it borders on sacrilege to criticize one of the Patron Saints of the Sacred Car Jones, especially with Shelby generously raising funds for his heart charity – he's had a heart transplant. (An *Automotive News* article appeared on July 23, 2007, with the telling headline, "Carroll Shelby's charity takes in plenty but skimps on the giving." The piece went on to say that Shelby's Children's Foundation Charity had given charitable grants of 6.2 percent, 4.3 percent, 13.0 percent and 8.7 percent over the previous four years. The Better Business Bureau says charitable grants should account for at least 65 percent of a charity organization's total expenses.)

Know this about Carroll Shelby: He may have been responsible for one of the most glorious chapters in the history of American racing, but the fact of the matter remains that he's been a nothing but a Texas-sized version of P.T. Barnum his whole life – and he's always managed to find willing "participants" to underwrite his various schemes.

He didn't give an armadillo's ass about the fate of his "beloved"

Cobra until he saw a bunch of people making money off of it – only then did the kit car Cobras become "offensive" to him, and only then was it was revealed that a miraculous discovery was made of enough components to make another 100 "original" Shelby Cobras.

Ol' Shel always went where the money was – and he still does to this day.

That's why it was so laughable to read about Carroll Shelby going after these kit car manufacturers for impinging on his "creation." The only thing they're guilty of is that they were smarter and more visionary than he was – and Ol' Shel hated getting outsmarted when it came to making a buck. They realized long ago that the Cobra was a timeless classic, when Shelby was too busy trying to come up with his next moneymaking enterprise – besides selling Texas chili mix, that is.

In spite of it all, for my money, the Cobra continues to be the very essence of what a high-performance sports car should look, feel and sound like.

A friend and I were musing recently about Shelby's historical desire to make money over just about anything else, especially now that Ford has produced a modern rendition of the Ford GT, and Shelby's name now adorns Shelby GT, GT500 and GT500KR Mustangs. He said, "I expect him to find 100 Ford GT40 tubs with matching serial number plates that he 'forgot' about in an abandoned warehouse any day now."

I wouldn't put it past him.

JIM HALL – THE BRILLIANT VISIONARY

The story of Jim Hall, the west Texas oil man and mechanical engineer, and how his personal vision engineered the transition of American sports car racing from the end of one era with his first front-engined Chaparral (which was a direct descendant of the magnificent Reventlow Scarabs) to the ground-breaking mid-engined Chaparrals is one of the great stories in all of motorsports history.

Some of the advanced technical concepts making their debut on the Chaparrals in the '60s were composite chassis technology (which Hall learned from his love of flying and what was being done in aircraft construction), the manual gearbox with an automatic clutch mechanism (commonly referred to at the time as an automatic transmission – a first for racing applications), the exploration of aerodynamic principles as applied to racing cars, including movable aerodynamic devices (driver-controlled front and rear-mounted wings) and the "black art" of ground-effects technology (this came to life in the Chaparral 2J, which used fans powered by an auxiliary engine to "suck" the car down on to the pavement to achieve unheard levels of cornering performance), and much, much more.

The fact that General Motors engineers, designers and aerodynamicists were knee-deep in all of this and contributed immeasurably to the Chaparral program makes the Jim Hall story that much more intriguing. It was during the time when GM was helping Jim through the "back door" of Chevy engineering that Ford was running its racing program out in the open. Even though I happen to prefer the Ford approach – competing openly and promoting its involvement – it still doesn't detract from what a few dedicated people were able to accomplish with the incredible Chaparrals.

It was an era when GM not only had prodigious talent and depth in their engineering staffs, but when they also had people running those staffs who appreciated the benefits that could be derived from competing – for the vehicles they would build in the future and for the people who would be working on those vehicles.

It was a different time and a different era, there's no doubt.

In the summer of 2002, Jim Hall brought all of the Chaparrals to Elkhart Lake's Road America for the vintage festival. Of all the automotive images and sounds I'll remember from that weekend, there is one that will always stand out the most...

As I watched Hall come into view on the track in the 2E, the high rear wing and gurgling sound of its V8 Chevy signaled his arrival before the rest of the car became visible.

And then for one brief fleeting moment, it seemed to hover there in the shimmering heat waves, its ghost-like white presence momentarily lost...somewhere in a blur of time...

It's no coincidence that the Chaparral adventure for Jim Hall and GM peaked right at the end of the '60s. The unbridled passion of a Bill Mitchell, the raucously successful cowboy-esque shenanigans of a Carroll Shelby and the visionary brilliance of a Jim Hall would soon give way to a darker and more somber chapter for Detroit.

And the "Glory Days" would be lost forever.

BLINDED BY ARROGANCE AND PARALYZED BY COMPLACENCY – DETROIT'S FORTUNES TAKE A TURN FOR THE WORSE

There's no doubt that the '50s and '60s were the epitome of Detroit's dominance of the automotive industry. Detroit was on the top of its game, and it reveled in its place as the Automotive Capital of the World. But the glory days of Detroit would soon begin to fade as safety and emissions regulations began dictating the tempo of the industry. And while Detroit set its cruise control on the "complacency" setting, scoffing at the foreign competition looming large in its rearview mirror, the die was cast for the beginning of the end of this country's domestic auto industry as we knew it.

The cocky, engaged, brilliant, seat-of-the-pants, go-with-your-gut Detroit auto executive from the '50s and '60s became the risk-averse, bottom-line-oriented, painfully conservative automaton of the '70s, '80s and '90s – with an unwelcome aura of arrogance thrown in for good measure. And even though they could see the Asian and German manufacturers gaining ground annually, the classic Detroit mindset wouldn't allow them to believe what was happening. It was inconceivable to these executives that the Motor City gravy train could ever be derailed – even though it was running off the tracks on their watch.

The problem for the Detroit automakers is that they never moved on from reliving their glory days, and while they were reveling in their gilded legacy, the automotive world irrevocably changed around them. Detroit's arrogant mindset blinded them to the rapidly changing realities of the North American automotive market. Detroit was slow to understand the real impact of the Japanese inroads into this market until it was way too late, just as they were slow to admit that the German manufacturers fundamentally altered the luxury car market. And on top of all of that, Detroit was painfully slow to realize that the quality/reliability component had become the basic price of entry in the new world order of the auto business.

The winds of change for Detroit really began rustling in earnest by 1966 – because of a man named Ralph Nader.

HOW GM CREATED RALPH NADER

Lost in the news of the passing of former President Ronald W. Reagan in June 2004, one of General Motor's former leaders passed on that same week too. James M. Roche, who started out with GM in 1927 at Cadillac and eventually climbed the ranks to become chairman and CEO of the automotive giant from 1967 to 1971, died at the age of 97. Roche was a good and decent man who did a lot of great things for the company and for the city of Detroit, especially after the horrific riots of '67 tore apart the city. Roche went out of his way to conduct himself in a caring and compassionate manner, and he was thoroughly devoted to helping get the city back on its feet and propel economic growth in the region.

But Jim Roche was also at the helm when GM committed one of the biggest blunders in automotive history, when, unbeknownst to Roche and his entire senior corporate staff (including my father, Tony, who was vice president in charge of GM's Public Relations staff at the time), GM's legal staff authorized hiring rogue private investigators to follow Ralph Nader around in Washington, D.C., in order to dig up anything that would discredit the young lawyer and burgeoning safety advocate.

Nader, who had published the book *Unsafe At Any Speed* in 1966 – a diatribe on the alleged handling problems of the Chevrolet Corvair – was gaining media attention and notoriety by the hour. And Nader's penchant for self-promotion and crowing to anyone in the media or otherwise who would listen had attracted certain Washington politicos, who were just itching for a cause they could sink their teeth into and further propel their careers on The Hill. And the louder Nader talked, the worse it got for Detroit – and especially GM. A senate subcommittee was formed to address the whole automotive safety issue, and the winds in Washington were stiffly blowing against Detroit and the entire automotive industry, thanks to the media firestorm unleashed by Nader's book.

Something had to be done – at least according to certain members of the GM legal staff, at any rate. Which is why they concocted their plan to "tail" Nader and find anything and everything bad about him that they could. Of course, they neglected to tell anyone of their plan or even seek some sort of permission, instead going off half-cocked on their own in their mission to bring down Nader.

Well, apparently the private investigators they hired weren't that good, or that discreet, for that matter, and Nader became suspicious that he was being followed. He was even able to ascertain that the people following him had been hired by General Motors.

Sensing an opportunity when one fell into his lap, he went to the media and blew the thing up to front-page status in *The Washington Post* and in other newspapers.

My father, Jim Roche and the rest of GM's top executives were dumbfounded. Not only were they not aware of such a plan or activity, they initially denied it because it seemed so far-fetched that it couldn't possibly be true. Only days later did they find out the truth, when GM PR's media contacts at the newspapers reported back that the private investigators had admitted that they were hired by the GM legal staff.

So, in a tense meeting that was called by my father, the head of GM's legal staff at the time reluctantly admitted to a room full of flabbergasted executives that he had indeed authorized the "tail" of Ralph Nader – without telling anyone.

My father had the unenviable task of not only telling his friend and boss, Jim Roche, what the legal staff had done, he also recommended – make that *insisted* – that Roche go in front of the Senate automotive safety subcommittee and apologize publicly to Ralph Nader, that it was the only proper thing to do. Which is what Jim Roche did, with my father sitting right behind him.

It was the most unpleasant memory of Jim Roche's career. This kind, decent and compassionate man had to apologize publicly to Ralph Nader before a Senate subcommittee – and the nation – because of a monumental lapse in judgment by his own legal staff. And it set into motion a series of events that fundamentally changed the course of the entire automobile industry.

Up until that point, Ralph Nader was just another young attorney trying to make a quick buck and a name for himself. GM not only put Ralph Nader on the map, they created his image and persona for him – and from that moment on Nader became a consumer advocate icon, the patron saint of every consumer product issue and advocate spawned from it for generations to come.

In one fell swoop, the whole automotive safety issue went from being a debatable issue and just something to do for bored Washington insiders, to a Federal mandate and a *cause célèbre* that would dominate the industry.

And the way it unfolded set the confrontational and suspicious tone that dominates Detroit and Washington's clashes over safety, emissions and fuel economy issues to this day.

The worst part of the whole episode? By 1965, the totally revamped rear-engine Corvair had become an outstanding car, one of the most distinctive designs ever to come out of Detroit. But by the end of the 1969 model year, the whole Nader debacle and the media firestorm surrounding it had killed the Corvair – for good.

From that point forward, the automobile industry became a blur of new regulations and ever-increasing challenges – while the burgeoning threat from Europe and Asia was just beginning.

PART TWO

MOTOR CITY BLUES

WHITE BOY CULTURE

Detroit is one of the strangest places on earth. It is dominated by the automobile companies. Ford in Dearborn. Chrysler in Auburn Hills. And, of course, General Motors, which is bunkered, appropriately enough, in the monolithic Renaissance Center on the Detroit River. And I mean dominated. People outside of this city can't comprehend how dominant and pervasive the automobile business is in this town. It is stifling. Oppressive. Demented. And flat-out crazy. Executive changes merit front-page space in the daily newspapers and lead stories on the local TV news. It is beyond being a "company town." It is a company philosophy. A company social structure. Company clubs. Company communities. Company morality. And, of course, company cars. And it isn't just the car companies themselves. It's the multi billion-dollar juggernaut suppliers like the Lear Corporation, all the way down to the guy who knew how to work a lathe pretty well, who is now knocking down a million a year out of some skanky building in one of the endlessly flat suburbs that fan away from the Detroit River. Yup, it's crazy alright.

Study the "Detroit deal" before the roof fell in on the domestic auto industry – and it's easy to see why Detroit managed to hasten its own demise. The typical middle level bureaucrat in this city at its arrogant peak was a narrow-minded, frightfully conservative study in extreme paranoia whose main job in life when he got up in the morning was to cover his ass. And when I say "he" – that's not to suggest that there weren't any talented women in the business because there certainly were – and they had been slowly (make that excruciatingly slowly) making their way up the corporate ranks. But one look at the executive rosters at the Detroit-based car companies even today, and there is a dearth of women executives. That's simply a fact – an unwelcome and flabbergasting one, but a fact nonetheless.

Getting back to our typical "he" in the bad old days of Detroit, the simple premise of "covering one's ass" dominated everything he did and every decision he made from the time he got up until the time he went to sleep. "He" was predominantly white, 35-55 years old, had a lovely wife, two adorable children, and, after an arduous ten-to-fifteen year journey that included such illustrious stops as the Kansas City Zone, had arrived back in Detroit, at one of the Divisions (unless he's a remarkably gifted financial genius, in which case he skipped that step and went right to Corporate). After rising at 6AM he is at his desk at the Renaissance Center (or at Ford's "Glass House" headquarters in Dearborn or in Auburn Hills at Chrysler headquarters) by 7AM. On the way into work, he listens to the same radio station every morning, a stunning monument to vapidity that goes by the call letters of "WJR" (AM760), the so-called "Great Voice of The Great Lakes," hosted by the unbelievably tedious "Paul W." Smith, a mediocre hack DJ from Philadelphia who was scrounged up as a last-minute replacement for the late and much-revered Joseph Priestly "J.P." McCarthy.

Smith's show is a turgid mix of cornball humor, an excruciatingly bad selection of contemporary "hits and oldies," news, talk, sports, birthday greetings and general jawboning about the city of Detroit. But the overriding subject is always the automotive industry: the people, the business and the "personalities" (and I use that term reluctantly). Smith fancies himself as some sort of "player" in the Detroit scene, which is absolutely laughable, because if he were plying his trade in any other town he'd be relegated to the graveyard shift without a second thought. But here, since he corrals an auto executive *du jour* and gets them to expound on pressing issues of the industry, he has carved out a niche for himself in this town – a niche that was handed to him, I might add.

This format was honed to a precision-like sheen by the late McCarthy, who relied on his deep social contacts made on his weekend golf outings and dinners at the Bloomfield Hills Country Club. As a result, never a day went by when J.P. didn't have some Detroit car executive on the air, either in-studio or by phone. It was also during this time that J.P. initiated a very strange ritual among these executives: the use of the descriptive term "brother" as a kind of knowing term of endearment. As in referring to an executive (usually his golf or clay shooting partner from the previous weekend) as "Brother Tom" or "Brother Jim" or "Brother Ben." This usually happened when the person was talking to an executive from one car company, but referring to an executive from another. And even today, if you listen closely in the meetings, or in and around the city, or at the restaurants (on the odd evening when people stray from the safety and security of their clubs), or even at the advertising agencies, you'll hear the term brother used to refer to the auto executives.

It is amazing to hear. And fascinating to watch.

It is a vaguely religious, almost "secret society" mantra that puts the definitive stamp on what this business, in this town, is all about. And it's equally amazing to see the hacks, flacks, butt-lickers and other sundry "hangers-on" from suppliers, ad agencies and what have you, frantically trying to sort out which "brother" is being referred to and whether or not that "brother" is "in" or "out" or just tolerated. God forbid they get caught on the wrong side of the "brotherhood." What's the point? The point is this: You can read all the glowing ink generated by the car companies as to how progressive they are. They can parade all the women executives out for all to see too. But the fact of the matter is it's a load of crap. The car companies, as defined here, operating in the southeastern region of Michigan, still function in an insular "White Boy Culture" – with its own set of values, moral codes, ritualistic behavior and lockstep thinking.

Is it any wonder the whole thing went south – literally and figuratively?

CAR COMPANIES AND THE DREADED "WHITE BALL" AFFLICTION

The biggest example of the Detroit mindset? The unnatural "affliction" that car companies have for sponsoring anything to do with golf. Having seen it over and over again through the years in the ad biz, the millions upon millions of dollars spent on professional golf by car companies around the world is just plain obscene.

Why?

Because there is little rational thought or solid reasoning behind any of the so-called sponsorship "deals" that the car companies commit to. The last time there was genuine thought put into the whole idea was probably the first big tournament sponsored by a car company that anyone can remember: The Buick Open in Grand Blanc, Michigan, which began as an idea in the late fifties. Since then, it has been a long, slow slide into doing it just because a certain car executive (at any car company you can think of) *likes* it.

Golf is the one thing that the ad agencies, the marketing firms and all the other hucksters roaming around sniffing for auto company dollars *never* have to sell. It's the quintessential "no-brainer." It's amazing what car company executives can get done when it comes to golf. There are minimal "reasons for doing this program" meetings. The approval process is usually a walk-through. And huge and I mean *huge* dollars are committed without so much as a "Hey, wait a minute!"

It's easy to see why too. Golf had, for the most part (pre-Tiger), been a predominantly middle-aged white guy's game. And if there was ever a last bastion of middle-aged white guy domination, it's the car business. And if there's "one true thing" that 95 percent of all white guy car company execs can relate to and believe in, it's playing a round of golf or watching a round of golf. If they're watching the Milwaukee Open at five o'clock on a Sunday afternoon, by god, *everyone* must be watching it!

The train of thought goes this way: A. I like to play golf. B. I *love* to play golf. C. Golf is on TV. D. Everyone must love golf as much as I do – hell, *everyone* I know loves it! And finally, E. It therefore must be a brilliant use of our ad/marketing/promotional dollars to spend it on golf! Sounds frighteningly like Chance the Gardener (Peter Sellers' character in "Being There"), doesn't it?

This, unfortunately, is where the poor ad agencies come in. All the typical teeth-pulling that takes place in their usual confrontational day with their client, while trying to get some immaculately researched and well-thought-out program sold, miraculously disappears. The client comes into a meeting and says, "We need to sponsor golf! Get me a golf deal!" And when the agency says, "We'll research it and get back to you," or something rational like that, the client usually goes berserk. "No need! This is a done deal! The big guy wants it! Research schmesearch! This is a *sold* program! Get on it!"

And thus begins a car company's odyssey with professional golf. It starts slowly, with advertising buys. Then, after "the big guy" and his minions are "special guests" at a PGA event (where they probably are giving away one of their cars or trucks that's floating magically in the water hazard on the 16th hole), the subject is broached about actually sponsoring *the whole damn shootin' match!* And as they wend their way back to headquarters, the grandeur of the program grows exponentially into test-drive incentives, promotional giveaways, even more ad buys, and before they or their ad agency knows it, a third of their total ad budget is being spent on golf.

And then it *really* gets interesting. One thing that even the most rational car executive goes gaga over and can't possibly resist is the actual *meeting* of a star on the tour. And better yet, actually getting to play a *private* round of golf with him! To the typical car executive who has made stops in every god-forsaken regional office around the country, and whose closest brush with celebrity was meeting the local weatherman with his kids once at the mall back in Iowa, playing a round of golf with Tiger or Ernie or Phil or Duval or whomever, is one of the best things to ever happen to him. At least that's what he admits to his wife. To his closest buddies and a few agency people, *it was the highlight of his life!* And what that usually translates to is a multi-million dollar, multi-year "personal services" contract with said golfer, the client's "new best friend."

After that, agencies just "duck and cover" as their client comes up with seemingly unlimited ways to "work my new friend Greg" (or Jack, or David, or Fred) or whomever into their advertising. The first stop is always their catalog or promotional programs, which is a convenient dumping ground for every lame-brained scheme (or scam) hatched by the client. It starts out simply. "Let's have 'Greg' stand by the vehicle" is all that's communicated. Then, before the shoot, the client wants to "do a little more" because, after all, he's now *going* to this lowly catalog shoot, and he will be playing another *private* round of golf with his new best friend after, so "can't you guys come up with something besides him standing next to the car?" (Understand, most clients will attend the occasional TV shoot, but if they're attending a catalog shoot, it's *only* because a celebrity is involved.)

So, the agency scrambles to work in "lifestyle" situations with the golfer, and if the golfer (or the golfer's management) is sharp, these situations become, amazingly enough, showcases for the golfer's personal line of clothes, balls, clubs or whatever else he has his name on.

And that's just the beginning.

Then, the client starts having the agency explore ways to work "his new best friend" into the print advertising. That, of course means more private rounds of golf and more meetings with the player's management so that their man is "portrayed properly." In effect, the player and his management now become sub-clients for the agency, always a lovely proposition. And then, the next logical step revolves around working the player into TV advertising, which usually means spots with inane "lifestyle" situations with the player, interwoven with golf action and vehicle driving shots. Sounds completely logical, right?

The net message of all this being – hmmmm – what *was* the message again?

All that appears to be accomplished with this is that the client gets to play private rounds of golf with "his new best friend." And the car company spends a *cajillion* dollars advertising to a bunch of white guys who probably either A. already work for a car company and have a company car, or B. are asleep on the couch, allegedly "watching" the tournament on TV (after playing their own round of golf that day, of course).

At that point, the company's agency is in complete turmoil. Any really good, community-based or new-wave experiential programs that have an actual chance of luring real live younger buyers to the brand have long since fallen by the wayside or gotten minimal amounts of spending. So that, ironically, because of golf's attraction to middle-aged white guys, nothing is done to turn around the fact that the company's owners and loyal buyers are aging, and even worse, dying off.

And of course, by then, the agency's entire creative department is ready to resign or strangle the client over some dispute about how "they weren't using his new best friend" properly, account people assigned to "golf duty" are busily schmoozing magazines about becoming media reps, and even some on the client side are quietly saying, "what are we doing?" And as soon as somebody starts "running the numbers" about what kind of impressions they're getting with their audience (and who that audience is exactly – a bunch of middle-aged white guy hackers who like to watch golf on TV), the whole thing starts to unravel.

Yes, I've seen it all over the years when it comes to the car companies' obsession with golf. Like the time we had to put Jack Nicklaus in the back of the Pontiac catalogs every year standing by a station wagon because he flew up once a year to play golf with GM executives at the local country club. Or the time a client renewed a million-dollar contract with a pro golfer without telling *anyone*, including his bosses, the people who worked for him, and needless to say, anyone at the agency, much to everyone's chagrin and dismay. And believe me, I could go on. Don't think this particular little "white ball affliction" is confined to the domestic car companies, either. The Japanese and Germans have fallen into the same trap.

But the car companies' never ending fascination with golf goes on, much to the delight of the PGA and much to the delight of your average star pro golfer, whose emotional involvement with his "new best friend" at whatever car company it is evaporates into thin air as soon as his G-550 goes "wheels up" at the local airport.

I have no idea when the car companies' infatuation with pro golf will end, or even wane just a little bit. Because as long as there are middle-aged white guys making the decisions, the money will keep pouring in like it grows on trees.

IMAGE MAKEOVER? THIS BUSINESS NEEDS AN ENEMA

Several years back – in the late summer of 1999, to be exact – then Ford Vice Chairman Peter J. Pestillo, speaking at Auto Conference '99 in Traverse City, Michigan, said that the automobile business "is on the brink of a devastating shortage of talent – on the plant floors, in our salaried ranks and at our dealerships."

He went on to say that "the perception is that auto manufacturing is a second-class industry," and that "we need to a better job of informing the outside world that our industry offers opportunities for *forward-thinkers*."

And then he topped it off by saying, "Today's workplaces need people who are flexible and adaptable, who have an intuitive ability to solve problems and work in teams, *who are independent, creative thinkers and can communicate effectively.*"

Well, which is it? Is it the ability to work in teams, or is it the independent, creative thinking? This comment just happened to nail this business right on the head, at least when it comes to recent Detroit car-making history.

The business/workplace environment in the "Detroit version" of the car business at the end of the '90s wasn't about independent, creative thinking at all. Not even close. Back then, the average car executive in this business woke up with a very short and concise agenda:

1. I must cover my ass from any and all possibilities of disaster, or looking bad.
2. I must make sure my boss either looks good to *his* boss because of information I gave him or something I did,

or at least *tell him* he looks good, even if I wasn't responsible for anything on that given day.

3. I must do what's minimally required to complete my
assigned tasks, with as little effort as possible. After all,
that's why I have assistants or, better yet, an ad agency,
to do my dirty work for me.

Note that the "I must reach deep down and come up with the
most creative solution for the tasks at hand today" point is mysteri-
ously missing.

Mr. Pestillo was either oblivious to the day-to-day working environment realities of his own company, or he had just returned from
some esoteric business course concocted by some "distinguished"
professor who hadn't seen the inside of a real live company since he
summer-interned at his dad's cardboard box factory 35 years ago.
Even worse, and heaven forbid, he may have just come back from a
personal, "laying of the hands" session with that living monument to
corporate stupidity and naiveté – Stephen Covey.

Except for a few, documented, brief fleeting moments of on-the-
street glory in this town (fill in your own list of the better vehicles to
come out in the last six years), it's a miracle that *any* vehicle escaped the
built-in labyrinth of the "Thank you, sir, may I have another" school of
day-to-day business back when it did its pirouette off the cliff.

Independent and creative forward thinkers? Back then, they were
missing in action in Detroit. That now thankfully defunct system
had been honed and manufactured by a long line of executives who
didn't have the first clue about what it took to do the right thing on
the job (except to engineer their promotions and stock options, of
course). I can count on both hands the cool and together people I
had as clients who were the genuine article in this business. That's
after nearly 25 years. The rest blur into a long litany of incompetent wimps, clueless empty suits, nasty double-crossers (with integrity levels that make some of the "stars" of The Best of The Jerry
Springer Show seem downright uplifting), manipulating weasels and
more flat-out losers than I care to remember.

My favorite game over the years? Try it for yourself in your given profession. Take the least favorite executive you can think of, and then think of what he or she would (or could) be doing if they hadn't stumbled on to their current positions. It was amazing what my agency friends and I came up with. There was one client I remember, painfully well, who we all agreed would have been hard-pressed to fulfill the attendant duties at a gas station, yet he was making pivotal decisions on how the company spent $400 million dollars of advertising money every year.

Another thing that Pestillo said in that now-famous speech was that "the auto industry has an image problem among so-called high-tech people." No shocker there.

The idea of an "image problem" gets at the very core of the fundamental problems of the way the Detroit auto companies conducted their day-to-day business back then. They didn't reward freethinkers at all. Rather, more often than not, they crushed them with a demotion and tagged them with the title of "troublemaker." That overused "team player" mantra in corporate America is a cover for "don't rock the boat and you'll go far"– and Detroit was the quintessential breeding ground for it. "March to a different drummer" in the Motor City back then and you would have been transferred to the Sioux Falls regional office so fast it would make your head spin.

Unfortunately, there are a lot of bright young kids out there coming out of school who know all about the way Detroit car companies *used* to conduct their business – and they're smart enough to know that they want absolutely nothing to do with it. And Detroit is having a terrible time convincing them that things have changed for the better.

The fact of the matter is that Mr. Pestillo got it all wrong when he said, "the *perception* is that auto manufacturing is a second-class industry." That is the *reality*, folks. The only way that the Detroit auto companies can even *begin* to think about informing the outside world that they are a haven for forward thinkers is to purge "the go-along-to-get-along" mentality and institute the kind of fundamental change that is necessary to develop a flourishing, vibrant, creative culture.

Until this happens, the car business in this town will forever be scrambling for talented people and chasing market share – and losing out to other industries that seem to operate just fine without the "duck-and-cover" school of doing business by intimidation.

THE "DEAL" ABOUT DETROIT

A lot of people who aren't close to this industry believe what's happening in Detroit is just a regional hiccup that won't have any effect on their lives, something that's just another filler story on the national news. Don't you believe it. This story is about the *real* cost to the nation's economy if Detroit continues its slide into oblivion and how it will affect every American – and not just those in the Rust Belt "flyover" states.

The adage used to be that one in seven jobs in this country is either directly or indirectly connected to the U.S. automobile industry. That figure has since been revised by some economists to be one in twelve to one in fourteen jobs, but needless to say, the writing is on the wall for this country's economy, and it's in the best interest for all of us to see GM, Ford and Chrysler survive. Ford and GM in particular are two of the most iconic companies in this country's history, and to see them struggling is a blow to everyone in this region. If their fortunes continue in a downward trajectory, it could be catastrophic to the U.S. economy overall.

I never relished writing about the blatant product and marketing missteps, the blind arrogance or the flat-out stupidity on Autoextremist.com because I knew that with the continued emergence of the European and Asian car makers and the correspondingly inexorable erosion of Detroit's market share that came with it – one day I would be writing about the decline and possible demise of Detroit as we know it. That day has come a lot sooner than even I thought it would.

PART THREE

SERIAL INCOMPETENCE – DETROIT'S TICKET TO OBLIVION

DETROIT'S BLUEPRINT FOR DISASTER

Designing, building and selling cars is one of the most complicated enterprises on the planet. It's filled with the potential for disaster at every critical juncture along the way. And many times, everything that can possibly go wrong – inevitably does. Why do some companies get it right and other companies consistently spin their wheels, wondering why their products are more popular with rental car fleets than with the public? Here are some of the sure-fire strategies for failure that Detroit has perfected over the years.

Don't Give Your R&D Staff A Big Enough Budget And Don't Allow Them To Be Creative. Companies that don't do their homework usually have trouble competing. Car companies that don't do their homework get buried. The companies that fund their R&D programs properly, hire good people and then encourage them to be creative are the ones that succeed. For most serious automotive companies, a "creative" research and development environment usually includes a serious racing program. Whether it's competing at the highest levels in a major racing series, or lending minds and bodies to more of a grass-roots effort, when you let your technical people out in the real world so they can see how things *really* work (or don't work at all), only positive things can happen. If a car company doesn't spend enough money on R&D and deprives their in-house technical community of outside stimulation, you don't get creative and inspirational "what ifs" – you get predictable "me too" solutions and safe answers. Car companies that chain their advanced engineering and technical people to the lab (and to their computers) get exactly what they ask for – cold, calculated, black-and-white thinking and predictable ideas. Honda learned this lesson very well and learned it a long, long time ago. They understand and embrace the creative R&D development process. Example? The engineers churning out brilliant solutions for their production cars today were the same ones working on their Formula 1 racing program a decade ago.

Don't Let Your Design Staff Do Its Job. There is no bigger turn-on in the world if you're a true car freak than to be given an advanced preview of an upcoming model at a car company's design staff offices. The security is palpable – you sense that if you stray a few feet beyond your assigned area you'll be shot – and the smell of the modeling clay is intoxicating. The first thing you start noticing are the wild drawings and things all over the designers' workstations: futuristic racecars, dramatic renditions of current models and blue-sky renderings of their pet vehicle concepts. And then you turn the corner and come face-to-face with the car that's supposed to reverse the company's lagging fortunes but is nothing more than a four-wheeled monument to mediocrity. What the hell happened? How do these people, with all of their obvious talent, deliver a vehicle that is so stunningly unappealing that it's almost incomprehensible?

Well, to begin with, for each new vehicle the designers are given a white paper or "deck" the size of a phone book, which includes brand positioning, target market info and painstaking research on the alleged "buyer" of this new vehicle – everything from demographic data and social tendencies to minutiae such as what toothpaste these people are likely to use and what TV shows they watch. This document is frighteningly narrow and relentlessly rigid, its message is "signed-off on" by the brand marketing people, and it is so etched in stone that it not only effectively kills the spirit of early design experimentation, but it also actually shortens the time given to blue-sky thinking altogether. It is the most frustrating thing you'll ever witness if you're the least bit into cars – and it was a specialty of the Detroit carmakers, up until only recently.

Don't Follow Your Gut – Just Research And Clinic Everything To Death Until Your New Product Bores The Public To Death. I've been to every kind of auto clinic and focus group imaginable, and they all start with the same flawed premise: *The majority of people invited already own the company's current model, and the rest are predisposed to buying that type of car.* And the results are heavily skewed with the weight of these people's comments. So, for instance, if you're a domestic "intender" (and you already own the current model of the vehicle in question) being brought in to see the upcoming version of that particular car, then your comments will be positively noted and given more weight than those of someone who is an import owner and who couldn't care less about domestic cars. For some domestic manufacturers, the priority *has* to be to sell their current owners first, because they know that the likelihood of actually "conquesting" customers from the imports is virtually nonexistent. And inevitably, the import "intender" thinks the new domestic car they're being exposed to is a piece of crap, to be blunt. I can't tell you how many times I've sat next to clients who will animatedly describe a research group as a "good" group. And what constitutes a "good" group in their minds? It's a group filled with domestic "intenders" and current owners of that client's particular vehicle who are so "gaga" about seeing the future version of their beloved sled (while getting $100 *and* free food!) that they can't say enough great things about it. And what do you think would constitute a "bad" group to these same clients? That would be a group consisting of import owners and "intenders" who have absolutely *nothing* good to say about the product under review, usually peppering their comments with bitingly accurate comments like "out of touch," "dated" or "I wouldn't buy one." I've even witnessed clients go so far as to order the moderator to cut one of these offending groups short and send them packing because they were so negative (and true).

Years ago, the domestic manufacturers (particularly GM) found out that *any* focus or research group in the state of California was so openly hostile to their products (except for trucks) that they abandoned doing serious research there altogether. Is it any wonder that

GM nearly went out of business in California when it came to selling passenger cars before cooler heads prevailed? Domestic car companies will even seek out areas of the country that are known hotbeds of domestic intenders in order to do their research – just to make sure they hear what they want to hear. I once suggested to a client that maybe we ought to send all of the groups home who are predisposed to buying the particular model we were testing and instead spend all of our time grilling the import intenders to find out exactly what they *don't* like about the product in detail. As you can imagine, the suggestion was scoffed at and met with blank stares. And so here we had these companies, making cajillion-dollar judgments based on the comments of people who already think their products are too cool for words anyway, blissfully ignoring the fact that there are millions of people out there driving imports who couldn't care less about what they're building, and who have no interest and absolutely no intention of giving them any serious consideration at all. What a way to expand your markets, huh?

Now, I'm not suggesting we go back to the bad old days when manufacturers had the attitude of "screw 'em – they'll buy what we make," but product testing and research is just another tool, no more, no less. Truly breakthrough products will *never* come out of a focus group or a clinic. If Bob Lutz and Company had waited for some kernel of info from a research group hinting that there might be interest in a car like the Pontiac Solstice, it never would have been built. Cars like the Solstice (and countless other "hit" vehicles you can think of) simply wouldn't exist if they had been left to the typical car company research process. It takes guts, gumption and *real car people* with a genuine feel for what's going on to bring out breakthrough products that are well ahead of the curve.

Don't Trust Your Dealers' Judgment, Especially When It Comes To His Or Her Local Market. The age-old battle between car companies and their dealers has been going on since Day One. From the car companies' perspective, dealers should be thankful that they're given any products to sell at all, that if it weren't for the car companies, most of them (the dealers) would be out pounding sand somewhere. According to the car companies, dealers should shut up, do what they're told and be grateful that they're given such "stellar" vehicles to sell. After all, a good bunch of them became multi-millionaires thanks to the car companies anyway.

From the dealers' perspective, car companies are stocked with incompetent carpetbaggers who have never had a real job in their lives and who have no clue what it's like to deal with a legitimate profit/loss statement or in-your-face consumers who aren't exactly enthralled with the intermittent quality of their new BelchFire 8. Car companies make stupid decisions that cost the dealers money, they make dealers take the brunt for flawed products and poor sales strategies, and they generally only really care about dealer problems in the first few months of a new executive sales director's reign "down at the corporation." Not exactly a match made in heaven, is it?

Car companies that abuse their dealers usually get *exactly* what they ask for. If you keep them in the dark about upcoming product strategies, ignore their input, treat them like incompetent fools who couldn't possibly understand their local market as well as "headquarters" does and generally just take them for granted, the next time you really, *desperately* need their help – they might just tell you to go fly a kite. When things go wrong for a car company, you can bet the relationship with their dealers is either deteriorating or has already gone bad.

Don't Treat Your Ad Agency Like A True "Marketing Partner," Just Treat It Like Another Supplier. The biggest joke in Detroit is how the car companies started calling their ad agencies "marketing partners" years ago, as if the relationship was some sort of "touchy-feely" lovefest just bursting with good times, brand "symmetry" and breakthrough creative ideas that ultimately benefited both parties. That certainly sounds good on paper, but it is about as far from reality as you can get. Agencies are "marketing partners" for their clients as long as everything is all sweetness and light with the car company's fortunes, which is never for very long, by the way. The moment those fortunes turn, watch out. The asshole-buddy "off-site" meetings with the faux camaraderie and euphoric bonding sessions are the first things to go. Then, the client's "enlightened" attitude and his or her receptiveness to new creative ideas go next. Then, "Take your time, we want it to be good" becomes "I want it yesterday." Then, "We're stepping up to the plate on this one, just tell us how much you need" becomes "It costs too damn much." Then, "It makes me feel uncomfortable, so that means it must be good, right?" becomes "I don't give a shit whether you think it's breakthrough or not, I just don't like it." Then, "We want you guys to reach for the stars, we want you to be successful, we want to see our agency win some awards" becomes "Don't tell me about art, goddamnit – we need to move some iron!" Which is then followed by a complete breakdown of civility and professionalism.

And guess what? Those "sacred relationships" with their trusted "marketing partners" are completely gone. Come to think about it, that's exactly the way a "bad" car company treats the rest of their suppliers, isn't it? There's an old axiom in advertising that clients ultimately get the kind of advertising they deserve. And when you're doing things wrong as a car company, it's very, very true.

The next point may be a no-brainer but it's probably where all of the bad juju in the car "biz" got started to begin with, and there was no greater living, breathing example of this than General Motors in its brand management heyday in the mid-to-late '90s...

Don't Promote A "Car Freak" Culture, Just Let Newly Minted "B-School" Foot Soldiers Run Wild. One thing that car company executives forget along the way to pleasing their shareholders and increasing the size of their year-end bonuses is that *everything begins and ends with the product.* You could gather all the top MBAs and P&G brand marketing "experts" in the world and unleash them on the car business, and you still wouldn't be able to make a load of shit look like Shinola. You can strategize and analyze until the cows come home, but if the executives ultimately making the decisions don't have a basic "feel" for what makes cars or trucks inherently appealing to people, then they will bring products to market that are totally out of touch. This is *exactly* what happened to General Motors at the height of the John Smale regime, which was nothing but a glorified, transplanted P&G "love-in" that did nothing but promote ill-equipped people into positions that they had no business being in and then having these same people make crucial product decisions with absolutely no clue as to what they were doing or why they were doing it. The only things these so-called brand marketing "experts" brought to the party were impressive resumes. To top it all off, they actually prided themselves on the fact that they *weren't* "car people," that they were ultimately smarter than "car people" because they could make their decisions in a cold, analytical way based on rea- soned, logical and proven P&G brand marketing methods.

It was an unmitigated disaster.

The amazing thing about GM is that it took years for them to admit the fact that they had systematically destroyed any vestiges of a "car freak" culture. Sure, there were *always* pockets of irrational exuberance within GM, which against all odds *did* bring excellent cars and trucks to the marketplace. But they did it *in spite* of the system, not because of it. And this was sad, because at one point in this was a company populated with some of the most legendary car freaks in the business.

When there's a cultural void at the top in the car business, things usually go wrong. And even though there might be intermit- tent "home-run" products, the net-net of all of this is that products brought to market in a dumbed-down, B-school-polluted environ- ment are inevitably, and by and large, mediocre. Reliable and safe maybe, but vehicles that generate about as much excitement and "buzz" as the first quarter of a typical NBA game.

Finally, Whatever You Do, Don't Let The "Car Guys" Have Their Say. There is an obligatory descriptor that's been around the car business for as long as anyone can remember that categorizes a car executive, man *or* woman, as a "car guy." Now in *some* car com- panies, it's someone who shows up at a press gathering or a cheesy auto show product intro with either a short leather jacket or one of the company's racing team jackets on. This person makes a few broad-based (and heavily scripted) pronouncements about "performance," "youth marketing" and "edgy appeal," and then throws out a few comments to indicate that he or she is "hip" to what's happenin' out "there" on the street – when in fact they have no clue as to what they're talking about or why they're saying it. Some misguided PR-type will term that person a "car guy" and that's the end of it. From then on, that person has some sort of borrowed interest "car guy aura" attached to them that they don't deserve in the least. These phony "car guys" usually end up destroying a car company's momentum by playing politics and trying to do things with mirrors instead of having a gut feel for the nuts and bolts of the business. These people populate every car company, but it's when they fall through the cracks and fail upward that the real damage is done.

With other car companies (at least the ones that have their shit together), *everybody* is a "car guy." From the entry-level plebe to the person at the top, the company eats, breathes and sleeps car stuff, all day, all the time. It's not something you can manufacture, and it's not something you can approximate with a few well-meaning MBAs in borrowed corporate racing team jackets. It has to be part of the very fabric and culture of the company, something that never has to be said by anyone but rather shows up in the kinds of products it actually brings to the street. You can pretty much name the companies right now that have the car freaks in control rather than the B-school refugees, can't you?

Here's a little story to demonstrate what I mean. Ed Cole, one of the fathers of the legendary Chevrolet "small-block" V8 and one of the industry's most talented and respected engineers, ended up being the head of General Motors at the end of the '60s. Cole was heavily enamored with developing a sophisticated version of the Wankel rotary engine for GM passenger cars. He assigned a crack engineering team to the project and asked them to let him know when they were ready to have him test-drive their handiwork. One day, when they thought they were ready, they invited "Mr. Cole" out to the Milford Proving Grounds so he could evaluate their progress. For the next several hours, he literally drove the wheels off of the prototypes (one engineer used the expression "drove the living shit out of 'em"), running them harder than anyone had up to that point, and when he was finished, he handed them a list of "things to do" that was twice as long as what they started with. He left a bunch of young engineers with their mouths open in his wake, but he had made his point. *That*, believe it or not, was General Motors at the end of its previous heyday. A company with the biggest "car guy" in the business at the helm. A company that was as formidable a competitor as you could possibly imagine in design, engineering and market savvy. A company that was actually worried about having *too much* market share and was afraid of attracting "break up GM" talk from within the U.S. Government!

Hard to believe, isn't it?

BENCHMARKING: THE INSIDIOUS DETROIT DISEASE

When I'm asked if there's just one thing that has contributed to the decline of the Detroit-based car companies over the years, my answer is always "no" – because there are many, many things that have contributed to Detroit's lack of competitiveness and alarming loss of market share. But on the list of things that have contributed to Detroit's continuing downward spiral I reserve particular ire for the insidious habit of product benchmarking. I have observed up close over the years, as well-meaning executives, engineers, designers, and marketing and advertising people have become caught up in this fool's errand – which amounts to nothing more than chasing a moving target – and which has resulted in putting the Detroit-based car companies further and further behind the eight ball with each passing model year.

Benchmarking occurs when a manufacturer aims all of its resources and talent at meeting its competition head-on in a furious effort to gain a competitive foothold in a segment. They dissect every last inch of their competitors' vehicles, they find out what suppliers are used, how they do things, where they spend their money, and, after all of that investment in time, energy and effort, they focus all of their energies on meeting or beating that competitive vehicle in terms of performance, design, ride and handling, fit and finish, interior materials, etc., etc., etc.

But while that manufacturer was furiously trying to capture their competitor's "magic in a bottle" – that competitor had already gone on to develop an all-new version of their benchmark. And the result of the time, effort and money spent on benchmarking by that manufacturer trying to catch its competition? A perfectly competitive vehicle to *last year's* segment leader.

Sounds deceptively simple, doesn't it? Well, believe me, benchmarking has been a plague in Detroit ever since the emergence of the Japanese and German manufacturers in this market.

I can't tell you how many ride and drives I've been on where executives have gotten up and told the assembled media (who were still choking down their complimentary breakfasts, of course) that "these new BelchFire 8s are equal to or better than the existing and acknowledged industry standard in that segment in every way," or words to that effect. And then these magnificent new machines would be trotted out for the media to drive, complete with the competition's vehicles there to drive back-to-back, so that you could see for yourself that these new BelchFire 8s were indeed, really something special. Except that, inevitably, the competitive vehicles were "cherry-picked" to reflect option configurations that no one ever ordered, so that they would surely fall short of the newer cars.

The deeper problem was that most of these same journalists had just come from another media preview, where they in fact drove an all-new version of the competitive vehicle in question. The comparison was then painfully obvious for all to see – and the new BelchFire 8 was flagrantly obsolete before it even hit the showroom.

This went on all through the '80s and '90s like clockwork. Detroit would trot out its latest offerings – benchmarked in a hermetically sealed vacuum, free of original thinking and inner inspiration – and they would land with a thud (except for a few shining exceptions) on the assembled media and a subsequently underwhelmed public. Do this long enough, and you'll surely get behind and never be able to catch up – and the denizens of corporate Detroit were absolute masters at it. They ended up releasing a series of mind-numbingly uninspired, "me-too" products that were supposed to be "as good if not better!" than their European and Asian competitors, but instead were monuments to mediocrity and lowest-common-denominator thinking.

I recall one memorable product ride and drive in the great South-west, where we spent a couple of days reveling (allegedly) in a certain manufacturer's latest offering for a mid-size car. We were immersed in presentations that boasted how the new "great hope" from this particular manufacturer would finally turn the tide back in Detroit's favor and beat their Asian competitors at their own game. They showed us all of the numbers that clearly played up their advantages (More performance! Quieter! Better Fit and Finish! Roomier! Better Handling!), and then they let us drive the cars. They of course included competitive vehicles, which were supposed to show just how far this manufacturer had come and just how good their new mid-size challenger was.

The only problem was that these new vehicles weren't any better than the vehicles they were aiming at. Yes, there were glimmers of competitiveness, but the net effect of the cars was that they were designed with a mixture of ingredients and targeted numbers – not from a cohesive philosophy and a focused point of view. And to top it all off, the competitive car that they expended all of their time and energy to beat? The all-new version of it was being previewed to the media – three weeks from that exact date.

The bottom line is that Detroit careened its way through the '80s and '90s, benchmarking their way to oblivion. With each successive model introduction, Detroit kept falling further and further behind, while their competitors poured it on with new thinking and new products that captured the hearts and minds of the American driving public. Yes, there were exceptions, as Detroit kept its vise grip on the light-truck market. But even that has begun to slip away in the New Age of Fuel Economy.

The concept of benchmarking is far from dead, unfortunately. Spend enough time in the halls of Chrysler, Ford and GM, and you will inevitably hear the phrase, "Audi has the best interiors, we're going after that level." Or, "BMW has that elusive 'feel' we're looking for." And this is exactly where it starts to go wrong for Detroit. Why does inspiration for a vehicle's interior design or "feel" always have to come from another manufacturer? Where is the original, visionary thinking in that? Yes, of course, you have to acknowledge who's considered "best in industry" – at this point in time, you'd be foolish not to. But then at that critical point, the manufacturer must put that aside, walk away – and then go its own way in order to ultimately succeed.

Car companies that do their thinking in a vacuum and fail to stretch the existing envelope end up bringing "me-too" products to the street that are out of touch and obsolete before they even hit the showroom. They may be competent and reliable, but they're inevitably devoid of character and personality. And then car company executives are left scratching their heads and wondering why their new vehicles end up populating rental fleets before their first birthday.

The interesting thing that's happening is that Detroit is finally rediscovering one of the axioms that fueled this business from the very beginning. And that is that there is no substitute for an original idea, creative thinking or a willingness to take risks. Cars like the original Corvette Stingray, the Mustang, the first Buick Riviera and the original Pontiac GTO (just to name a few) best exemplified that.

Today's offerings like the Ford Mustang and Fusion, the Buick Enclave, the Chevrolet Corvette, the Cadillac CTS, the Saturn Sky and Chevrolet Malibu are the latest and greatest examples of that kind of thinking. They shine because they come from visionary thinking that originated from within. Yes, these companies acknowledged their competition, but then they captured what *they* wanted to do instead of blindingly mimicking their competitors.

Great cars get built because of vision, creativity and old-fashioned guts. And fortunately, the aforementioned cars are only the tip of the iceberg as Detroit continues to unleash a torrent of new vehicles that have the distinct air about them of "marching to a different drummer."

Will it be enough to stem the tide? We'll see.

But at this point, I would settle for the more modest goal of just stopping Detroit's market share erosion – and not hearing the term benchmarking ever again.

MEDIOCRITY IS *NOT* BLISS
– IT'S JUST MEDIOCRE

After benchmarking, the most loathsome term in this business is *"engineering to the lowest common denominator,"* but it's difficult for the casual observer to really understand what it means, exactly. Quite simply, it means that a purchasing decision is made – with the tacit approval of the engineering department – to spec a part on a vehicle that is "marginally acceptable" for the task at hand. Whether it's a tire, a suspension piece, the overall capability of a braking system or whatever else you can think of, it means that an acceptable margin of safety or performance is agreed upon (based on vehicle use, class of vehicle, cost, etc.) and then built in. It's a subtle balancing act between cost and performance, and too often in the past vehicle manufacturers have erred on the side of merely "adequate."

To give you a specific example, braking systems on light trucks were notoriously *inadequate* for years. It was common to make decisions about those systems based on what was "adequate" for typical use, instead of what was needed out in the real world. But with more and more people using trucks for daily commuting, it was obvious to many that "adequate" wasn't going to cut it anymore. When GM completely redesigned their full-size pickups recently, they paid particular attention to the braking system – giving it a huge upgrade in feel and a corresponding leap in overall performance. It was long overdue.

"Engineering to the lowest common denominator" is one of the most despicable practices in the entire automotive industry. And it is something that is deeply rooted in the purchasing-driven, profit-oriented "culture" of the American automotive business. I have heard the argument for years (from serious-minded engineers, no less) that goes something like this: "With our roads and our typically lower speed limits, we just don't need all that stuff that you enthusiasts keep demanding. It just adds unnecessary cost to the vehicle."

Oh, really?

It's that attitude that has allowed the German manufacturers to run roughshod over their American luxury car competitors. I remember sitting in car company conference rooms in the late '90s and hearing engineers spout off about how the Germans were "masters of overkill" in the way they design their cars. That people are stupid for "buying into the hype."

What does it all mean? For instance, does the typical Mercedes-Benz or BMW owner in L.A., who will never drive his or her car over 85mph for the entire time they own the car, really need all the performance capability that machine has built into it? I would argue that yes, in fact, they do. For the one time that person decides to drive his or her car to Santa Barbara for the weekend, and for all the possible "worst-case" scenarios that could ensue out on the open road, its built-in performance and safety margins are worth every dime. Or, it might just prove its worth on the 405, in a simple fender bender. The fact is that the Germans, who have traditionally understood and appreciated high-performance capability, also understand the scope of the safety margins needed to go along with that performance capability – not just to "adequately" compensate for things, but to actually make it part of the overall performance equation. And obviously the American consumer buys into the calculated marketing that goes with that too.

"Engineering to the lowest common denominator" is a practice that many would argue is on the wane in the U.S. car industry (and there are certainly some excellent American cars being made right now that seem to point to that fact), but the fact remains that there are pockets of stupidity still operating unfettered in certain segments of these companies.

I humbly suggest that the following be taped to every engineer's desk in the car business:

1. Cost should never be the single deciding factor in a part or a system. Only *after* quality, performance, reliability and safety are factored in should a "number" be formulated.

2. Never spec tires for a vehicle that are simply "marginal." If there is a "worst-case" scenario, rest assured that it *will* happen at some point. This isn't a purchasing decision; it's a *life* decision.

3. "Affordable" transportation should never mean cheap tires, underperforming brakes or "adequate" anything. Tell the statisticians to sit down and shut up, and then think about it this way: Would you want someone you love driving around in a vehicle with "adequate" brakes or tires?

4. The last time I checked, a car company's purchasing department should be involved in getting the best deal for the company only *after* the engineers have signed off on what they feel is necessary to do the job properly, with all possibilities factored in. It's obvious to a lot of people that that hasn't necessarily been the case in the past.

5. Mediocrity is *not* bliss or something to aspire to. It's just mediocre.

The fact remains that "engineering to the lowest common denominator" is a cancer, a plague and a practice that simply must be terminated. "Adequate" should never, *ever* be good enough. And in order to purge this kind of thinking from a car company, the attitude must start changing right from the top.

To put a finer point on things, why is it that when you sit in a BMW, Mercedes, Porsche, or Audi, etc., no matter what the price point, there are consistencies in what you're looking at? That there seems to be a certain "way" that they go about doing things? It's because there is a clear-cut, active and forceful design and engineering philosophy at work in those companies. *It's just the way they believe things should be done.* And that's just with the things you can see, feel and touch. That consistency extends throughout the machine you're sitting in.

American car companies? They're all over the map. When it's a "performance-oriented" vehicle, you usually see signs of intelligent life everywhere – even in a particularly well-thought-out truck interior. But consistency? Not nearly enough to mention. The "affordable" cars always seem to have been sick the day they doled out engineering "philosophy." That's because there still isn't a consistent design/engineering philosophy at work in these companies, even though they would vehemently insist that I'm wrong. Well, I guess I'm wrong with one company in particular – GM's interior design philosophy does seem to have progressed beyond the concept of "Sea of Gray" – I'll give them that.

The bottom line? Good enough isn't good enough anymore.

And this just in: It *never* was.

IN THIS "AGE OF ENTITLEMENT" WE ALL GET SCREWED

Imagine, for a moment, that you're the head of an advertising agency with a long history with one car company. The relationship has had its ups and downs over the years, but for the most part, it has been a mutually beneficial and respectful one for both parties. Your agency does excellent work for them, including providing myriad support services, and they reward your agency handsomely because of it. Even with the cost-cutting maneuvers that have slammed your fee structure and the business in general in recent years, the relationship has held up strong.

But lately, you've noticed how things have started to change – drastically.

There's a new breed of marketing manager let loose at the client, people with no background in the car business, with not even a whiff of gasoline in their veins – and very proud of that fact too. They are arrogant, insensitive and rude, whether it's to a junior account executive/gofer or to one of your most trusted senior executives. They are abusive in meetings, make ridiculous demands and expect the agency to not only bend over backwards, but also to just do things "gratis" for them because of their belt-tightening efforts. But that's not all. There's a mercenary aspect about these people that you're just not familiar with. You hear about it first as it filters up through your senior people – about how one of the new clients demanded a huge effort on a very small piece of collateral business – and then at the last minute, not only awarded the job to another agency, but took your agency's ideas and had the new agency use them. And rather than this being an isolated incident, the problem becomes more and more common. Maybe not resulting in the work going somewhere else, but considerable time, effort and energy are being expended to appease this new breed of so-called "manager."

So you start to poke around. And you begin to realize that these new people are basically operating unchecked, spurred on by "instant success" dreams and a new hierarchy at the client that not only just doesn't care, but that is actually setting the tone. You hear little off-the-cuff remarks like, "That's just the way it is now" or, "It's a new day" or, "Get used to it," or, "You guys just need to start thinking outside the box more." But you also know this isn't the business passing you by, either. Because these people have about as much business evaluating advertising as a typical NFL scout has in evaluating candidates for The National Ballet Company.

No, it's something else – something that feels much more ominous.

But you don't have time to dwell on all of this because you've been asked to pitch on a new piece of business for your client, a new truck that will be launched in the near future. So, you shift your troops into high gear and have your best people work day and night to craft the finest pitch in the agency's history. Then, presentation day comes, and you knock their socks off. You're proud as hell of your agency, and you lead a low-key "thank you" celebration for everyone. And it's one of those days that you still feel good about being in the business...

The next day, you're notified that it's between your agency and a new, upstart agency that was formed by three "hot" creative executives who did award-winning work for a "dot com" brand before they went on their own. All right, you're thinking, we're still in it, this is good. Then, the next day, you take a call from your client, and he informs you that the marketing/advertising manager for this new division is coming over from the very same company/account that the creatives from the competing shop worked on. And that this person will be involved in the final decision and that "it's still very much a jump ball." You feign that everything is fine, and you exchange pleasantries and say how you'll look forward to working with them, but as soon as you hang up – you smell a rat.

And then two weeks later, the roof caves in.

Instead of hearing it from your client, you're informed by a reporter for the local newspaper that you didn't win the jump ball. And then you realize that you've been had. You've just spent a couple hundred thousand dollars in expenses and people hours on a project that consumed your agency to the detriment of everything else – and it was all a set up, all just window dressing. The decision had nothing to do with "out-of-the-box" thinking at all. It was nothing but an old-fashioned backroom political deal, and you were flat-out misled from the very beginning. You take the call from your client and act like you didn't already know the news. You don't miss a beat and say, "It's just another day in advertising," and you clench your teeth and say cheerily, "We'll look forward to the next one." And then, while saying "how great you and your people are," your client has the nerve to say, "As a matter of fact, we're going to use most of your strategies because they clearly were the best – and it will give us a leg up on the task at hand." You sit stunned for a moment, exchange more conversation-ending pleasantries and then you hang up the phone. You walk out the door at 11:30 and don't come back. You call your right-hand person from your car and inform her of the decision, and you drive home in a daze.

Should we be shocked? Oh hell, no. This little fable actually happened. McCann-Erickson, GM's lead corporate agency and also the agency of record for the Buick account at the time, was the ad agency that participated in a pitch for GM's Hummer account against an upstart ad agency named Modernista. The Modernista agency was formed by a trio of creative executives who had left the Arnold agency, where they had worked on the VW account at the time. The new executive hired by GM to lead marketing on the Hummer? She was a woman by the name of Liz Vanzura, who coincidentally just so happened to have been VW's advertising director – where she had worked with the trio of creatives as their client on the VW account. GM dragged McCann into the Hummer pitch whereupon McCann came up with the definitive strategy for the brand. But the die was cast the moment Liz Vanzura was hired for the Hummer advertising job – and GM burned McCann by misleading them into thinking that they had a real shot at the business. Just another beautiful day in advertising on a car account in the Motor City.

McCann would later lose both the GM Corporate (to Deutsch/LA) and Buick advertising accounts, as GM "consolidated" its business with Leo Burnett – a controversial decision, to say the least. It was one thing to consolidate the "behind the curtain" business operations of three divisions like GM had done with Buick-Pontiac-GMC, because that makes all the sense in the world, especially since no one at GM seems to be able to come to grips with this "too many models, too many divisions, too many dealers" thing. But consolidating your advertising accounts with one ad agency to mirror the divisional business structure? Not so much.

GM marketers pulled the Buick account from McCann Erickson and the GMC account from Lowe, New York (both Interpublic agencies) and gave them to Publicis Groupe's Leo Burnett Detroit without a review (Burnett already has Pontiac) effective October 1, 2007. And GM did this because…why, exactly? Ironically, Leo Burnett Detroit was the same agency that wasn't good enough to do Cadillac just a little over a year and a half earlier – and now it was good enough to handle *three* GM brands? Wow, I'd certify that as some sort of miraculous recovery, or else there was a potent gaseous version of delusional thinking being pumped through the HVAC vents at GM headquarters.

What was wrong with this picture? It's not as if Leo Burnett Detroit had exactly distinguished itself with any rock 'em, sock 'em creative for Pontiac. As a matter of fact, Pontiac had had the *most* mediocre creative – bordering on the completely irrelevant – of any GM division for the last several years. They latched on to one visual gimmick three years ago and beat that to death, managing to make an art form out of not lighting the cars so as to prevent anyone from actually seeing them. On the other hand, maybe that *was* genius – after all, if you have nothing to show except for the Solstice, why not? And then Pontiac marketers fell head-first into Second Life, which was fine, man – as The Dude might say – but what did that do for the brand, exactly, other than to guarantee that the Pontiac marketing brain trust got invited to join lots of advertising industry panels to talk about how to become a "hip" marketer?

This was an ill-advised, bush-league bullshit, bean-counting-oriented move on GM marketing's part, plain and simple. Burnett pitched a low-ball offer to handle the business that GM just couldn't refuse – end of story. Because if it had anything to do with the actual quality of the work, Leo Burnett Detroit would have been consoli-dated *out* of the GM agency mix a long time ago. And at the end of the day, it's supposed to be all about the work, isn't it? Uh, well, not in this case, apparently. That old advertising adage about clients ulti-mately getting exactly the kind of advertising they deserve? Transla-tion for GM marketers? Not good.

This episode was just the latest example in a long line of classic Detroit screw jobs as automobile company ad agencies (and auto company suppliers) can attest to and know so painfully all too well. Anyone who makes a living in this town, whether it's at an ad agency or at one of the huge mega-suppliers, is unfortunately intimately familiar with this kind of treatment. You can carve out the exact same scenario for every parts supplier in town too. They've all been through it. In their case, it goes something like this: get beat up relentlessly on your price, whittle your quote down to the bone – to the point that it's literally not even worth it to do it – and then watch as the client not only awards the job to a competing supplier, but hands over your concept/technology/design to your competitor.

Does any one Detroit carmaker have the market cornered in this regard? No, not by any means, because they all conduct themselves in exactly the same manner when given the opportunity. It's just nothing but "business as usual" in the Motor City. These companies throw around the term "partnership" with their agencies, suppliers and dealers, but no one ever really believes it. Ask any ad agency or parts supplier executive how many times in the past their company has contributed ideas, strategies, products or creative solutions to their long-term clients at the car companies – only to see these com-panies take their ideas and then turn around and award the business to someone else – and you will see grown men and women who are normally mild-mannered citizens display the kind of genuine rage and frustration only reserved for one of Joe Pesci's characters in *Good-Fellas* or *Casino*. Add to this the fact that they might find out that their client *knowingly* had already "pre-made" their decision, but were willing to see their so-called marketing or manufacturing "partners" expend vast quantities of time, people power, money and effort on their behalf and then turn around and suck the very life (and ideas) out of them at their whim, and you have a bunch of people who would make the term "going postal" seem charmingly quaint.

What have we learned from all of this, as Jerry Springer might say? What we can learn is that when it comes to plagiarizing ideas or cutting costs, the Detroit car companies will stop at nothing to get what they want and outrageously enough, actually feel that they're *entitled* to whatever it is they want.

Oh, how I have grown to *loathe* that word as it applies in Detroit as well as in modern day American society. It's everywhere. And we've all heard it: I'm *entitled* to this. We're *entitled* to that.

For example: "I was minding my own business driving 90mph in my SUV talking on my cell phone and drinking scalding hot coffee while steering with my knees when this giant semi truck appeared from nowhere and forced me off the road and then I rolled over fourteen times, and oh, yeah, I'm sure my tires came apart before that so I'm gonna get Geoffrey Fieger and sue the car company, the tire company, the company who paved the road and the trucking company and anything and everything that moves because I'm *entitled* to get as much money as I possibly can out of you."

Or this: "Yeah, you gave me a scholarship to play football and that was nice and everything and I know you're the coach but I don't like to be yelled at when I screw up and all you do is yell at me so I'm gonna call my mom and we're gonna get a lawyer and we're gonna sue you and the university for a whole bunch of money because I'm *entitled*."

Or how about this: "Let's make one thing crystal clear here – I'm your goddamn client and if it weren't for me you'd be selling newspapers out on Woodward Avenue and your kids would be models for UNICEF ads and if I want you to make a nickel instead of a dollar or I want to put you though a glorified dog-and-pony show knowing full well that there isn't a slim chance in Hell of you ever getting the business that's just too damn bad, and oh, yeah, by the way, if you do happen to come up with anything that's actually worth a shit I will take it and do whatever I want with it because I'm *entitled* to it and don't you ever forget it."

Yeah, it's business as usual in the Motor City, or "The Big Ugly" as we sometimes affectionately like to call it, and no one ever said it had anything to do with honesty, integrity or common sense.

I'm sure that when the "brainiacs" down at the RenCen and over in Dearborn and out in Auburn Hills read this, they'll choke on their cornflakes and Starbucks.

After all, they're *entitled*.

ACCOUNTABILITY? IN THE MOTOR CITY?

Late fall is usually a time of reflection for most people. The withering of the late summer foliage, the leaves bursting in one last defiant splash of color before floating silently to the ground. Apple cider. Football. Crisp days and chilly nights. But in the car business, especially in Detroit, it means time for the car companies to assign blame for all their missteps, boondoggles, mistakes and bad management decisions during the year.

It's a simple formula really, and it goes like this: Dumb Decisions + Corporate Boondoggles + Bad Management x Short Sightedness = Uh-oh, we gotta make some cuts to pull our asses out of the fire on these year-end numbers! Now!

No one plays the blame game better than the Detroit-based auto companies. They've taken the ritual to a higher art form. Bumbling executives who made horrific judgment calls back in May become artful dodgers who deftly slide blame off to anyone they can, which inevitably leads to a supplier in most cases. There's nothing mentioned about the boondoggle media event orchestrated in some far-away exotic place that cost $3 million, or the dim-bulb media expenditure that turned out to be an embarrassingly expensive flop, or the incentive-mad marketing strategy that sucked the profitability out of the entire year. Nah, not a chance. Someone else will get blamed one way or the other. After all, accountability is a concept in short supply in the Motor City.

The target for all of this blame from the car companies is a long list of the usual suspects: There are always the money-grubbing suppliers (who are already scraping by on such absurd profit margins that it would even raise eyebrows at Wal-Mart headquarters). There are the dealers, of course. "Oh, why not?" seems to be the prevailing attitude from the manufacturers. After all, didn't we help put them in business and allow them to make a ton of money thanks to us? Or how about the ad agencies? There's a perennial whipping-boy target. After all, if it weren't for us, they'd all be out on the street, and besides, they make too much money anyway (of course, even though ad agency fees have been sliced to the bone, the car companies still demand "perks" from their agencies whenever they can get them, and agencies have to deal with constant incompetent management "guidance" from ill-equipped car company "suits" for their troubles too).

Yes, with the car companies, it's always something or someone in the fall: It's our competition, it's the Asians, it's the economy, it's Katrina, it's the lousy stock market, it's those idiots in Washington, it's the suppliers, it's our stupid incentive-happy sales environment, it's our thankless dealers, it's our whining ad agency and on and on and on...

What you'll never hear: It's our basic lack of planning, our dim-bulb marketing, our frightfully lame styling, our incompetent "executives," our bad product decisions, our bloated and cumbersome bureaucracy, our total lack of vision and foresight, our clinging to out-of-date attitudes, our continued arrogance, our relentless stupidity, etc., etc., etc.

When Detroit gets on the cost-cutting bandwagon, everybody pays. Except for the car companies themselves.

Accountability? You must be joking, right?

JUST HOW MUCH LONGER CAN DETROIT EXTRACT BLOOD FROM A STONE?

The renaissance of Detroit – what's left of the Not-so-Big Three, or as Toyota-istas like to refer to it, the "Detroit Three" – continues. Or does it? Yes, the new product is coming on strong from Chrysler, Ford and GM, and the next 24 to 36 months will be the closest thing they'll get to a total product revolution in this decade. And with new designs bordering on the spectacular, and the engineering substance underneath undeniably bristling with genuine vision and excellence in some cases, there is reason to be cautiously optimistic about Detroit's prospects. But *how* Detroit is getting there is an issue that just won't go away.

Detroit continues to operate under the assumption that suppliers will somehow "make do" as it continues to extricate more cost cuts on top of the brutal cost cuts that have already been enacted over the last several years. In what clearly amounts to a strategy of intimidation based on fear, Detroit is trying to fuel its return to profitability on the backs of its suppliers. And in the course of doing so, they're setting into motion a process of erosion that threatens to hollow out the guts of its recovery, so that all that will be left will be an outer structure of limited success – one in critical danger of crumbling from within at a moment's notice.

Car company executives will argue convincingly that forcing the absurdly low profit margins (or in some cases negative profit margins with the promise to suppliers of being awarded more business "down the road") is the only way Detroit will be able to ensure its survival – and that suppliers must take the hit and suck it up in order for the "greater good" of getting the Motor City back in the game. But when suppliers are going under at an alarming rate, and even the largest supplier conglomerates are starting to question how much longer the whole "game" can continue – talk of the "greater good" of the industry doesn't carry much weight.

It would be easy for the suppliers to buy into the notion of taking one for the "team" – if the team in question demonstrated a modicum of understanding as to what they're doing and why. Instead, Detroit has created a mindset in its engineers and purchasers that begins with the basic premise that they're not responsible for their predicament in the least. That Detroit's long, 35-year slide into mediocrity was not *their* fault and that accountability for their actions, past and present, will never be a topic for discussion as they go forward. As a result, suppliers will do what's asked, "or else."

Now, the manufacturer-supplier relationship (at least in this town) historically would never be mistaken for a hand-holding, touchy-feely, skip-through-the-morning-dew kind of a deal. No, it has always been a ball-busting, at times flat-out adversarial standoff that has left little room for pleasantries or for the weak of stomach, for that matter. But with the Detroit-based manufacturers having successfully instilled this attitude of no accountability in their robot-like minions assigned to the task of finding cost "efficiencies" – the suppliers are finding themselves in an untenable position.

There are literally thousands upon thousands of examples out there in today's cutthroat manufacturer-supplier environment, and I'm not going to attempt to go into them, but the net-net of all of this is that Detroit is trying to shortcut its way to profitability before their competitive new products hit the street – by having the supplier community take the hits.

This doesn't exactly foster a notion of trust or a feeling of partnership between the two parties, as one might imagine.

But Detroit is continuing on its path of more and deeper cuts in its quest to gain even more efficiencies, with little attempt at building partnerships with suppliers except in the cases when they just can't get the job done without them. And even then it's done with a grudging acknowledgment instead of a sense of appreciation.

In the midst of all of these maneuverings is the reality that the manufacturers are looking to China as the Holy Grail for reduced supplier costs, and they're willing to leave longtime contributors to their efforts broke and busted at the side of the road if they have to.

Executives in Detroit continue to scratch their heads as to why Toyota is seemingly unstoppable. They point to the obvious product and marketing successes, but they never mention the fact that Toyota has developed a legion of loyal suppliers based on a relationship of mutual respect – and not one of intimidation or threats. And lo and behold, suppliers actually *want* to work for Toyota. They want to give Toyota their best creative thinking because they enjoy a level of trust in their professional relationship that Detroit can't match.

Yet Detroit continues to do just the opposite. And while conducting business with their suppliers on a foundation of antagonism, contentiousness, threats, fear and relentless intimidation, they wonder why they can't command the respect they feel they deserve in the overall scheme of things.

Yes, it's still about the product in this business, and it always will be. It also takes laser-accurate brand positioning and smart marketing on top of that in order to succeed.

But for Detroit to pull out of its "death spiral" of eroding market share, they will have to convince consumers that their products are finally worth considering again. And if Detroit can't even convince the people who help them get these new products designed and built in the first place that it has fundamentally changed – how are they ever going to convince anyone else?

Unless Detroit fundamentally changes its approach to the whole supplier issue, they will end up bottom-feeding for parts around the world and throwing their lot in with the lowest-common-denominator supplier/flavor of the month that will give them exactly what they ask for and deserve.

Just how much longer can Detroit continue extracting blood from a stone?

OBSOLETE AND OUT OF TOUCH, THE UAW IS DESTINED TO BLOW ITS ONE CHANCE FOR RELEVANCE IN THIS NEW CENTURY

In typical fashion, the UAW has deemed the healthcare cost crisis battering the Detroit-based auto companies as not significant enough for them to consider offering any meaningful help, other than incremental steps. When the subject came up of the possibility of the UAW reopening the national contract early in 2007 to help the Detroit automakers, they went on record saying that they weren't asked – and they weren't offering, either. Not that anyone was expecting anything else from the UAW. After all, this is an organization that has prided itself on "getting what's coming to us" regardless of what the current business climate is – or what the future implications might be – even as jobs and the focus of the world automobile industry continue to walk right past them and right out of this country.

You could give a list of reasons to the UAW as to why the Detroit automakers are facing the most serious set of challenges in their history, and they would spew a standard set of pat answers completely absolving them from all responsibility.

Healthcare costs out of control? The UAW will say something like, "We see no need to renegotiate anything. Yeah, we may agree to pay a nominal co-pay, but we'll make you scratch and claw and beg for us to give up that much. Anything more than that and you can forget it."

With the UAW, it's always somebody else's problem – either because "the car companies have plenty of money and we're *entitled* to our fair share," or, "it's Washington's problem – it's up to the lawmakers in Washington to protect our way of life and slap tariffs on these imports if they have to."

As much as Detroit wishes that they will get some relief at some point from Washington, no one is holding their breath that this will actually happen. The Detroit automakers must do everything in their power to get these costs under control on their own, because waiting for Washington is not a value-added activity in my estimation.

And this is where the UAW comes in. They absolutely need to stop their usual routine of looking three feet in front of them and start understanding the Big Picture here. And the Big Picture isn't pretty. The continued market share slide of the domestic-based automakers doesn't look like it will flatten out anytime soon, and the very existence of this industry and the way of life of this entire region are being seriously threatened. Add to this the fact that the emerging nations of China and India are turning the world automobile market upside down – and you have a scenario for disaster.

So, this is no time for the UAW to pull their usual obstructionist pontificating, yet they persist with their antiquated thought processes and "What, Me worry?" cluelessness – insisting that things aren't all that bad and that they'll just worry about it when they have to. After all, why take responsibility for the future of their very livelihood when they can blame somebody else for their predicament a little while longer?

But then again, accountability as a concept has always been MIA in the UAW mindset, and at a time when true visionary thinking on their part is sorely needed, they're incapable of answering the bell.

Case in point is Ron Gettelfinger, the UAW President, who is waiting for comprehensive national healthcare reform, according to statements he's made on the record, which means he'll be waiting for a very long time. Gettelfinger is, in no way, shape or form, the visionary leader that the UAW so desperately needs right now. He is simply way over his head and hell-bent on protecting what once was for the UAW instead of adding positively to the discussion about what is and what will be.

The incremental steps that the UAW favors aren't going to help Detroit one iota. That's a multi-million dollar non-solution to a multi-billion dollar problem that grows more dire by the day.

And it's too bad. The UAW had a golden opportunity to prove its relevance going forward into this new century by helping Detroit automakers grapple with the healthcare issues that threaten to bring down an entire industry. Instead, by clinging to the past and pretending that things aren't really all that bad, they're demonstrating to everyone that they're obsolete and out of touch.

And they're not only blowing it – they're hastening their own demise.

THE SMALE/ZARRELLA REIGN OF TERROR DECIMATES GM

GM has always created some sort of weird diversion to keep them from dealing with any "backs-to-the-wall" realities. By diversions I mean GM's strange habit of embracing outsiders, or corporate "messiahs," who, for no apparent reason, are given the keys to the whole shebang and let loose until they screw it up too much for everyone to ignore, so that they then have to be removed or asked politely to leave (with plenty of money left in their pockets for their trouble). GM's history is filled with people who were supposed to lead the company back to the "promised land" whenever they were confronted with really desperate times. Remember Ross Perot? I certainly don't need to add any more about him, do I? How about Elmer Johnson, the little-known lawyer from Chicago who tried to give the corporation a conscience, but ended up getting sucked in to the GM power elite just like every other outsider who joins up? And then there was the infamous John Smale and his legions of brand management loyalists, led by Ron Zarrella, who was brought over from Bausch & Lomb.

Ron Zarrella's legacy at General Motors will always be that he was the wrong person for the wrong job in the wrong industry at the wrong time. But before we get too carried away, Ron was only the chief functionary, a glorified puppet and nothing more than a conduit for one man's vision – and that man was the P&G Prophet, John Smale. More damage was done to GM under the regime of this former chairman of the Board of Directors than at any other time in their long, storied history.

In seven years (from 1995 to 2002), Smale and his minions, led by Ronnie Z and his merry band of packaged goods lightweights, almost succeeded in bringing this once-proud company to its knees with their particularly insidious form of brand marketing. The most horrifying thing to realize about the ill-fated Smale/Zarrella reign of terror at General Motors is that the Smale doctrine, when boiled down to its most basic elements, really revolved around one simple but maniacally warped premise: That brilliant marketing strategy alone could sell anything and overcome any obstacle – even an inferior product.

Not only were they completely wrong, but they also failed miserably trying to prove it – almost destroying the corporation in the process.

John Smale was directly responsible for some of the most egregiously bad decisions in GM history. His "brand management" philosophy set GM back 25 years, which isn't good, since they were perpetually operating five to seven years behind the rest of the industry as it was back then anyway. A busload of Smale/Zarrella acolytes was unleashed on the moribund bureaucracy at GM, a particularly offensive bunch who spewed forth B-school-infused, P&G-laced mumbo jumbo, and who took great pleasure in not having even the slightest clue about the car business – at times even reveling in the fact – while they ran the brands they were charged with well and truly into the ground.

It was one of the sorriest chapters in the history of the automobile business.

Zarrella didn't stop with just being incompetent, either. He also had the grating habit of regaling all of the "Neanderthals" stuck here in Motown with how he would be teaching Detroit a thing or three about the High Art of Brand Management and how he would show how it's done the "proper" way. He made bold, emphatic pronouncements about stabilizing and even improving GM's market share, only to see it continue its inexorable march southward. Zarrella and his minions cultivated a very bad habit of blaming everyone and everything else from the Japanese, to the Government, to the economy – stopping just short of blaming sunspots – for GM's poor market performance. It was galling to Zarrella and his troops that virtually every single shred of success that GM had under their watch was due solely to the fact that a few product "hits" slipped through the cracks – in spite of, and not because of, their oppressively gross incompetence.

As this bunch of frightfully misplaced outsiders went about stumbling through bad decisions of their own, the outrageously unqualified people who were already in place at the various divisions (and whom Zarrella promoted) were wreaking havoc too. Chevrolet, for instance, was a clearinghouse for some of the most gloriously incompetent stumblebums in the industry. They were rotated through Chevy sales and marketing, for instance, just long enough to do their damage and then promoted to even *bigger* jobs at other divisions by Zarrella and his yes-men (and women). Because of John Smale's delusional brand management "vision" as executed by Ron Zarrella, GM slid completely off track.

In GM's glory years – when it controlled nearly fifty percent of the market and dictated to the public and the rest of the industry what people would buy, in terms of everything from product segment and design, right down to the colors offered – GM could be forgiven if a little arrogance crept into the equation. But that was more than 35 years ago. That they actually were led to believe for a time that they could get the public to buy into the narrowly defined product distinctions of brand management only revealed that the insular, "blinders-on" mentality of the GM corporate culture was still there, in all its ill-conceived glory, just repackaged for the '90s in a P&G doctrine that was obsolete before GM ever got hold of it.

GM's problems were deep and severe by the time the full impact of the Smale/Zarrella era took hold. The whole exercise of brand management only served to underscore the fact that a basic reluctance existed on the corporation's part to deal with a business that had changed dramatically. GM was always quick to blame someone or something else for their problems. It had almost become the company motto, sort of an Alfred E. Neuman-toned, "What, me worry?" excuse for everything. But the reality of the situation is that they were operating within a structure that had been made obsolete by smarter and tougher competitors – companies that had been willing to start over because their backs were up against the wall, and they had no choice but to change the way they did things.

The painful lesson learned from the Smale/Zarrella era at General Motors was that the car business wasn't about soap or toothpaste or disposable diapers. And all of the marketing models and Cincinnati-bred P&G lingo in the world couldn't disguise the fact that brand management was an abject failure for GM. The fundamental difference between a P&G-soaked culture and the car business? One was dealing with heavy metal, the other theoretical "what-ifs?"

The Smale/Zarrella Brand Management strategy was such a failure that General Motors lost seven points of market share in seven-and-one-half years. It paralyzed the individual car and truck divisions with one "reorganization" after another – to the point that GM became a reorganization company, rather than a car company. Wave after wave of woefully ill-qualified people with no experience in the automobile business were hired for key, powerful marketing positions and then given *carte blanche* to do whatever they felt like.

And GM's meager product selection was carved into neat little segments of demographics and brand personalities that made little or no sense – while adding even more layers between GM management and what was really happening in the trenches.

After all of GM's pronouncements over the years, all of its posturing about how "we've finally turned the corner" and how everything would be just fine "once we do this," or "fixed that," or "settled" that, or "put our new marketing strategies to work," or "streamlined our structure," the fact remained that under the Smale/Zarrella reign of terror they studiously avoided mentioning the one secret ingredient that the whole damn business is based on to begin with: The Product. How to make it better. How to make it desirable. How to make it fun. How to make it the talk of the street. Nope. Never mentioned. Not once. Not ever.

There has never been and never will be a time when brand management mumbo jumbo will serve as an effective substitute for the integrity of the product. Unfortunately for everyone associated with GM, it took a painfully long time to understand that basic fact.

I'm reminded at this point of Alfred Sloan's famously arrogant statement about GM, "We're not in the business of making cars, we're in the business of making money." And lord knows GM made boatloads of money in its heyday, in spite of itself. But American history is littered with corporate ghosts that were so big and so powerful that everyone thought they'd go on forever. And then the whole thing came crashing to the ground. I got the same feeling about GM at the end of the Smale/Zarrella era. GM had all the looks of a corporate Gulliver about to be tied down permanently by its own ineptitude and arrogance.

"WE HAD A PRETTY DOGGONE GOOD YEAR HERE AT GM"

That statement by GM chairman Rick Wagoner in December 1999 represented the last vestiges of the "old" GM for all to see, with its legendary arrogance and incredible capacity for delusional rationalization intact. This was the same automobile company that two years later would adopt a suicidal incentive strategy that would turn Detroit upside down and suck all of the profitability (at least what was left of it) out of the business in one fell swoop. This was the same company that believed that an all-out incentive marketing strategy would actually *gain* back market share – when instead it accelerated Detroit's Doom Train.

GM was at the definitive crossroads in its history.

Instead of pissing away time and money on a failed incentive marketing strategy, what GM really needed to be doing at that point in time was a total rethink (with a large dollop of reality thrown in while they were at it) of who they were and what they planned to be doing as a company five, ten, even fifteen years down the road. And that self-reevaluation should have been undertaken with the realization that not only would it not be the biggest company in the world – it wouldn't even be the biggest *car* company in the world. But alas, it wasn't meant to be.

GM had slipped by with their "Aw, shucks, we had a pretty doggone good year" routine one too many times. The reality for GM by then was that it was a fading company, one that had fiddled and fumbled over all the wrong things while their *very* narrow window of opportunity for actually changing their course and charting a new direction for success in the twenty-first century had closed to a slit.

It was unconscionable that this company had allowed itself to be led down the primrose path of mediocrity by a pathetic bunch of self-righteous, so-called marketing "experts" over the previous decade. And the fact that their illogical and convoluted strategies had been allowed to continue unabated in spite of the fact that their market share needle had only trended downward even made it that much more ludicrous.

GM was in crisis, and crisis normally has bred fundamental change in corporate America. But it was oh so slow coming at GM. Even though GM's problems were deep and severe, the fact of the matter remained that there was a basic reluctance on the corporation's part to deal with a business that had changed dramatically over the last 35 years. They were always blaming someone or something else for their problems, but the reality of the situation is that they were operating within a structure that had been made obsolete by smarter and tougher competitors.

The GM bureaucracy was the real culprit here. It had layers upon layers of people paralyzed in abject fear of making a decision – knowing full well that there's at least a 50-50 chance of that decision being blown out of the water – even if it's right. How was any real change going to come to a culture this cancerous?

How can the words *passion for the product* have a snowball's chance in hell of surviving – let alone thriving – in that kind of environment?

With seriously good products finally now starting to emerge from GM and Detroit for the first time in a long time, you have to wonder why it's always feast or famine in the auto business as practiced in Detroit – these car companies are constantly subjecting themselves to wild swings between doing great things with their products and wallowing in the Sea of Incompetence – with seemingly nothing in between in the way of a happy middle ground. After more than 22 years of working up close with auto industry executives and another eight years writing commentary on Autoextremist.com, I have some reasoned hypotheses to offer about why this happens.

Could it have something to do with the fact that so many car executives range from the merely average to the downright awful? Am I being negative? Hardly. After observing every kind of auto executive behavior and level of competence imaginable over the years, I can assure you that truly outstanding auto executives are few and far between. Perhaps this assessment could be applied to all of corporate America, but I prefer to stick with what I know here.

There have been countless long-winded explanations about why mediocrity seems to run rampant in Detroit, but most of those fall short of getting to the heart of the matter. First of all, as I've said many times before, the car business doesn't necessarily smile on those with exemplary B-school grades or successful track records in other business endeavors. The sterile, philosophical environment of a classroom or demonstrable success in marketing other products often doesn't count for much or translate into great performance in the car business. You only have to look as far as the dismal failure of brand management at GM to see that.

The real reason for chronic mediocrity? Quite simply, the "system" breeds it.

Too often, good people with great potential get lost in the Byzantine bureaucratic systems that are not only alive and well at most car companies, but thriving. When the first order of business is to not make a mistake, then all subsequent decisions are hopelessly compromised. This self-perpetuating cycle breeds the kind of mediocrity that was once widespread at the Detroit-based car companies – at every level. This "fact of life" in the auto biz was either constantly at or below the surface, and it affected every decision made – both internally and externally – as outside suppliers will gladly testify.

If you *are* considered a success in the "system" – it might have nothing to do with your level of competence. As a matter of fact, there's a good chance that it could mean the direct *opposite*. Instead of being recognized as a stellar executive who knows what he or she is doing, a promotion could mean that you have been successful only to the degree that you've figured out the "system" – what your boss needs and wants, when to keep your head down, and what you need to do to further solidify your reputation as a worthwhile contributor to the effort. On the advertising and marketing side of the business, in particular, this usually means taking credit for an idea that originated at the ad agency or promotional agency, and using it to create one more visible feather in your cap, which then tags you as a "comer" in the organization.

This is exactly why, in a lot of cases, the incompetent get promoted, and the wrong people get hired in the first place. And if you're an auto executive under the age of 45 whose only claims to fame are cutting costs and taking credit for someone else's ideas while being in the right place at the right time – you sure don't deserve "whiz kid" status in my book.

So, if the "system" is so pervasive and still has such a stranglehold on the business today – *how does anything good get done?*

That's an excellent question. In GM's case, nothing much *did* get done during the reign of terror brought on by brand management. All of the bad things that happened have been well documented. Too much time, people hours and effort were put into making the brand management religion stick – meaning the focus was on the process and not on the real job at hand – which, allegedly, was to build cars and trucks that were competitive and that people actually wanted to buy. But GM wasn't alone. Chrysler and Ford had their own particular set of problems within their "systems" too.

Before the German takeover, Chrysler had a massive, company-wide "flu" that had people from every discipline taking their eyes off of the ball. Costs got out of hand. The good people either retired or left, and then the wrong people were left to make the bad decisions – and eventually the whole thing crumbled under the weight of the company's own serial incompetence.

For Ford, it was buying into one man's grand vision, only he, too, turned out to be another wrong man, at the wrong time, for the wrong company. Jacques Nasser's idea for Ford was to turn it into a "consumer-focused" company that delivered all things to all people. And it looked and sounded good – for about 12 months. But in the end, as everyone now knows, by turning the company away from its core business of building desirable cars and trucks, his ideas and programs helped put the company in serious financial jeopardy. Yes, of course, there were other obvious things involved – like the Explorer-Firestone debacle – but Nasser's personal "vision" almost destroyed the company from the inside out. Bill Ford Jr. and his new management team headed by Alan Mullaly are still trying to recover from Nasser's tenure, almost eight years later. To say Jacques Nasser's impact on Ford was disastrous is the understatement *du jour.*

But let's get back to how good things get done in the car business. Good things get done in this business when all of the organizational distractions are eliminated or at least muted, either by chance or by force. This means when all of the impediments to the organization finally play themselves out (executives leave, retire or are fired; or the Board of Directors somehow musters the *cojones* to say "enough is enough"). Then, as if by some miracle, and in spite of the ongoing drudgery created by the self-perpetuating mediocrity, cracks appear in the system, and great ideas surface against all odds. In other words, things can only get so bad before the pendulum starts swinging back toward the direction of positive accomplishment and achievement. A perfect example of this in the car business is when GM's design concepts started to show some real vision and reach seven years ago – almost out of the blue.

That means the poseurs and the bureaucratic system "experts" were either jettisoned or "iced" and put on the shelf in favor of those who had the "fire" and the gut feel for what needed to be done – otherwise known as the genuine "car guys."

It's moments like these when the incompetent, "going-through-the-motions" executives know that it's time to keep their heads down and do a slow fade back into the labyrinthine woodwork of the bureaucracy, waiting for the next "lull" in the action, only to surface again. And when does this occur? The pendulum inevitably starts swinging back in the negative direction again when a car company achieves great success and then spends too much time resting on its laurels, patting itself on the back and lingering too long over its gushing media clippings – and then it loses focus – only to initiate a slide into a tailspin where mediocrity reigns supreme once again. A perfect example of this is what happened to Chrysler before the Daimler-Benz buyout. Too many good people left or retired, and then the mediocre ones took over and bungled the decisions.

GM, Ford and Chrysler have each had their turn in the figurative barrel, with various internal and external pressures and missteps keeping them from focusing on the job at hand – which, last time I checked, was to design, engineer and build the best damn cars and trucks they can possibly put on the road.

GM got over their precious philosophical lovefest with the process of brand management and got back to focusing on the product, and not surprisingly, good things started to happen almost immediately. They actually started doing it well before the New Lutzian Era, but now "Maximum Bob" Lutz is enjoying being the catalyst and accelerating the process.

At the Chrysler Group, Dieter Zetsche and Wolfgang Bernhard stabilized the sinking ship and refocused the organization on their cars and trucks before moving on to bigger and better things – and good things happened for Chrysler – at least for a while (that is until the wheels came off in grandiose fashion).

And at Ford, the struggle to reinvent itself continues. The ex-Boeing management star Alan Mullaly has had his hands full changing Ford's legendary moribund culture – a culture largely rooted in the past and still holding the company back as you read this.

All of these companies are focused on one thing now: product, product and more product. And none of these companies has any reason to pick their heads up for even a whiff of the roses, because there's still a long, long way to go. But at least everyone seems to remember what business they're in these days – and believe me, that's a refreshing change from recent Motor City history.

In the end, I'll venture to say that no business does a better job at sabotaging itself than the denizens of what's left of the "Big Three." Hiring and promoting the wrong people, letting the "system" and the bureaucracy drive the process and become the focus of the organization, taking their collective eye off the ball and off of the job at hand. It's a miracle that anything good comes out of the whole mess at all.

And it's why this business, as it's played out in the Motor City, has always suffered through these wild swings between "Happy Days Are Here Again" and "The Eve of Destruction."

Fortunately, as long as there are still people around who have the fire in their bellies for the product, and who still not only believe in what they're doing but who also understand why it was, is, and always will be about the product – then the pendulum will always swing out of mediocrity and into greatness…if only for those elusive and fleeting moments in time.

SNATCHING DEFEAT FROM THE JAWS OF VICTORY – THE SAD SAGA OF SATURN

How GM floundered and bungled their way through the handling of Saturn and Oldsmobile and dropped the ball on the Camaro/Firebird are stories worth repeating, because they ultimately provided the cautionary tales that finally got Detroit to realize that it was on the edge of disaster.

Every summer at the beginning of July, GM has a quaint little ritual, a two-week "shutdown" across the board, when their employees aren't paid, but rather, encouraged to go away and contemplate the wonders of life. This move was originally put in place in the early '90s, when GM was precariously close to bankruptcy (closer than anyone ever knew, or could even imagine, for that matter). Let's turn back the clock for a moment when that pitiful, slumbering giant that was once-mighty GM actually had the future in its hands, and then crushed it with its own bureaucracy and misguided logic. This is a story about jealousy, greed, stupidity, shortsightedness and ultimately, bad management.

You remember Saturn, don't you? The little car that almost saved GM from its own bad instincts? The little car that rose from a simple concept for a new way of manufacturing to become a marketing exercise in corporate reinvention? The GM division that has now been resurrected through a series of shrewd product decisions after years of neglect? This is the inside story of how GM blew it and literally almost destroyed the Saturn franchise

Let's not forget the original facts for a moment. The whole concept for Saturn started within GM as a new way of making cars, which meant Job 1, to borrow Ford's hackneyed phrase, was putting the plant as far away from the UAW as possible, which happened to be a big empty field in Spring Hill, Tennessee.

And let's be realistic, the original Saturn was a mediocre product at best, with a truly obnoxious little four-banger for power, one that rivaled a decent Briggs & Stratton riding lawn mower for output (but actually suffered in a noise comparison when it came to the dulcet tones of a lawn-eater at full chat). The gimmick, of course, was the plastic "no-dent" body panels, which GM first field-tested on the late and lamented Pontiac Fiero. But that was basically it. Any number of cars were better, in every way.

The magic came after the project was well and truly a "go." Much to everyone's chagrin, the powers that be ignored GM's roster of corporate mirror-image ad agencies in Detroit and went with the genius behind the then-famous Bartles & Jaymes wine cooler commercials: Hal Riney. However this happened, it was a fortuitous aligning of the planets, because Riney and his troops created perhaps the greatest advertising campaign ever done for an automobile (in terms of what it actually meant to the overall image of the brand), and one of the greatest for *any* product, for that matter.

Riney didn't just create a traditional ad campaign and brand image. He created a magical "aura" that everyone strives for, and few ever accomplish. He turned this basic little uninspiring four-door appliance into a state of mind that, even if you couldn't relate to it quite yet, you just *knew* you had to go there. And the genius of the Riney campaign congealed with the isolated visionaries at hand within GM to create a dealer selling environment that combined hugs and high school rah-rahs to give America a most unique car shopping and buying experience.

Well, it worked like new rope. Saturn not only survived, it thrived and fulfilled every marketer's dream: it became a true cult. But in classic preordained GM fashion, they didn't know what to do with it once they tasted success.

During the development and launch of the Saturn, Oldsmobile, was on the ropes. Finding that the American car buyer had finally gotten tired of that division's formula for sales success, which amounted to throwing a half-vinyl roof on everything they had and calling it a Cutlass, Oldsmobile executives, led by then divisional General Manager John Rock, started to hear the drums beating loudly: Olds was yesterday's sorry-ass news, the "weak" link, and Saturn was the *future*. There was even serious talk about eliminating the Olds division completely – so more resources could be directed toward Saturn.

Well, if nothing else, John Rock was a fighter. He also happened to be brilliant, and his maverick, shoot-from-the-lip-style was like a beacon of light in the faceless, gray corporate bureaucracy that GM had become. He spoke out. Loudly. The press loved him, and the dealers worshiped him. He was going to save Olds from the wolves, by god, and he would not be denied. He was a cowboy, and "They're trying to shoot my horse out from under me," as he was quoted.

Meanwhile, the Saturn lovefest rolled on. Having studiously avoiding equating Saturn with GM in any way shape or form during its development, GM was discovering whole legions of Saturn customers didn't even know there was a connection. The shrewd insiders realized this was a *very* good thing. A whole new generation of buyers was in GM hands, and they were actually *happy*.

And remember, all of this was accomplished from scratch, without the benefit of a cult history, like the New Beetle enjoyed at its debut.

But GM's internal wrangling and hand-wringing kicked into high gear. There was a bigger and even more influential faction waiting in the wings to weigh-in: Chevrolet. GM's premier moneymaking division had fallen on hard times. Their products were tired. Their dealers were beyond agitated, and every day they picked up the newspaper, there was another reminder of the wonderful world of Saturn – either in the ads themselves, or in feature articles about the ads in the business sections, or even worse, actual editorial content about happy people and their love affair with their Saturns. And all that the Chevrolet faction knew or assumed (correctly) was that Saturn, that *non*-division of GM, was getting engineering and marketing money that they could desperately use.

At this point, GM had a decision to make. The popularity of Saturn caught them off guard. They needed to commit massive amounts of money to develop extensions to the product line, because they knew that these initial buyers would soon be ready to buy their next new car. And they wanted them to look at Saturn first. Saturn planners were chomping at the bit with their wish list: A mid-size four door. A people van. A full-size sedan. All with the Saturn "magic" baked-in.

Then the wheels came off the whole thing.

The flamboyant and eloquent Rock, brandishing his catchy phrases and witty posturing in the media in the fight of his career, convinced the corporate-types that they absolutely had to save Oldsmobile. He actually made them believe that Saturn customers *could* and *would* shop and buy Oldsmobiles after their little "fling" with Saturn. He marshaled the dealers, retirees and everyone else he could think of, and they all weighed-in on Rock's side.

Then Chevrolet, even without a gifted front man, rightfully asserted its place in the divisional pecking order and laid claim to the money it desperately needed (and in their minds deserved), relent-lessly hammering their point home with the corporate honchos too.

The result?

Oldsmobile survived and got new development money. John Rock, after fighting the good fight, retired, his legacy intact. Chev-rolet survived, but suffered another five years before any serious money was committed its way.

And Saturn? They had a couple of re-skins on the sedan and coupe. But that was it. No bigger Saturn was ever developed for their rabid customers to move up to. The magic, if not completely worn off, was severely tarnished. As if GM needed to be reminded, the American car-buying public is fickle. Even card-carrying Saturn-istas just aching to bathe in the "glow" again had nowhere to go. They wouldn't be caught dead in an Oldsmobile showroom. And they wouldn't even think of going to a Chevrolet dealer, either. And Saturn floundered even further – with the pathetic "L-Series," which ended up being a nonstarting dud of massive proportions in the market.

But now we all know the rest of the story.

GM killed-off Oldsmobile, wasting all of the time, money and effort marshaled to save it. And Saturn languished in limbo with a horribly antiquated product line that almost killed it off too. It was only after Saturn was on the ropes in 2002 that GM committed massive amounts of money to resuscitate the brand. In 2006, GM finally rolled out two new Saturns: the sleek Sky two-seat roadster and the contemporary Aura mid-size sedan, with the impressive new Outlook crossover making its debut in 2007, along with the revamped VUE and other vehicles developed in conjunction with GM's Opel division in Germany on the way. Now, Saturn is one of GM's star divisions again, but it certainly took a long, strange trip to get back to where it needed to be.

After all of the *sturm und drang*, Saturn had been resuscitated through a series of shrewd product decisions (and a serious infusion of development money), surviving years of neglect.

Funny, it always comes back to the product, doesn't it?

NO ONE DID SELF-FULFILLING PROPHECIES BETTER THAN GM

Late in 1999, the Associated Press released a story saying that the Chevrolet Camaro and the Pontiac Firebird would be discontinued after the 2000 model year. They later retracted the story, because the cars ended up being around through the end of 2002. The news back then, of course, was not that the cars would be discontinued, because it had been common knowledge within the corporation for at least three years that there were no plans for either nameplate after 2002. The real story was that the Camaro/Firebird situation was another little peek into the empty hole inside GM, where a corporate soul should have existed.

Back in 1965, after the overwhelmingly successful launch of the Ford Mustang was well into the record books, Chevrolet started planning the launch of a counterattack for 1967, using the new "Camaro" nameplate. Though obviously playing catch-up, the new "pony car" entry from Chevrolet had a contemporary look all its own, and for Chevy loyalists and Americans in search of the "next" thing, the Camaro did very well. The Pontiac Firebird was equally distinctive, and the Firebird launch was handled by GM's hottest ad agency at the time, McManus John & Adams, which came up with the memorable "The Magnificent Five" campaign, for the five Firebird model/engine combinations. The GM entries in the pony car war were so well received that even the Sports Car Club of America took notice, forming a new class of racing called the "Trans Am" Championship catering to the new pony cars.

The Mustang vs. Camaro Wars (with occasional involvement of Firebird) fueled a crosstown rivalry that was everything good and fun about the glory days of the car business in Detroit. And it marked an era that probably will never be repeated. Many consider the Trans Am series races from 1966 to 1971 to be the greatest American road racing ever staged on the continent. The unlimited Can Am series was spectacular, but nothing could touch the tooth-and-nail clawing and scratching that went on in the Trans Am. With full factory participation and America's greatest drivers (Mark Donohue, Peter Revson, Parnelli Jones, George Follmer, Dan Gurney, el al.), anyone who witnessed the racing has to be still in awe of what took place on tracks all over North America in those years. And the fact that the factories were squaring off with each other in the showrooms and on racetracks yielded dividends for enthusiasts who were looking for affordable performance on the street with a slight bit of versatility.

Although the pony cars were mere caricatures of themselves by the late '90s, the fact that they were an integral part of the American landscape was undeniable. And one company realized it. Ford looked back at the Mustang and what it meant to the very fabric of their company and set out to put the nameplate on a path of revival that's bearing tremendous dividends today. GM, on the other hand "maintained" their franchise, not taking chances or leading, but doing enough to keep their entries somewhat fresh, particularly with sensational engines that delivered incredible performance for the dollar. But then a few years ago, the "death spiral" started. You could see it and feel it in the fact that Ford never stopped developing the Mustang as a concept, while GM, except for the engines, never bothered to work on the next generation "F" cars. I know, because I was at Chevy's ad agency to watch it, firsthand. No one does "self-fulfilling prophecies" better than GM.

When sales of the muscle-oriented pony cars started to slow, the juxtaposition of the two car companies' philosophies was painfully obvious. The talk around Chevrolet was that Camaro sales were "in the dumper." What did GM do? Instead of regrouping and trying to rethink and perhaps push the segment in new directions, they started withholding development funds. Then, the sales team at the division stopped allocating advertising and promotional money to the

Camaro. At that point, it became a dead duck. At the ad agency, we ended up working on Camaro advertising and promotional concepts that went nowhere (except for a few notable instances). Instead, we watched them get lost in the labyrinthine halls of Chevrolet sales/marketing. Next, we attended advanced product meetings and saw that the Camaro was dropped off the calendar after 2002. And finally, we watched as GM Motorsports pulled factory funding from Camaro Trans Am teams. The "death spiral" was well and truly set into motion. Of course, the fact that GM abandoned development on a new, worldwide corporate rear-wheel-drive platform in the early '90s didn't help either. That gave everyone at the corporation just one more reason to let the Camaro/Firebird die off.

Over at Ford, it was a remarkably different story. The freshened '99 Mustang was a decent sales success for Ford, but they had no intention of resting on their laurels. On the contrary, Ford unleashed an all-new Mustang in 2006 that harkened back to Ford's glory days but pushed the vehicle into a contemporary, harder-edged groove. And now, this new-generation Mustang is a roaring sales success and has brought all kinds of attention back to the Ford brand. It's all about knowing where you've been, with a true sense and understanding of history and tradition. And it's all about knowing where you want to go, given that sense of history and tradition. Ford's dedication and perseverance with the Mustang have done justice to a true American icon. And they're continuing to keep the flame burning with a passion and a purpose that are truly admirable in these cynical times. The Mustang is part of Ford's corporate soul, and as long as that remains true, they will be bringing great cars to the street worthy of the name for a long time to come.

The Camaro/Firebird went away in early 2002. Bloated like a pair of former heavyweight champions on the Las Vegas casino "meet-and-greet" circuit, these proud names faded away, miserably. And in what seems to be a recurring pattern in GM history, GM only realized what they had in the Camaro/Firebird when they were gone. GM always seems to learn the hard way.

In January 2006, a hot new Camaro concept made its debut

at the North American International Auto Show in Detroit. It was unveiled to massive acclaim and excitement, and now the new version is expected to hit the street in the first quarter of 2009. Will anyone care by then? Who knows? But there will be yet another all-new Mustang waiting in the wings to counteract it, you can count on it.

RESURRECTING "THE STANDARD OF THE WORLD"

A perfect microcosm of Detroit's predicament in the early years of the twenty-first century was the Cadillac Division of General Motors. After stirring from its more than decade-long slumber several years ago, Cadillac woke up to find that the luxury-car landscape had changed so dramatically that virtually nothing worked for them anymore. Overrun by an onslaught of BMW, Mercedes-Benz and Lexus models, Cadillac had to literally start over. And rather than starting over with a bang, they sputtered along in fits and starts – spinning their wheels and digging themselves into an even bigger hole with a series of not-ready-for-prime-time products, one monumentally embarrassing ad campaign and an ingrained lackadaisical attitude in their dealer body that just wouldn't go away. Old-time Cadillac customers began to have their heads turned by the latest and greatest offerings from the German and Japanese luxury automakers. And even worse, the much sought after younger affluent buyers didn't even bother to look at Cadillac, because it was so far off of their radar screens that the brand never even occurred to them.

By the time GM killed off its Oldsmobile division in the spring of 2004, GM had fallen into a downward spiral that it was having difficulty pulling out of. Refusing to deal with the realities of a changing market and continuing to conduct their business with a paralyzing bureaucracy fueled by a debilitating combination of arrogance and complacency, GM was quite literally on the ropes.

The time for GM to kill off Olds was years before that, and GM management's steadfast refusal to deal with the realities of a world that had stopped revolving around their whims and wishes had cost them and everyone associated with them dearly.

General Motors had spun its wheels and pissed away *billions* upon *billions* of dollars trying to act like the dominant company it once was. GM chased its tail, threw good money after bad and generally squandered every opportunity handed to them, while treating the prevailing gale-force winds of a new automotive world order as if they were just warm summer breezes.

Up until the time they eliminated Oldsmobile, the people at the very top of General Motors had been flailing around trying to keep the proverbial balls in the air, while completely missing the most basic and obvious point: GM had too many models and too many divisions. And they couldn't possibly support them properly in the cutthroat automotive market that exists today. If Chevy needed a push, Cadillac suffered. One marketing dollar spent on GMC was another dollar not going to Chevy Truck. If Saturn got money and product, Olds had to drop off the table. If Buick needed to do a proper launch, where was the money coming from – at the expense of Pontiac or Chevrolet?

When a GM nameplate caught a cold, another nameplate inevitably ended up with the flu. When would it stop? Remember, this was such a competitive automotive environment that a company like Toyota would spend $100 million in marketing, advertising and promotions just to launch a new Camry, while the marketing "experts" at GM continued to believe that they could cover all the nameplates they have in each division by spending less than half as much on a typical launch. And at that point, they were not only just blending into the advertising/marketing woodwork – they weren't even generating a blip on the radar screen. It was utter folly, and the only people who couldn't seem to see it back then were the people in control of the reins at General Motors.

At the time, the Oldsmobile decision seemed to be a pinpoint of fiber-optic light at the end of the tunnel, but in reality, it was just a momentary blip of sanity.

GM had made money hand-over-fist for so long on sheer inertia alone that a lot of their top executives *still* couldn't believe things were all that bad. But more savvy GM insiders were painfully aware that GM couldn't conduct its business the way they had been any longer. Not even for one more day. They knew they couldn't compete in today's market in their current configuration – and if they were going to turn around Cadillac, then things would have to change once and for all.

Smart insiders within GM had finally gotten religion about its new reality in the automotive pecking order. And although it had been a painfully arduous journey, they had finally come to the realization that GM needed to attack the product side of the car business if they were to survive – let alone thrive. And they finally understood once and for all something that had been true since the days of the first horseless carriage – Product is King – and anything that distracts their focus from that simple premise should be deemed inconsequential and irrelevant.

There were too many people at the top of this once-great corporation who didn't know what they were doing and who had no clue what the car business was really all about. They may have been smart in the hermetically sealed textbook sense, but they were absolutely lost when it came to understanding what the essence of this business was. They weren't taught the subject in business school, and the laws of packaged goods didn't necessarily apply either – as they painfully found out. And they had to go.

GM found out the hard way that it wasn't about numbers or business models or some theoretical claptrap from the latest checkout lane, book-of-the-week "guru." You either have The Fire in your gut, or you don't. And finally, the people at the top of GM had it.

Cadillac and GM marketing gurus set about to desperately crack "the code" – the code that would propel Cadillac out of the swirling maelstrom of mediocrity that had plagued the brand for years. But it wasn't easy.

Cadillac, once one of the most revered brands in the world, started down the primrose path of mediocrity back in the early '70s, when they made the mistake of almost doubling the number of dealers and started selling Cadillacs like they were Chevys – in other words, by "pumping up the volume" to the point of absurdity. This worked absolutely heroically in the short term by making mind-numbingly huge profits for the corporation and making multi-millionaires out of countless Cadillac dealers across the country. But in the process, everybody involved lost sight of the Big Picture and started churning out Cadillacs that had lost their desirability, their quality and most important – their distinctiveness.

At that point, Cadillac had become just another car adrift in the GM system.

And while GM had been struggling to restore the Cadillac brand, new, formidable competitors had come out of the woodwork. In no time, Lexus, Mercedes-Benz and BMW had supplanted Cadillac in terms of prestige and street "cred."

The really stunning fact in all of this is that the name Cadillac – even after years of enduring GM's built-in bureaucratic bumbling and relentless, systematic "dumbing-down" of the brand – still resonated with people like few brand names did. Which is incredible when you really think about it – after all, we're talking *years* of egregious mishandling of one of the world's great names – and it *still* had enough juice behind it to get people's attention.

The powers that be in charge of putting Cadillac back in the game had a yeoman's task in front of them.

The GM system had become a morass of mediocrity, where everyone was responsible for a little piece of something but ultimately accountable for nothing – where underqualified generalists and so-called "experts" from the dreaded packaged goods world had been let loose on the car business and allowed to run amuck with impunity. It was the new GM "way." John Smale and Ron Zarrella had unleashed a storm of bad juju throughout the company – a swirling maelstrom where non-car people were promoted and praised for their broader, more sophisticated "perspective" but in the end did nothing but permanent, if not fatal, damage to the little shred of what was left of the "car guy" culture that was already on life support in the company.

It had been 30 years since real car people ran GM. *Thirty years.* And by now, it was apparent to the Cadillac insiders with just a glint of something between the ears that you couldn't run the enterprise with accountants and smoke-and-mirrors hucksters at or near the helm. The perspective that was needed had to come from the car people – men and women who ate, breathed and slept cars – the kind of people who really loved what cars were and what they represented and what they could do and where they could take you.

The people charged with rejuvenating Cadillac had tremendous challenges in front of them. Tasked with restoring the luster to GM's most fabled division, they had to strike with bold strokes and make zero mistakes.

Shockingly enough, that's exactly what they did. GM pulled their most prestigious division up by the lapels and lavished billions of dollars on it – with a stunning combination of will, an aggressive new philosophy and a huge helping of flat-out guts. Led by the focused vision of one of GM's most talented executives, John Smith, GM unleashed a new wave of Cadillac models over a six-year period that transformed the division from a frumpy, "lost in the '70s" fading Detroit icon to a contemporary, high luxury-performance, unapologetically proud American brand.

And in the midst of resurrecting Cadillac, GM stumbled upon the formula that it would use to transform the whole company – proving to them that when they really dig deep and put their minds to the goal at hand, they can, in fact, get it done.

GM'S PAINFUL REALITY – GETTING REAL ABOUT ITS PLACE IN THE NEW AUTOMOTIVE WORLD ORDER

Even though GM had come into the light with its resuscitation of Cadillac, reality had yet to play out for the once-invincible automaker. Watching GM's stock plunge in the spring of 2005 to its largest single-day share loss since the stock market crash of 1987 sent chills through the Motor City, the industry and the financial community. The loss was triggered by GM's announcement that it expected a loss of almost $1 billion with a capital "B" over the last six months of the year, after suggesting less than three months earlier that things would be tough in 2005, but not in the dire category.

Well, folks, this was seriously dire, and Wall Street reacted accordingly, coming down hard on GM. Danny Hakim, reporting for *The New York Times*, said that "The losses reflected an increasingly harsh reality: that General Motors, which three years ago was thought to be the healthiest of the Big Three automakers in Detroit, is now considered the weakest, primarily because it is not selling enough cars at home. The losses also raised questions about the strategy of the company's chairman and chief executive, Rick Wagoner." That was the most dire assessment you would hear from anyone about the situation, and GM spent the rest of 2005 under the gun and under the microscope.

The fact that GM was in such dire straits was shocking to many, but it wasn't surprising to those in the know. GM had been playing Russian roulette with its incentive-driven marketing strategy for the previous four years. What was a good and patriotic campaign in the beginning to "Keep America Rolling" after the horrific events of 9/11, turned into an obsessive-compulsive addiction that crippled

GM's ability to think rationally about the North American market. GM mistook a short-term marketing boost/gambit for a long-term marketing strategy, and they talked themselves into believing that they could actually take away market share from their competitors with it.

It worked for a while, but it also began a debilitating scenario in which GM slowly but surely cheapened their brands across the board, creating a "fire sale" mentality with the public that they're still finding exceedingly difficult to overcome. Except for the few instances of new hit products, GM had conditioned consumers to only consider its product portfolio when they were in search of a deal. And now that GM was bringing vehicles to market that were actually worth owning on their own merits for a change, they were still finding that a shocking number of American consumers couldn't care less.

In short, GM had put itself in a box – and they were running out of time to put things right.

I have been immersed in the history and the culture of this corporation since I was a very young boy. Legends like Harlow Curtice, Ed Cole, Bunkie Knudsen, Bill Mitchell, Zora Duntov and many, many others weren't just colorful characters from a GM history book to me – they were living, breathing individuals who were on a first-name basis with our family. In other words, I have had an intimate, up-close view of the inner workings of this corporation, and I probably have more of a perspective on what this company has meant to the auto industry – and to this region of the country – than just about anyone.

So to see GM in this situation was difficult – not just for me, but especially for GM veterans of the glory days and particularly for those at work down at GM's headquarters. But reality sucks, and this reality for GM-ers was anathema to their very core. For perspective, you have to remember that GM was once the New York Yankees of the automobile business. They didn't just win a lot of championships – they won the championship *every year*. At the peak of its powers, GM dominated the U.S. automobile industry, consistently capturing more than 40 percent of the market (think about that figure for a moment in the context of today's market, with GM struggling mightily to even maintain a 25 percent share).

GM was so dominant that it dictated every facet of the business to the rest of the industry, including the segments offered, the pricing, engineering features and design. You name it, and GM set the tone for it. GM's influence over car design was so overwhelming at one point that for one continuous stretch, from the '50s right through to the early '70s, it dictated design for the entire industry with two of the greatest automotive designers of all time – Harley Earl and Bill Mitchell. It was like having Babe Ruth hand off to Mickey Mantle. GM Design's influence was so overwhelming that they even dictated the *colors* offered from year to year by the Big Three.

But the problem for GM was that it never moved on from reliving its glory days, and while they were reveling in their legacy, the automotive world irrevocably changed around them. GM's arrogant mindset blinded them to the rapidly changing realities of the North American automotive market. I have already covered the long litany of mistakes that got GM to this point, but the time has come for me to delineate just what GM must do to survive, let alone thrive in the future.

Here are my key points for righting the listing GM ship...

GM must learn to make money while controlling a 20 percent share of the market. GM used to be the smug "overdog" back in the glory days when it controlled more than 40 percent of the market. The problem is that they retained a large measure of their arrogance when their market share fell through the 30s and into the upper 20s. There was even quaint talk a few years ago of regaining the 30 percent plateau, with Rick Wagoner sporting a "30" lapel pin as a reminder to his troops of his stated goal. Now, GM controls a very shaky 25 percent share of the North American market and that is by no means a solid number. Factor in fleet sales, and the "real" GM market share number is probably closer to 22 percent. And with the imports continuing to make inroads at a terrifying rate, it is not out of line to think that a more rational number for GM to target for its North American operations is a 20 percent share. If GM restructured its operations based on this assumption, it would be a dramatically different company, but it would have a much better chance of being a competitive factor again.

Operating at 20 percent of the North American market, it would be logical that GM right now has too many models, too many divisions, too many nameplates and too many dealers. GM stubbornly tried to prop up its hoary divisional structure and its bloated dealer body for as long as it possibly could, but this is the one aspect of the company that must be fundamentally and radically altered. GM has come to the stark realization that the good times – as defined by the olden days – will never return. GM has learned, albeit painfully, that it was okay to get smaller in order to regain their footing in this market, and now they understand that market share increases can slowly grow out of a leaner, meaner superstructure. For the near term, gaining market share is highly unlikely for GM, but a more attractive mix of fewer, more profitable, class-leading products will go along way toward stabilizing GM's fortunes. A more focused product portfolio is the key.

If GM is going to get real about its product portfolio, however, then its dealers will have to get real about their prospects too. GM cannot conduct itself as an "all things to all people" company at the divisional level any longer. The days when one division could boast a full complement of offerings ended a long time ago, but unfortunately GM and its dealers didn't get that memo until just recently. And I would also argue that the "old-think" GM was still way too active in the corporation for its own good, even as late as 2005. You only had to look at the fiasco masquerading as GM's minivan entries to understand my point.

How could one company take three years to develop a fourth-place minivan – and then knowingly distribute it to *four* of its divisions? Wasn't one mediocre minivan plenty? What's wrong with this picture? Did Pontiac dealers need a minivan? Confined within their own little myopic world and selling in a vacuum, yes, you could squint and say that on a good day and with the planets aligned just right, those Pontiac dealers indeed needed a minivan. But if you had stepped back and taken a good look at the competitive set of minivans in the market at that time, and considered GM's hopelessly also-ran position in that particular segment of the market, and also taken into account Pontiac's divisional brand identity (at least what was left of it at that point), there is no way in hell that Pontiac should have been given a minivan to sell.

Needless to say, I could devote the rest of this book delineating example after example of what GM can and should do, but for now it's safe to say that I'm not the one who should be worried about it. GM should be burning the midnight oil in preparation for executing these kinds of scenarios throughout the corporation. And GM dealers better be ready to set aside their 30-day mentalities long enough to realize that they will have to make fundamental changes in the way they conduct their business too. Yes, they have to continue to be responsive to their local markets, but they better ask themselves this basic question: Do they want to have fewer, class-leading products to sell, or do they want to continue to ride the incentive train to oblivion?

Fewer models, fewer nameplates and the biggest automotive advertising budget in the world – what's not to like? Right now, GM is *still* flailing around trying to adequately promote countless nameplates, while also hammering home the latest GM sales event message – and that just isn't going to cut it in this market. Cutting back GM's swollen product portfolio would have the immediate benefit of increasing its media throw-weight against the nameplates it retains. More advertising and promotional money for fewer nameplates? Sounds deceptively simple, and remarkably, it is.

Product, product, product. If there is one thing I was consistent about in my writings since Day One of Autoextremist.com, it's that The Product is, was and *always* will be King. For a manufacturer to

conduct itself with any less of an understanding of this fact is sui-
cide, or at least a ticket to a very bad time, as GM has discovered
at its nadir. GM found out the hard way that just covering a segment with a freshened product entry isn't going to cut it in this, the
most competitive market in automotive history. That its new and in
some cases outstanding products aren't getting the attention they
hoped for goes without saying, but why is that, exactly? For one
thing, they're still operating as if they control a huge chunk of the
market and can get away with propping up their now-obsolete divisional structure. But too many at GM also forget that out in the real
world, the customer doesn't care about GM's latest interpretation
of the Sloan model. They don't care about segment differentiation
or GM's "ladder" view of their product portfolio. The customer just
cares about being able to buy good cars and trucks with bulletproof
quality and reliability, excellent value and a modicum of style. If GM
hadn't been so focused on their old way of doing things over the last
20 years and in protecting the "sanctity" of their Neanderthal divisional structure, the market might not have flown right by them. But
it did and so here they are.

GM must change the fundamental way they approach this business. I'll give you just one classic example. The Chevrolet Equinox
was, by any measure, one of GM's new product hits in late '05 and
'06. It is smartly styled, properly priced and executed very, very well.
And miracle of miracles, customers embraced it without having to be
prodded by the Giant Rebate Stick.

Now, let's just imagine for a moment if Toyota had the Equinox
– what would they do? They would pore over the Equinox with a
fine-toothed comb. They'd improve the details, sweeten the mechanicals, refine the interior and make it better in every single way. Their
approach revolves around the concept of gradually improving and
refining a vehicle throughout its lifecycle to make it better in every
respect, and as a result, this is why Toyota is usually successful every
time out – in any segment they compete in. They build brand equity
by delivering relentlessly honed products that never disappoint.

What did GM do with the Equinox? Instead of seizing the opportunity of having a rare, potentially long-term product hit (the kind that doesn't come around very often in GM's world), and nurturing it by polishing it to a sheen and solidifying its place in the market with a clever big-buck marketing push – they made a few improvements to it and then gave Pontiac dealers a version called the Torrent.

If there is one vehicle scenario that encapsulated the old GM-think hanging on for dear life in the newly reinvigorated GM, the Equinox/Torrent example is it. GM must stamp out all remnants of that kind of thinking if they are to continue on an upward trajectory.

Yes, there are a ton of other problems that GM has to deal with. The crushing legacy costs, the nonsensical union contracts, the ridiculous healthcare costs, the relentless competition – but in the end, the reason GM put itself in this position is because of its ingrained recalcitrance and refusal to admit that what worked for the old, dominant, legendary version of GM makes no sense whatsoever in the cutthroat and globally chaotic automotive market that exists today.

Some people in this town cling to the belief that there's a rotation on the Detroit "roller coaster" that seems to follow this sequence – Ford gets in to trouble, then starts its comeback. Chrysler gets into trouble, stabilizes and starts *its* comeback. And the same for GM. The problem is that Detroit overall is running out of comebacks. With mounting competitive pressures emanating from the Far East and consumers refusing to give Detroit products the time of day (except for the obvious "hits"), the domestic car industry based here in the Motor City is facing the most serious crisis in its history.

As for GM, they can't continue to operate by just selling to their loyal buyers over and over again, because those buyers will slowly but surely dwindle each year. Until they convince the people who don't already drive GM vehicles to give their new products serious consideration, they will always be flailing about for little victories in the market – instead of getting the big, consistent hits they so desperately need.

GM's painful new reality will ultimately benefit the company in the long run. They know there are no shortcuts to respectability, no quick fixes and no awards for just showing up. Getting real about its place in the new automotive world order means focusing on the products it builds and never wavering from the commitment to that mission.

It's no longer a matter of fixing things so that GM can regain its rightful place at the top – it's a matter of survival, pure and simple.

SEVEN HIGH-OCTANE TRUTHS
ABOUT DETROIT

After hanging around this business long enough, I've compiled a list of auto industry "givens" that have emerged after years of up-close observation. It's still amazing to me that this business seems to operate too often as if the lessons learned in prior eras somehow don't apply today. And with each new crop of up-and-coming auto executives, there seems to be a trial-and-error learning curve that has to be played out before things start to sink in. It's also amazing to me how creative thinking, combined with a major dollop of common sense, can be so elusive in this business. But thankfully, every day is a new day – and as long as industry executives continue to ignore these "givens" – I'll continue to have plenty to write about.

There's no such thing as too much of a good thing – until there's too much of a good thing. The auto industry is made up of a bunch of "me-too" followers. Whichever car company manages to stumble upon a genuine hit first, others will immediately follow, even if the segment makes no sense whatsoever and they really don't have the platform architecture to properly compete. This kind of lemming-like thinking has led to any number of product disasters over the years, but suffice to say, just when a particular segment has "jumped the shark," you can bet there will be at least ten more product entries making their debut – long after it makes a lick of sense.

There's no practical substitute for cubic inches – or original thinking. That old hot rodder's adage is still true today, and you only have to look to the lingering popularity of the V8 for proof of it.

You can get more complicated with your engines, and certainly more expensive, but the most affordable route to performance is through larger-displacement engines. Period. And with modern electronic controls, these large-displacement engines can deliver stunning performance with acceptable levels of fuel economy.

As for original thinking, you only have to go back to my first point to understand the impact of an original idea in this business. The original Mustang was a perfect example of it. A great-looking car based on existing mechanicals, offered at a sensational price, equaled a monumental hit. Or consider the minivan from Chrysler, an original idea that was so eminently logical and practical – and so wonderfully executed – that it saved the entire company.

Today, Detroit has several examples of original thinking on the street. Take the Buick Enclave, for instance. Buick was close to being dead in the water, except for the mildly appealing and successful Lucerne, before the Enclave arrived. There was no street buzz, there was no media buzz, and Buick was threatening to fall off the radar screen completely. But now, at least, Buick has the American car-buying public's attention with the Enclave. Is Buick out of the woods yet? Not by a long shot, but at least they have a pulse.

It doesn't cost any more to do a great design than it does to do a mediocre one. Design is the single most important *initial product differentiator* in this business. As more car companies pile into more and more segments, design determines whether a consumer will even bother giving a product a second look. In short, design is absolutely crucial. And great design, inside and out, doesn't cost any more than mediocre design, either. It just requires outstanding creative talent, visionary upper management and a relentless insistence that "good enough" just will not do.

Spending a ton of money on advertising doesn't account for much if you don't know what you're doing – or why you're doing it to begin with. I can't think of any other industry where less has been done with more than automotive marketing and advertising.

I've basically been writing about this "given" ever since I walked away from advertising back in 1999 to start Autoextremist.com. For all the alleged smarts and all of the high-brow credentials that marketing executives bring to the table in this business, it's amazing how many of the same mistakes are made over and over and over again. Throwing too much money at a bad idea? It happens almost daily. Not putting enough money behind a brilliant strategy or not being able to recognize one in the first place? It's so predictable, you can bet the farm on it. The car business pisses away so much money on bad decisions and marketing strategies based on ego instead of reasoned logic that it boggles the mind just to think about it. One of the basic problems is that automakers have never really understood their place in the greater cosmic universe of advertising. The industry collectively has a staggering amount of money at their disposal to spend on their marketing efforts, but they spend most all of their time worrying about what their competitors are doing with *their* advertising, instead of looking at the big picture and understanding what their ads have to go up against for even minimal attention. In a nutshell, that's why so very few automotive ads are worth looking at.

Whenever there's enough time, there's never enough money, and vice versa. This applies to any business, but in the car business, at least as it applies to what's left of the Big Three, it has become standard operating procedure. When things are going bad in the car business, there's plenty of time, but there never seems to be enough money to get essential product programs done. But when things are booming, there never seems to be enough time to get anything done, as car companies try to chase after every long-harbored product wish at the same time. It's a never-ending cycle that sees some successes slip through, but there are a lot of failures too. It's just one of those "givens" in this business that won't go away – at least in Detroit. (Of course if you're a company like Toyota, this particular "given" doesn't apply. They have a ton of money at their disposal, and they keep piling it up every month. And they have all the time and money they need to go after any segment they choose to play in. But then again, Toyota has a habit of making a lot of the "givens" in this business appear obsolete.)

Auto company executives celebrate too soon and stick with bad decisions too long. This is a Detroit-specific affliction, it seems. String together a couple of good quarters in this town, and there's high-fiving going on in the hallways. It took Chrysler about ten minutes to start wearing that vintage Detroit "I told you so" smirk, thanks to the success of their 300C – but veterans in this business knew that it was just a matter of time before the folks in Auburn Hills ended up back in the dumper again. True to form, Chrysler soon crashed again in a nightmare of out-of-control inventory and a fundamental inability to do anything about it. The other Detroit-centric affliction in this business is the bad habit of sticking with bad decisions too long. Whether it has to do with a product or a particular marketing initiative, Detroit has a real problem with saying "enough" and moving on. Of course, this also has everything to do with the built-in culture in this town that has revolved around avoiding accountability since Day One.

Auto executives are too often incapable of giving a realistic appraisal of their own products. This is a universal truth in the car business. It's a rare auto executive who will admit, in no uncertain terms, that one of his or her products is somehow deficient. Some admit it in behind-closed-door, internal meetings, but few will admit it to the media or to their competitors. And it's too bad, because if auto executives were more blunt and honest in the assessment of their own vehicles, they might be able to come up with the kind of original thinking necessary to succeed in this, the most competitive market in automotive history.

PART FOUR

THE UNITED STATES OF TOYOTA

THE SLOW, PAINFUL DEATH OF
AN ALL-AMERICAN BRAND

Forty-seven years ago, I remember being glued to the television set for the season debut of "Bonanza," the most popular show on television, which back then garnered ratings numbers comparable to today's Super Bowl. This episode would be special, because not only would it be in full color for the first time, but Chevrolet, the show's sponsor since its inception, was withholding all commercial messages until the end of the show (a bold and unexpectedly dramatic move for those times). Instead, it would run a five-minute film on the entire lineup of all-new Chevrolets for 1960.

Things *were* different back then. A Western about a widower and his three sons on the Ponderosa was the number one television show. Chevrolet was, far and away, the most popular car in America. It was truly one of America's "All-American" brands, an icon, along with Coca-Cola. And its theme, "See the USA in your Chevrolet," went on to become one of the most memorable and popular themes in automotive advertising history. GM was on its way to flat-out dominating the American market, and Chevrolet dominated almost every segment it competed in, with a remarkable combination of style, performance and value that no other car company could match.

But a lot has happened to America and its car market since then. The dawn of safety regulations began in 1966. Emission controls became a real factor in 1971. And the Japanese onslaught began in earnest in the early '70s as well. Today, the American automotive landscape is fundamentally altered. The Japanese carmakers are part of the American automotive establishment. They build their cars here in factories all over the country, with American white-collar and blue-collar labor. The Europeans, led by the Germans, have taken broad swipes out of the performance and luxury segments in this country too. In 1979, GM controlled 48 percent of the domestic car market. In 2007, they're struggling to hang on to 25 percent of it.

And the most glaring change? The most glaring change is that, for all intents and purposes, Chevrolet has been usurped and replaced by Toyota in the hearts and minds of the American car-buying public. Toyota is *everywhere*, dominating in a wide range of segments. Toyota has even established a highly visible presence in NASCAR – the American manufacturer's traditional racing playground – and promotes that involvement with a withering barrage of advertising. And Toyota has taken Chevy's traditional high-visibility role on television with its mind-numbing but effective seasonal "sales event" campaigns – and has marginalized Chevy's efforts at every turn.

GM corporate executives didn't help, certainly, starving Chevrolet of new product and underfunding their budgets along the way. But Chevrolet and its ad agency, Campbell-Ewald, managed to make it easy for Toyota to waltz in and steal its thunder too. For almost 20 years, Chevrolet and Campbell-Ewald careened around trying to put as much distance from the classic mid-to-late '80s "Heartbeat of America" campaign as they could, even though it was the spiritual and logical successor to "Baseball, Hot Dogs, Apple Pie and Chevrolet" and the famous late '50s, early '60s iconic call-to-action campaign – "See the USA in Your Chevrolet" – as if there were something wrong with being identified as America's brand. And after Chevy wasted their time on a series of forgettable campaigns that did nothing but erode the brand, Toyota stepped in and stole Chevy's thunder – becoming "America's car" literally overnight. You could chart Toyota's soaring sales success with a corresponding decline in Chevrolet's fortunes, all because Chevrolet (and GM) forgot who they were, what they represented and where they needed to go in the market. Chevrolet and Campbell-Ewald fought back with the "This is our country, this is our truck" ad campaign featuring John Mellencamp's music in the fall of 2006, but it wasn't enough.

To be fair, GM's premier, high-volume division wasn't alone in its serial incompetence, Ford and Chrysler performed similar marketing face-plants that accelerated Toyota's gains in the market too. And while GM, Ford and Chrysler were rumbling, bumbling and stumbling their way to mediocrity, Toyota was making few, if any mistakes.

And Detroit's death spiral was put in motion.

IN THE LAND WHERE IMAGE IS EVERYTHING, DETROIT IS PRACTICALLY OUT OF BUSINESS

It's America wide open. It's boulevard dreams and Technicolor schemes. It's the long lost drive-in and some of the world's best damn scenery. It's an up-at-dawn, pedal-to-the-metal, cross-country sprint in a fuel-injected, chromachromed, fat-tired baby. It's no apologies, no regrets and free refills, all day, every day. It's open 24/7 and go-cups bigger than a redwood. It's hip dancin,' gum crackin,' give your dog a bone prancin' on an uptown Saturday night. It's a red, white and blue, shoot for the stars – soaring into a cobalt sky. It's aiming for the fences and goin' deep on a wing and a prayer. It's palm trees and movie stars, black snake roads and concrete canyons. It's every-thing good and bad about America, rolled into one giant movie set.

Los Angeles, undeniably, is the car capitol of the world. Cars may be built everywhere else around the globe, but it's here where they live, breathe, shine or fade into the woodwork. If you can't make a four-wheeled statement here, you can't make one anywhere else. In the land where image is absolutely everything, it doesn't matter if you've never had your Ferrari 599 over 80mph – the most important thing is that it looks *sensational* when you're pulling it up to the valet at the restaurant of the moment.

It doesn't take a genius to see what's happened to the American car industry over the last 30 years – all you have to do is drive around L.A. for a few days to understand. Where are the American vehicles? You see Lincolns and Cadillacs for the limo fleets. The occasional Corvette, Mustang, Chrysler 300, Pontiac Solstice, Saturn Sky and Cadillac V-series performance cars. And pickups and SUVs, of course – particularly the obligatory black Cadillac Escalades used as security limos. Other than that, except for a few domestic loyalists, if you see a car from a Detroit automaker on the road, there's a good chance it's a rental.

In L.A., Toyota replaced Chevrolet years ago as the standard American car. As a matter of fact, for all intents and purposes, GM as a whole is precariously close to being a non-factor in the California market. They've been trying desperately for the better part of a decade to reverse the long, painful erosion of their market share there, but it remains to be seen if they can halt the downward slide with a slew of new-think products. But it's not just GM. Ford and Chrysler haven't exactly lit up the charts in L.A., either.

Detroit is damn near out of business in the car-consuming capitol of the world.

How did this happen?

It's a long story, or it could be a short story with a series of long explanations. Suffice to say that Detroit's almost preordained knack for doing the absolutely wrong thing at the wrong time, combined with the Japanese manufacturers' remarkable ability to come up with the right products and the right marketing strategies at the absolutely perfect time, has turned the automotive world in the U.S. upside down.

In 1995, Toyota's market share in North America was just under 8 percent. By June 2007, that number had increased to nearly 17 percent. By contrast, Detroit's market share had declined to less than 50 percent – an all-time low. Even more staggering, Toyota's market cap was nearly as much as that of the entire Western car industry. On November 13, 2006, *The Wall Street Journal* reported that the market caps of BMW, DaimlerChrysler, Fiat, Ford, General Motors, PSA Peugeot-Citroen, Renault and Volkswagen added up to not much more than Toyota's $222 billion.

How integral is Toyota to American society? An August 2005 study from the Ann Arbor, Michigan-based Center for Automotive Research (CAR) showed that Toyota's investment of $13.4 billion in its U.S. operations contributed 386,300 jobs and $14.4 billion in wages to the U.S. economy in 2003. According to the study, Toyota's

U.S. manufacturer-related operations directly employed 29,135 people that same year. Those workers represent employment in manufacturing operations, sales, marketing, distribution, research, development and design, headquarters, and all other operational activities within the company, including the five manufacturing plants, located in Buffalo, W.Va.; Georgetown, Ky.; Huntsville, Ala.; Princeton, Ind.; and Fremont, Calif.

Another 74,060 workers were directly employed in new vehicle dealer-related operations, including sales, service and marketing-related activities. Add in the number of supplier jobs and the number of spin-off jobs (defined as jobs resulting from spending generated by Toyota's direct employees, dealers and their suppliers), and the total was 386,300 workers.

CAR also estimated that the San Antonio, Texas, plant, which opened for business in the fall of 2006 to manufacture the Tundra truck line, will generate approximately 9,000 additional total jobs and $460 million in annual compensation in Texas once it is fully operational. During the long-term construction phase of the plant, extending from 2004 through 2008, that number is expected to rise to 10,600 as a result of the construction labor required to complete the $850 million facility.

"Toyota's longtime motto is 'to enrich society through building cars,'" said Dennis Cuneo, senior vice president, Toyota Motor North America (TMA). "We are proud to be an integrated part of the American economy and an integral partner to the communities where we do business."

Longtime motto encapsulates Toyota's approach better than anything I could possibly say. The concept of time and how Toyota approaches it hits squarely on one of Toyota's key strengths and an area of enduring weakness for Detroit. It all starts with a fundamental difference in thinking...

TAKING THE LONG VIEW

The emergence of Toyota as the industry's leading automobile company is without question the most significant development in the automobile business of the past 25 years. Poised, polished and relentless in their pursuit of building quality cars and trucks, Toyota has been absolutely uncanny in their ability to not only identify a segment – but also in their ability to exploit a given segment with spot-on products that instantly become best in class right out of the box. Toyota has demonstrated that they know how to cultivate momentum in the market with savvy marketing and public relations strategies, along with the assistance of a deeply talented dealer body, and they are absolutely vigilant about not falling into complacency. And now that they have decided to build excitement into their products with a new emphasis on design and performance, it's logical to assume that Toyota will be at the top for a long time to come.

You only have to look as far as how Toyota launched its Lexus brand in the U.S. to understand the differences between the Japanese and Detroit approach to the car business. When Toyota introduced their Lexus brand in the U.S. in 1989, they willingly took a loss on every single one they brought in this country in order to gain a toehold in the luxury segment. Back then, the prevailing competition from BMW and Mercedes-Benz was in the $50,000 range, but Lexus came in with "lowball" pricing at around $35,000 at introduction – because the company made a calculated decision that they would have to take radical steps to "crack" the German automakers' stranglehold on the premium luxury segment in the U.S.

Today, Lexus is not only an integral part of the Toyota juggernaut striving for dominance in the worldwide auto market, it has become a gold standard brand in the U.S. Toyota's lowball strategy with Lexus didn't go unnoticed, of course, and they endured heavy criticism for it. The word "dumping" was used in print in more than a few stories in the media, because there was a vocal faction in the auto business both within and outside Detroit accusing Toyota of selling their home-built, luxury segment entries in this country at a huge loss and intentionally disrupting the market. Toyota took great umbrage at the suggestion that they were doing this, issuing a flurry of the appropriate denials, but the fact of the matter was that was *exactly* what they were doing with the launch of their Lexus brand.

And in hindsight, it was a brilliantly executed strategy.

But Toyota's Lexus strategy also points to one of the inherent fundamental differences between the Asian manufacturers and old-line Detroit-think (a mindset that is thankfully finally receding into the woodwork). The Asian car companies are perfectly willing to take an initial loss to gain a foothold in a market, especially the all-important North American market, and they're not only willing to invest in a long-term strategy, they allow themselves to invest in the concept of patience too – something the Detroit car companies aren't allowed the luxury of doing. Especially when the Detroit car companies are haunted by 30-day sales reports and a hostile financial community that questions their every move – fueled by the relentless din of the "doom and gloom"- tainted journalistic spin that seems to be all the rage whenever Detroit is referred to in the media.

It does help, of course, that the financial health of the Asian car companies is such that they can afford to adopt this kind of strategy to begin with, but it still takes a lot of balls to float your whole business on future profits down the road. One-way money going out is not a concept that makes for settled stomachs – no matter what the language.

But this is just one key to Toyota's success – there are plenty of other reasons too. Like their calculated manipulation of the media – and the media's blind willingness to take everything Toyota says as "gospel" – while questioning Detroit's motives down to the use of paper clips.

The bottom line is this, however: Toyota got where it is because of a near-perfect storm of events – their own skill and their relentless devotion to quality played a huge role, to be sure, but we would never be having this discussion if Detroit hadn't squandered every last opportunity to get their act together in a mind-numbing series of missteps and rampant incompetence.

LOST IN THE "GO-ALONG-TO-GET-ALONG" CULTURE

The reasons for Detroit's inexorable slide – from the top of the automotive world to very nearly a footnote in automotive history – are as simple as they are complex.

While Toyota was keeping its head down and taking the long view on the road to success, Detroit collectively took their eye off of the ball for the last 25 years. And in that time, the Asian and German manufacturers waltzed in and pulled the rug right out from under them. Detroit not only lost a generation of customers, they also lost the confidence of the car-buying public in this country. There are simply too many ugly stories about bad car experiences involving Detroit-branded products floating around "out there" in the real world – and that lingering stench of mediocrity is not something that will go away with a snap of the finger or a few exuberant auto show intros of "gotta have" products.

To a large degree, the Detroit car companies put themselves in the position they find themselves in today. Yes, there were several other contributing factors – the pervasive "not invented here" syndrome. The "go-along-to-get-along" bureaucratic mentality that strangles the life out of any decent idea that manages to escape the din of mediocrity that is the perpetual corporate soundtrack in the Motor City – the quintessential Detroit mindset that stifles any chance of true creativity and genuine vision from ever emerging on a consistently effective basis. The serial mismanagement and rampant egos that allowed Detroit executives to "assume" that they could hold off any challenges from their Asian and German competitors, even though the erosion of their market share continued unabated quarter after quarter.

But the bottom line is that Detroit collectively lost sight of the "Two P's" – *Product* and *Passion* for the product – and everything else associated with making cars and trucks the best they can be.

A car company revolving its efforts around the product – and vigilantly pursuing building great products with passion – requires an unwavering organizational focus and a relentless desire to do everything necessary to succeed (see BMW). Detroit lost sight of that and is ultimately responsible for the precarious situation it finds itself in. And it has been painful to watch as Detroit slowly but surely sinks into the Abyss.

Toyota is the Inexorable Force that must be reckoned with. Their products cover all niches and all perspectives without getting tangled up in missteps or with each other. They have an innate sense of what will be attractive to the mainstream buyer without totally alienating the fringe. They do it all with the most consistent quality in the business. And as they address segments in which they've been lacking, with higher performance machines on one end of the spectrum and more hybrids and cool entry-level cars on the other, I don't see anyone stopping them.

The concept of a downward slide simply does not apply to Toyota. They will just keep doing what they've been doing – because they've been doing it better than anyone else in the world for a long, long time.

But is Toyota an American car company? In a word, no.

THE HUNGRIEST CAR COMPANY IN THE WORLD

I first referred to Toyota as "The Juggernaut" several years ago – and for good reason. We're talking about an automobile company that earned just over $13 billion for their fiscal year completed at the end of March 2007, while Ford and General Motors failed to make money. Amid the mind-numbing numbers Toyota keeps delivering is the stark realization that it has the kind of momentum in the market that hasn't been seen since the glory years of GM's heyday. Toyota sales in North America set records nearly every month. And Toyota's worldwide sales climbed to 9.34 million vehicles in 2007, up almost 6 percent from the previous year.

Besides the fact that Toyota is about to surpass GM as the world's number one automaker, what does this all mean, exactly?

What it means is that success breeds more success in the car business, and because of Toyota's advantageous position and unbelievable cash flow – they can press their advantage in every segment they choose to compete in, address their real problem areas and take some "flyers" in the market that the other car companies don't have time to even think about.

For instance, Toyota will spend more than $6 billion on research and development – the very lifeblood of this business – in 2007. That means they can spend more and do more with their resources than any other car company in the world. Nothing fuels a car company's momentum like a generous research and development budget – and in this case, Toyota is going from strength to strength with no letup in sight.

Look at what Toyota has done in the youth market with Scion.

They could afford to spend whatever it took to "seed" the Scion brand in the North American automotive landscape. While other car companies are scrambling to carve out their own piece of the small car market, Toyota can attack subsegments and chase nuances – that's what deep pockets in this business will allow you to do.

Again, when you have cash flow, you can assess and address weaknesses, and even explore and experiment – without fear of stubbing your toe. Maybe that also explains why Toyota is one of the few car companies in the world right now that can compete in two major racing series – Formula 1 and NASCAR – at the same time.

Add to all of this the fact that Toyota can recruit the best talent in the business, from designers, engineers, managers and quality assembly people, right down to the finest dealers available, and it's easy to see why Toyota's stated goal of capturing 15 percent of the worldwide market by 2010 – which would tie GM as the world's largest car company – is a goal that absolutely no one doubts they'll achieve.

But perhaps the biggest luxury that comes with Toyota's momentum?

While other automakers are reeling just to make their "numbers," Toyota has the kind of financial stability that enables them to take some chances – something other car companies around the world that are teetering on the edge of solvency simply cannot afford to do.

Toyota is a car company the likes of which this industry has never seen before. They are not content to rest on their laurels – not by any stretch of the imagination. They're even deathly afraid of getting too "big" in attitude, like so many other car companies have before them. Which is why they remain ever vigilant in their quest *not* to lose their way.

As a matter of fact, Toyota is the hungriest car company in the world right now. They're using their success to do more research and development, chase down their flaws, explore new segments and fine-tune the details – all in order to build upon the eye-opening success they've already achieved.

In short, Toyota just *wants* it more than everybody else – and unless it completely blows up somewhere along the way, it will be "The Juggernaut" for many years to come.

THE MASTER MANIPULATORS

If media coverage of Toyota were encompassed in a news/talk radio station, it would have the call letters WTOY (or KTOY on the West Coast), standing for "All Toyota, All The Time." The kick start that really launched the media barrage for Toyota was *The New York Times'* reporter Micheline Maynard's book, *The End of Detroit: How the Big Three Lost Their Grip on the American Car Market*. The buzz about her book, which focused much of its content on Toyota's "way" – and why it is so successful, started in September of 2003, and this in turn focused other journalists' attention on the Toyota story, too, so that when Toyota delivered their ball-busting financial numbers shortly afterward, it created something akin to the "perfect storm" of media coverage for the Japanese automaker.

They were on an unbelievable roll, as the headline on a *Business Week* cover blared, "Can Anything Stop Toyota?" That was the question on everyone's mind in the "biz" – and it would remain there for the foreseeable future.

An *Automotive News* headline, "Toyota passes Ford as No. 2," only added to the impact of Toyota's staggering sales numbers. For the first time in history, Toyota passed Ford in worldwide sales, and the Asian giant served notice that they would be the force to be reckoned with in the automotive world. Passing Ford for number two was not only a *fait accompli* for Toyota – it was just one more step in their calculated plan for domination of the world's automotive market.

Although much of the Toyota media coverage is, in fact, deserved, there's an extra component to their success that involves more than just sales numbers and outstanding quality. That's because Toyota's dominance isn't just limited to their manufacturing expertise or their sales numbers. It also involves an equally crucial ingredient, one that few people even think about – and that is that Toyota has absolutely dominated the Public Relations wars too.

Automobile companies seem to go in cycles when it comes to their PR staffs and the job they do. The ones that get the PR function right – and do it consistently – are the companies that seem to be one step ahead of the others. But that's no easy task. Building a professional PR staff that meshes together seamlessly, delivering a "one voice" approach on a broad spectrum of issues is an extremely difficult challenge. The companies that involve PR in their core strategic product planning from the very beginning seem to be the ones that always have a leg up on their competition. This demands that the people making up these auto company PR staffs be extremely product savvy, which, as insiders in the "biz" will attest, isn't always the case – but the companies that get it right inevitably have the most success.

Of the Detroit-based auto manufacturers, GM's PR staff is clearly the deepest and arguably the most talented group operating today, but that still hasn't prevented them from having their hats handed to them by Toyota PR on a frequent basis. Steve Harris, GM PR's Chief, is known for his strategic acumen and for being an outstanding crisis PR manager. But it's hard to fight the pro-Toyota faction in the media – journalists who can't seem to find one redeeming quality within a Detroit-sourced car or truck.

The Ford Motor Company, on the other hand, has been all over the map. Bill Ford, the Chairman of the company and the man with his name on the door, flits in and out of his role as the face of the company. On the one hand, he's an eloquent spokesman for his company and his family's interests. On the other, he's reluctant to be in the public eye and to draw attention away from his executives. Ford, the company, has lived in this Public Relations Limbo for a long time. The net-net of it though is that when Bill Ford is "on" and engaged on the company's behalf, Ford always benefits. Now that Alan Mullaly has been given the reins of the company, Bill Ford has stepped back and allowed Mullaly to run interference. I'd give Ford an "incomplete" on the whole Public Relations function, because they're forever reacting instead of acting. And until they change that, Ford will continue to deliver an erratic performance when it comes to PR. Again, Toyota's PR troops don't have that problem and take every advantage of it.

In the case of Chrysler, Jason Vines, an auto industry veteran, heads up the PR function for the folks in Auburn Hills. Vines is smart, articulate and has a great sense of humor – and he uses it effectively in the course of his role. Vines can also be belligerent, blindly loyal and susceptible to gross overhyping. He can adopt an attack-dog persona at the drop of a hat if he feels his company's interests are being unfairly portrayed, too, which many journalists have encountered over the years. Because of the Dark Side of Vines' personality, he is sometimes unable to see the Black Forest for the trees, but he's always "on" for his company and at the end of the day, someone who represents his company's interests – and his profession – very well.

Toyota PR has done an unbelievable job of consistently getting the media to not only help tell their story – but to tell their story with all of the nuances of the Toyota "spin" completely intact. And Toyota has been hands-down the clear winner in the PR wars over the last decade because of it.

Toyota hasn't just executed a masterful PR campaign, it has crafted an aura for itself that somehow manages to combine the dream-induced stupor that Hal Riney originally created in order to sell the perfectly ordinary Saturn with a "touchy-feely" environmentally responsible image of a benevolent, automotive Jolly Green Giant – one who presides over a beautiful, green, patchwork-quilt valley filled with shiny, happy people all driving flawless and environmentally benign Toyotas.

So, while Toyota has become the irresistible force on the factory floor, in the showrooms, in the J.D. Power surveys, with the financial analysts, and in the hearts and minds of the American people, it's important to understand the absolutely key role Toyota PR has played in their rise to automotive stardom too – because it may have been as important, if not more so, than any of the other factors.

TOYOTA = GOOD, DETROIT = BAD. HOW THE MEDIA GOT SEDUCED BY THE TOYOTA PR HYPE

Analysts expect Toyota to blow by GM in terms of world market share by 2010, but make no mistake about it – they've already achieved it. No, they haven't exceeded GM's numerical world market share of 15 percent, but they've already exceeded GM in terms of product development capability, marketing strategy, and dealer development, and they've won the hearts and minds of American car-buying consumers to boot with the most successful PR and image campaign the automotive industry has ever seen. Toyota has slowly but surely usurped their way into a position of being "America's car company" – pulling the rug right out from Detroit. They should be praised for that, too, because they've been truly brilliant at it (an overused and overhyped term, but in this case "brilliant" is the only applicable word).

But in the course of doing all of this, Toyota has gotten a "free pass" from the media. You'd have to have been living under a rock not to have noticed it. Toyota not only can do no wrong with the media, journalists have swallowed the Toyota Kool-Aid willingly for years, glossing over things that Toyota does (or doesn't do), while heaping derision on other car companies – especially Detroit-based car companies – for the exact same things. The most glaring example of this is how the media has bought Toyota's manufactured "green" persona hook, line and sinker. Read the articles, and it's amazing that some journalists get away with what they write, bestowing Toyota with the equivalent of corporate sainthood whose technical brilliance will save us all – and the planet, too – while they're at it.

The breathless, almost frenzied coverage given to the Toyota Prius by certain card-carrying members of the anti-car, anti-Detroit intelligentsia in the media quickly became embarrassing – with their theory being that this is the latest example of how Detroit is once again missing the boat on what's "next" in the market. In what amounts to a complete rollover by certain members of the media to the hype of Toyota's PR machine, "the rest of the story" – when it comes to the realities of hybrid ownership – was late being told. Things like the discrepancy in the real-world mileage of the Prius versus the "projected" numbers touted in the advertising. Or the fact that absolutely no one was speaking about the high costs of a battery replacement facing buyers who plan on keeping their cars. Or that hybrid vehicles are one idea for a transition step to this country's transportation future – but they're certainly not suited for everyone's needs (or pocketbooks) by any stretch of the imagination. The Prius is certainly a smartly executed piece, but if you paid too much attention to some of the drivel being spouted by the media, you'd get the impression that it is the greatest thing since sliced bread. Well, guess what? It's not, but we'll all have to continue to weather the sniveling media rhetoric canonizing hybrids – at least until they move on to telling the next chapter of the Toyota=Good, Detroit=Bad story.

But Toyota's posture is a duplicitous one. Their "We're the most environmentally conscious car company in the world" mantra – which they spout at the drop of a hat, while they continue to churn out gas-guzzling trucks and luxury SUVs at a prodigious rate – is transparent and blatantly untrue. And nary a negative story is being written about it. When Toyota took the wraps off its giant, full-size pickup truck concept at the Detroit Auto Show in 2004 – the FTX – it was amusing to see Toyota drop its precious "We're so green, we're sickening" persona as they reveled in big-truck adjectives that talked about size, strength and power. It was not so amusing, however, to see the mainstream automotive press continue to give Toyota miles of slack when it came to this glaring contradiction – giving Toyota gushing coverage of its Prius, yet refusing to call them on the carpet for the fact that they were shortly going to begin building the biggest pickup truck on earth at a new factory in San Antonio.

Perhaps the most egregious example of the media buying into Toyota's hype came from *The New York Times'* Op-Ed columnist Thomas L. Friedman, who clearly embarrassed himself royally in a June 2005 column entitled "As Toyota goes..." He opened his column with this sentence, "So I have a question: If I am rooting for General Motors to go bankrupt and be bought out by Toyota, does that make me a bad person?" From there, he proceeded to embark on a ridiculous diatribe against General Motors and Detroit, suggesting that GM should be taken over by Toyota because of its incompetent management, saying "Indeed, I think the only hope for G.M.'s autoworkers, and maybe even our country, is with Toyota. Because let's face it, as Toyota goes, so goes America."

First of all, I was shocked to learn that Friedman had become an instant expert on the automobile industry overnight. Secondly, I was even more shocked to learn that he was capable of indicting the U.S. auto industry and GM in particular in a column that was based entirely on dubious technical facts. Oh hell, let's call these "facts" what they were – flat-out fiction.

Friedman's entire premise revolved around the fact that in his opinion, GM management's behavior had bordered on the criminal and that "Having Toyota take over General Motors – which based its business strategy on building gas-guzzling cars, including the idiot Hummer, scoffing at hybrid technology and fighting Congressional efforts to impose higher mileage standards on U.S. automakers – would not only be in America's economic interest, it would also be in America's geopolitical interest." As if those accusations weren't ill-informed enough and just simply untrue – for the record, GM has spent more money on environmental and advanced emissions research (including hydrogen-powered fuel-cell vehicles) than any other car company in the world – Friedman officially veered into dim-bulb territory with his assertion that "Toyota has pioneered the very hybrid engine technology that can help rescue not only our economy from its oil addiction (how about 500 miles per gallon of gasoline?), but also our foreign policy from dependence on Middle Eastern oil autocrats."

Wow, we could wipe out the industrial Midwest, solve our energy problems and be on course to have energy independence in no time – just by buying a Toyota? Who knew?

Friedman touts "Geo Greens" as the answer to all of our prayers – people who "seek to combine into a single political movement environmentalists who want to reduce fossil fuels that cause climate change, evangelicals who want to protect God's green earth and all his creations, and geo-strategists who want to reduce our dependence on crude oil because it fuels some of the worst regimes in the world." And then, in order to back up his assertions, he says that with the vision of the "Geo Greens" our world will be a much better place. Friedman then identifies "Gal Luft, co-chairman of the Set America Free coalition, a bipartisan alliance of national security, labor, environmental and religious groups that believe reducing oil consumption is a national priority..." as his be-all and end-all source for all things having to do with the automobile.

I have a hot tip for Mr. Friedman – and maybe *The New York Times* can unleash legions of reporters to help him uncover what I'm quite sure he'll deem as the biggest cover-up in the history of industrial America, seeing as he seems to gravitate toward such conspiracy theories. There once was a magical carburetor in the '60s that delivered 100 miles per gallon. It was so revolutionary that it threatened to transform the automobile industry. But the inventor was stymied in his attempts to get Detroit to buy his invention, because, after all, it would fundamentally change their cozy little business model, and it would ultimately cost them money. So, the Big Three got together and purchased the rights to the invention for $10 million, bought up all the existing tooling and sample carburetors – and then promptly took them to a smelter and melted the whole lot down into metal, which was later reused to make cars and trucks. And the "magic" carburetor was never heard from again. Yes, Tom, it was an evil conspiracy – and if you'd just dig deep enough into the story, I'm quite sure there'd be a Pulitzer Prize in it for you.

I only throw that mythical little fable out in order to give you a sliver of an idea of just how wrong-headed Friedman's column was. For an esteemed journalist like Friedman to lapse into a blatantly misguided diatribe – which sounded for all the world like the wild-eyed bleatings of a delusional hack, by the way – and then, on top of that, to have the temerity to suggest that it's The Gospel and that he's just solved the United States' – and the U.S. auto industry's – problems overnight with a few keystrokes, was simply inexcusable and unforgivable.

I know that Friedman fancies himself as a geopolitical expert, but I have an excellent suggestion for him: *he needs to stick to writing about what he knows* (and no, riding around in yellow cars with lights on their roofs or in black "hired" sedans doesn't constitute having accrued knowledge about the automobile business), because 1. It's clear he knows nothing about the automobile industry or the technology involved in building automobiles, and 2. He also doesn't have a clue about the technological resources and vast amounts of people power and money that GM spends (or Ford and Chrysler spend, for that matter) on advanced research into fuel efficiency and future automotive propulsion systems.

GM, for one, has spent billions upon billions of dollars to reduce emissions and to search for more innovative technological solutions to our nation's long-term energy needs. One living, breathing example of this that exists right now is the hybrid propulsion system that has been developed at Allison Transmission, a former division of GM. This exceptionally innovative hybrid propulsion system has allowed GM to focus on larger vehicles – conventional buses – in order to make them more commercially viable. If Friedman had bothered to ask, he would have discovered that by the summer of 2007, there were more than 400 GM-hybrid-equipped buses operating in about a dozen North American cities – saving more than one million gallons of fuel a year. And, as GM has pointed out, if America's nine largest cities were to replace its existing fleet of 13,000 transit buses with hybrid buses, the nation would save approximately 40 million gallons of fuel a year.

What, GM has hybrids? To certain ill-informed members of the media, it may come as a surprise, but yes, they do. As a matter of fact, there are automobile companies in Detroit and around the world *other than Toyota* that not only have hybrids, but future-think hydrogen-powered fuel-cell vehicles too.

I'm just wondering out loud here – but how could GM's management possibly find the time and money it does to devote to furthering the advancement of the automobile and securing our nation's future transportation needs when they – according to Friedman – are so completely preoccupied with a business strategy based on building gas-guzzling cars and scoffing at hybrid technology?

Yes, Toyota has done a wonderful job with their hybrids, but Mr. Friedman's column flippantly dismissed the countless talented men and women at work at General Motors (and by association, Ford and Chrysler) who spend their entire working lives coming up with *real-world* solutions to improving the efficiency of our cars and trucks. And frankly, Mr. Friedman owes all of them an apology.

Weaning this country off of our dependence on "Middle Eastern oil autocrats" for our energy needs is an urgent and noble goal. But much to Mr. Friedman and the "Geo Green" movement's chagrin, there are no "500-mpg" magic bullets out there just waiting to be discovered that will solve all of America's geopolitical problems overnight. And there is no "Geo Green" Happy Dust available that we can all inhale that will suddenly fix everything, either.

The long-term, big-picture thinking required to solve our country's future transportation and energy needs requires the talents of serious, knowledgeable people immersed and engaged in coming up with innovative, real-world solutions. The kind of practical and effective solutions that will set this country on a course to energy independence – without impeding our economic growth.

The wild-eyed bleatings of "instant" experts add absolutely nothing to the discussion – and are flat-out irresponsible.

Friedman's column remains the quintessential example of how Toyota's "Master Manipulators" in Public Relations basically created an aura for the company in the media's eyes that is seemingly impenetrable. The company can absolutely do no wrong – because members of the media have liberally imbibed in the Toyota Kool-Aid to the detriment of accurate reporting. To see it in print, however, from someone of Friedman's reputation, was shocking – and still is.

But unfortunately, Friedman wasn't through...

In June 2006, Friedman went after General Motors again (in what now has become an annual ritual, apparently) in a piece entitled, "A Quick Fix for the Gas Addicts" with this opening line: "Is there a company more dangerous to America's future than General Motors? Surely, the sooner this company gets taken over by Toyota, the better off our country will be. Why? Like a crack dealer looking to keep his addicts on a tight leash, G.M. announced its 'fuel price protection program' on May 23. If you live in Florida or California and buy certain G.M. vehicles by July 5, the company will guarantee you gasoline at a cap price of $1.99 a gallon for one year with no limit on mileage. Guzzle away."

Comparing GM to a crack dealer was irresponsible enough, but what has now become *de rigueur* for Friedman, America's newest auto expert went on to abandon the facts completely and accuse GM of financing our enemies in Iraq and Afghanistan by "...subsidizing its gas-guzzlers, but not a single member of Congress, liberal or conservative, will stand up and demand what most of them know: that we must have some kind of gasoline tax to compel Americans to buy more fuel-efficient vehicles and to compel Detroit to make them."

The fact that Friedman could go out of his way to equate a simple cash rebate for vehicle purchasers cloaked in a fancy wrapper with sponsoring terrorism would be laughably absurd in and of itself – if it weren't so pathetic.

GM and the rest of Detroit make plenty of vehicles that get terrific gas mileage and in fact are adding more and more models every day to their fleets. The Detroit automakers are also spending billions on advanced propulsion and powertrain research, too, but those facts are completely lost in favor of the gushingly positive cacophony generated about Toyota by the sycophant media.

Detroit's problem – at least to Friedman and his pals – is that they also make the larger and heavier vehicles that help the hardworking people of this country do the work that needs to get done, which, when you really think about it, is something that a *New York Times'* Op-Ed columnist like Friedman couldn't possibly be familiar with or understand.

Much to the Detroit-haters' chagrin, this country simply couldn't function without the wide array of vehicles that the Detroit car companies make. Period. And Friedman also chooses to conveniently ignore the fact that Toyota makes large, oversized, gas-guzzling vehicles too – vehicles that actually deliver worse mileage than the new offerings from GM. And, to top that, Toyota opened a brand spanking new plant in Texas so that they can build the biggest pickup truck in their history. It's funny, but Friedman is strangely silent about those facts, but then again, why let facts get in the way at this point?

Friedman's simplistic view of the world would be just another part of the media "white noise" out there if it weren't for the fact that too many people pay attention to what he has to say – even if they should know better – and even if it is wrong-headed, illogical and supported with purported "facts" that only he seems to have access to.

What's really going on here is that Friedman has now appointed himself Supreme Commander of the Anti-Car, Anti-Detroit Intelligentsia in the media and in Washington, and also for the Dan Beckers of the world and others of his ilk who share Friedman's laughable, Toyota=Good, Detroit=Bad mantra, and who would have us all driving clown cars made out of balsa wood, hugs and a smile, if they had their way – with Toyota emblems on them, of course.

Fortunately, America isn't ready to become Rickshaw Nation. Questioning Friedman's motives in all of this or giving him the benefit of the doubt is a monumental waste of time. Linking GM and an entire American industry that supports 1 out of every 12 to 14 jobs in this country with financing terrorism and in turn demanding the destruction of it, along with the countless livelihoods associated with it is not only reprehensible, it borders on sheer lunacy.

In the meantime, Toyota continues to get a "free pass" in the press. How long will it continue? It's up to the rest of the establishment media to decide.

A JEKYLL & HYDE PERSONA – "MR. GREEN JEANS" VERSUS WORLD DOMINATION

Okay, by now you're getting the fact that Toyota is the Greatest Car Company in the World. They have raised building quality cars to an art form, they have an uncanny knack for nailing market segments right out of the box, and they've managed to convince millions of Americans that the rolling equivalent of automotive vanilla is preferable to just about any other cars and trucks out there, becoming, in effect, "America's car company." On top of all of that, they've even managed to redefine the luxury and near-luxury segments with Lexus, they've turned the entry-level market segment upside down in their spare time with Scion, and they've brainwashed everyone who will listen that they're the only car company in the world capable of building hybrids. When you have all of that going for you, what's left to worry about?

Plenty, apparently.

Companies dealing from this position of overwhelming strength are usually concerned about things such as maintaining their focus, keeping from falling into a pattern of complacency or improving the designs of their products – all of which Toyota is doing as you read this.

There's one overriding issue that keeps Toyota executives in Japan awake at night, however, and that is the fear that a protectionist political movement might gain momentum in Washington, because Toyota is steamrolling through the U.S. market seemingly at will, while Ford, General Motors and Chrysler are slumped against the ropes. In order to counteract any winds blowing in the protectionist direction, Toyota has taken great pains over the last 25 years to build factories and an organizational structure here employing thousands of Americans and in short, doing everything in their power to convey to consumers and legislators alike that they are, in fact, an American company. They've done a damn fine job of it too.

And therein lays the rub with Toyota. I don't begrudge them the success they have at all. Toyota is focused, they're unbelievably consistent, they are relentless in identifying what people want, they execute almost flawlessly, and they simply do things better than just about everyone else in the business. I happen to equate 99 percent of their products to motorized pabulum, but apparently anesthetized transportation rings true for a lot of people in this country – and so be it.

But Toyota has a very annoying habit of talking out of both sides of their corporate mouth.

On the one hand, they try to project themselves as being the Ultimate Green Car Company, seducing every half-baked Hollywood type and underachieving media slacker into thinking that their hybrids are singularly brilliant and that no other car manufacturer in the world can touch them. On the other, Toyota builds a growing number of large, gas-gulping SUVs and trucks that they conveniently neglect to talk about – as if no one will notice. And for the most part, they get away with it.

And on the one hand, Toyota keeps opening cans of Whup-Ass on America's hometown automakers, exploiting their built-in price advantage for all it's worth, while on the other, they turn around and try to make nice by putting a creative new spin on an old tactic.

The evidence? According to a report in the *Asahi Daily* (June 2005), Toyota was planning to raise the prices of its new cars in the United States by an average two to three percent in October of that year because the company was "concerned" with its struggling U.S. rivals. Even though Toyota spokespeople took great pains to deny any such action was imminent at the time, then Toyota Chairman Hiroshi Okuda had been telegraphing the fact that this was coming for months, going on record a couple of times that Toyota could "help" America's struggling automakers by raising the prices of their cars and trucks.

An altruistic gesture on Toyota's part? *Right.*

First of all, it's no secret that car and truck prices are raised to a varying degree at new model year introduction, which is still predominantly in the fall. Car companies annually factor in higher material costs, more standard equipment and whatever else they feel like covering in their sticker prices – and prices go up. Lately, some car companies have even resorted to raising prices just so that it can appear that they are giving deeper discounts.

So, Toyota's move was not only nothing special, it passed for standard operating procedure in the car biz. Not only that, but by raising prices, there's the built-in little side benefit that Toyota would make even *more* money. How convenient.

Yet, Toyota was hell-bent on convincing anyone who would listen that they were raising prices strictly out of the goodness of their hearts in order to help out poor, downtrodden Detroit.

But it just didn't wash.

Toyota raising their prices and then saying it would be for Detroit's own good is like going to the dentist and hearing, "This will sting a little bit" just as they start a root canal.

Even Toyota's "Master Manipulators" were unable to overcome this major *faux pas*. And there was no concealing the fact that this stunt pegged the stupid meter – big time – no matter how hard they tried to spin it.

IS TOYOTA UNSTOPPABLE?

It's easy to get lost in the "local" stories in Detroit – the continued renaissance at GM, the battling comeback for Ford and the not-out-of-the-woods-by-any-means-yet Cerberus-owned Chrysler, but the fact of the matter remains that Toyota has basically been hammering these companies on all fronts for at least a decade.

So what is it about Toyota, anyway?

Not only does Toyota do everything well, it's their *consistency* that separates them from the rest of the pack. It's not unusual for an automaker to do a few things well and enjoy some notable successes while doing it – every manufacturer can boast of at least a few bright spots (well, almost every one, anyway), but every classification of vehicle that Toyota touches seems to be at or near the top of every segment they compete in right out of the box. That type of *consistent* excellence is unrivaled in the business today.

And that's just the beginning. Along with its obvious strengths in product development, Toyota brings savvy marketing and out-standing strategic thinking to bear on behalf of their efforts too. They not only built American plants, they became part of the local communities, conducting themselves as an American company. And well they should, since the majority of Toyota's profits are derived from the American market. And despite the fact that Toyota *isn't* an American car company, there are plenty of people who insist that the exact opposite is true – that Toyota *is,* in fact, an American car company. That's an indication of how consistently brilliant the Toyota marketing and PR strategies have been over the years. And it doesn't hurt that helping Toyota execute its message and strategy is a superb group of dealers who "get it" and who understand that Toyota has now become a part of the American fabric – and they conduct themselves accordingly.

I've made fun of the "Toyota-thon" mentality in the past, but make no mistake – what Ford and Chevy used to do as a nice year-end sales gimmick, Toyota has turned into a quarterly event that dominates the airwaves and other media. The ads have become so ubiquitous and such a part of the media landscape in this country that they have sunk into the American consumer consciousness, which, ironically is exactly why the GM's "Employee Discount for Everyone" campaign was so successful. Toyota had reminded GM of the "formula" that GM used to do best once upon a time, and that is to keep the message simple and powerful – while making sure the products deliver what's promised. And nobody executes that winning formula better than Toyota.

As if to put an exclamation point on Toyota's efforts, there is the one thing that they continue to lord over the rest of the industry like a badge of honor – and that is their expertise in quality. As soon as the industry gets a little closer to their top quality numbers, Toyota finds a way to raise the bar again. It has been going on like this for years now. The amazing thing is that the other car companies are building some excellent products right now, but since Toyota has such a clear-cut quality leadership image with the American consumer and continues to reap all of the benefits of that leadership position – the other car companies find themselves trying to convince the American consumer that they're well within range, and consumers are having none of it.

Simply put, Toyota is intent on world domination of the automobile business. They're competing at such a high level that they're steamrolling anything that gets in their way.

Other car companies, more often than not, are barely able to keep up. Toyota can present their "good corporate citizen" routine to all who will listen, but there's no question that they intend on being the largest and most successful car company in the world one day.

Toyota is focused, they are relentless, they rarely make mistakes and even when they do, they seem to have an uncanny knack for recovering from them almost immediately.

But are they unstoppable? Not necessarily…

PRECISION-CRAFTED BLANDNESS

As I like to say, Toyota does bland so well that the concept of a "design language" for Lexus or Toyota is irrelevant. Toyota has specialized in delivering an alluring blend of bulletproof reliability and unfailing quality in their cars and trucks to the U.S. market, and after experiencing this reliability and quality firsthand, almost an entire generation of American car buyers has turned away from the traditional Detroit-based domestic automobile manufacturers and has never looked back. But if Toyota wants 15 percent (or more) of the world's automotive market by 2010, they know that what they've done up until this point isn't going to be enough.

Toyota's emphasis on quality and reliability has gained them legions of buyers, but for the most part these buyers tend to view their cars and trucks as just "transportation" or worse – as mere appliances. And even though Toyota has produced wonderful engines for the street and has been heavily involved in racing over the years – the bottom line is that Toyota vehicles for the street have been beyond bland. So now Toyota is hell-bent on changing that perception.

But in my estimation, they have a long, *long* way to go.

Using the word "bland" in conjunction with Toyota doesn't do justice in describing just how vanilla most of the vehicles Toyota has unleashed on the streets and byways of America really are. They're coldly colorless to a fault, relentlessly antiseptic in their demeanor and elicit little more than what your average toaster does in terms of an emotional response. I take that back – some of the heavily art-directed contemporary toasters are fascinating to look at, and I've never said that about a production Toyota.

You only have to look as far as what Toyota has done with Lexus to gain a full appreciation of the predicament they're in. Lexus vehicles border on being flawlessly executed, with sumptuous appointments and all the luxury accoutrements you'd expect of vehicles in that class. But they're totally devoid of personality. Buyers are supposed to revel in their flawless execution and "no surprises" functionality, and for some (actually, for a *lot* of people, with Lexus sales climbing), that's enough. But for others looking to spend in that price range, it will never be enough – and those are the kinds of buyers Toyota is desperate to reach.

Lexus has been a brilliant marketing and customer service exercise, but their automobiles and sport utilities fail to engender much in the way of passion. There is no question that this formula appeals to a growing list of people, but even Lexus knows that they can't live by latte lounges and shiny happy service greeters forever. That's why Lexus has a full-court press on right now to redefine itself as a stylish design leader in the luxury class, although ironically, its much-touted new LS460 imparts the same sort of coolly detached, non-involving design language that Lexus has always delivered.

For now, however, Lexus is a state of mind, a beautifully screwed together appliance that appeals to people who have no real reason to go out of their way to use the words "passion" and "automobiles" in the same sentence. And Lexus has made an absolute killing on that premise.

Several years ago, Toyota tried to engineer passion into the Lexus SC430 – the sports/luxury coupe/roadster with the retractable hardtop that was supposed to be Toyota's expression of sensual luxury wrapped in an emotionally drawn exterior shape. In true, earnest Toyota fashion, they even sent their design team to the south of France to soak up the sun and the atmosphere to help jump-start their creativity. But they missed the mark by a bunch. Yes, the SC430 ran flawlessly and was bathed in luxury features, but it provided about as much of an emotional connection to the driver as a Camry. And its painfully overwrought design, with its ungainly turns in the metal, did nothing to help its cause. If this was Toyota's best stab at delivering emotionally satisfying vehicles to the street, well, that's what I mean about them having a long, *long* way to go.

But how do you teach soul to a car company?

Much to the chagrin of more than a few executives, there isn't an MBA curriculum on the face of the earth that offers it. It's just not that simple. In recent years, car companies were brimming with financial and marketing types who went through a few performance-oriented "ride-and-drives" orchestrated by company gearheads and emerged as "car guys" virtually overnight. It was a magical trans-formation, and all of a sudden the entire industry was overrun with freshly minted "car guys" who didn't have the first clue as to what the hell they were talking about. If donning the obligatory khaki Dockers and a sporty polo shirt complete with racy company motor-sports logos was all it took to become a certified "car guy" – then we'd all be bewildered by the countless exceptional cars we'd have to choose from in the market today.

Again, it's just not that simple.

Toyota must be secretly wondering what they have to do to grad-uate from being flawlessly reliable to becoming wildly desirable. I'm sure they'll go about it in their usual fashion – conducting exhaustive studies revolving around interrogating enthusiast buyers, desperately trying to capture the mindset and the details that trigger their every nuance, smile and sigh of satisfaction. And they'll tout their various racing involvements as proof of their legitimate "DNA" (that ridicu-lously overused and overhyped expression that's spread like wildfire throughout the industry) to add credibility to their quest. And then they'll somehow try to quantify where they want to go by distilling it all down to an intricate formula and then challenging their product design team to execute that formula down to the last digit.

But in the process, Toyota is bound to learn some very hard les-sons about themselves.

For instance, they'll quickly find out that you can't instantly instill passion into an organization whose entire culture revolves around the mantra of coldly calculated, precision assembly. Toyota isn't a company like BMW, which has performance as part of its basic MO, and it isn't even a "Motor" company like Honda. Rather, it's a car company whose sole claim to fame is its manufacturing excellence, and it's hard to extract a passionate idea out of that.

Toyota's quest will not be easy, by any stretch of the imagination. They can't achieve it with money or sheer marketing muscle. They can't call on their mega dealers or their awesome distribution system to help with it, either.

No, Toyota is going to have to find that passion and soul deep within themselves (if it exits at all) and allow it to come to the surface without it getting buried in their "system" or tainted by one of their patented digital formulas for success.

Unless and until they do all of that, they don't stand a chance of altering their dowdy image in this market.

Oh, and one more thing – in order to succeed in their quest, somewhere and somehow along their journey Toyota will have to come to understand one of the irrefutable laws of the car biz:

You can't put a number on a car's soul.

BASEBALL, HOT DOGS, APPLE PIE AND TOYOTA

Toyota has become ingrained in American society to the point that Americans working for Toyota, whether it is at factories or dealerships, consider it to be an American company. And it's easy to see why, what with Toyota selling more vehicles in the U.S. than it does in Japan on a regular basis. A lot of people would even argue the fact that it really doesn't matter anymore who owns Toyota, that it's a moot point and that nationalistic concerns should have nothing to do with it. Add to this the fact that to people in cities across the U.S., where Toyota is in fact *the* reason they are able to feed their families, pay for their kids' education and make a comfortable living, it doesn't matter to them who Toyota really is in the global scheme of things, because to them it's a local company, it's involved in their local communities, and it provides them with a comfortable standard of living. And if you look at it that way, they're absolutely right.

But I offer a different perspective.

And no, this will not be some maudlin, jingoistic "Buy American" diatribe, either. I'm certainly not going to dispute the fact that the American automobile companies brought their current predicament upon themselves – because they absolutely did. They ignored the seriousness of the competition from their Japanese competitors for so long that by the time they woke up to the reality of what was happening, it was way too late. The Japanese products were better, more reliable and – before their inroads into the luxury market – often cheaper than anything from the traditional Detroit automakers. And in most cases, this is still true today, because although the quality "gap" has grown smaller between domestic and import manufacturers, the fact that the Japanese can build their vehicles for far less cost means that the domestic manufacturers from Detroit will always be playing catch-up in a market that has no time for catch-up.

Every day of every week, Detroit auto executives get up to face a daunting disadvantage against Toyota. Toyota's cost structure allows them to operate with a revenue per vehicle number that is as much as $6,000 per car better (depending on the vehicle) than that of the typical U.S. automaker. This is a result of Detroit's daunting health-care cost burden of $1,500 per car, its monumental legacy costs from thousands of retirees' pensions and the oppressive union contracts negotiated in Detroit's last "heyday," which prevented the automakers from closing plants unless they paid the displaced workers 85 percent of their wages. Detroit's inability to cut their costs enough prevents them from even remotely competing with the Japanese cost struc-ture. Add the Japanese government's orchestrated manipulation of the yen designed to benefit "Japan Inc." at every turn, and you have a laundry list of horrors for Detroit auto executives that is crushing in its scope. But Detroit is culpable too. As a matter of fact, Detroit has hastened its slide to oblivion at every turn.

So really, it's not that hard to see why Toyota has supplanted Chevrolet as "America's car." GM's dismal mishandling of its pas-senger car brands over the last 20 years has permanently damaged the one brand they absolutely couldn't afford to damage – Chevrolet. I saw it for myself while at Chevy's ad agency, how GM siphoned off huge amounts of dollars away from Chevrolet marketing and advertising so that they could prop up Saturn's remarkably average product lineup – a lineup that they could not, or would not – for the life of them figure out how to expand. I saw major Chevrolet product launches given a token amount of money almost as an afterthought, just so that Saturn could get one more enhanced promotional pro-gram under way.

And I was there to see Chevrolet's market share literally fall off the radar screen out in California (except for trucks) as Toyota basi-cally became the "people's car" for a majority of consumers on the West Coast. GM's willful and intentional dismantling of Chevrolet has to be one of the most egregious mishandlings of a brand in auto-motive history. GM marketing blunders literally destroyed the quint-essential American automobile franchise in less than 20 years.

But GM wasn't alone. The domestic manufacturers squandered their dominant position in the U.S. market *en masse* because they were consistently the highest-cost, lowest-quality producer in a game that the Japanese had single-handedly redefined to be as one of lowest cost, highest quality. And now we are well into the *second* generation of buyers, who, thanks to the Toyotas of the world, have *never* owned a domestic brand of car or truck.

During this time, Toyota never wavered from their game plan. They slowly and methodically wove themselves into the American economy. Complaints of taking American jobs away were met with an emphatic rejoinder – they simply built plants here and hired American workers. And their suppliers built plants here too – and hired American workers. And they recruited local business people to buy and run their dealerships. They sponsored motorsports and other sporting events on a national level. And they sponsored little league teams on the local level. They sponsored the arts in cities across America and contributed to a wide range of charities and edu-cational programs too. They've done an absolutely superlative job of winning the hearts and minds of the American people.

It's no wonder people consider Toyota to be an "American" car company – because for their money, and their communities, and their educational and cultural institutions, and their charities, Toyota, for all intents and purposes, is an American car company. As a matter of fact, no other car company – Asian or German – has so blatantly promoted itself as an American company. Yes, of course, Honda has been assembling motorcycles and cars in Ohio for nearly 30 years, but they haven't gone as far as Toyota has in adopting an American persona. The same is true for BMW and Mercedes-Benz. They build cars here, and they participate in community affairs, too, but the lines never seem to blur between the origins of the company and their U.S. outposts.

But Toyota has always been a different story. Some of the most respected business leaders in communities all over America are Toyota dealers. Or work for a Toyota suppliers. Or sell Toyotas. Or work for Toyota directly. Roger Penske, for instance, owns the world's largest automobile dealer, Longo Toyota, in California. There are millionaires (and a few billionaires) all across America who have made their fortunes either directly, or indirectly, from Toyota. Look around you. People all over your local community drive a Toyota or Lexus and think nothing of it. Your friends, your neighbors and your coworkers. To them, Toyota is more American than Baseball, Hot Dogs, Apple Pie and Chevrolet. Hell, most people don't even *remember* when Chevy was any of that. Toyota has become an accepted part of the American fabric. It's just no big deal. After all, if Detroit can't compete, too bad and tough. It's a dog-eat-dog world, and only the strong survive, right? And why should I buy an American car when they're just not as good, right? Well, yes and no. On one level, that's certainly all true. Buy what you like. Like what you buy. And get the best quality for your money. If that happens to be a domestic brand, fine, but don't sweat it if it isn't. After all, Detroit is ultimately responsible for their predicament, and it's not my problem, right?

Maybe so, but let's not forget one key point.

Toyota may provide for comfortable livelihoods all across America. It may even be your own car or truck of choice. It might have even provided you with a scholarship to go to school. But after all is said and done, there is one simple reason why Toyota never has been and never will be an "American" car company:

Well, 13.2 billion reasons, actually.

Toyota earned $13.2 billion net profit in 2006. And where, exactly, did those profits go? It seems there's one very big thing that *isn't* American about Toyota, and that is where those profits go at the end of the day. To me, that makes Toyota a Japanese company, plain and simple. A company that is now inexorably woven into the fabric of this country, but a Japanese company nonetheless.

THE END OF LIFE AS WE KNOW IT?

In the late spring of 2005, Toyota Motor President Fujio Cho, called General Motors a "wonderful" company at a media conference in conjunction with the Tokyo Motor Show and dismissed suggestions the Japanese automaker was trying to overtake its bigger rival. "We honestly don't intend to and we're not aiming to overtake GM," Cho told an industry conference in Tokyo, also attended separately by top executives from GM, Ford and other major automakers.

"For us, GM and the 'Big Three' have always been a presence beyond our reach, way beyond the clouds in the sky, and now we feel we've finally reached a position where we can see them somewhere in the distance ahead," said Cho. Let us offer a collective *right* for all the people who heard his speech in person and who probably muttered it under their breath. Cho's touchy-feely "Mr. Sunshine" speech flew in the face of reality, as Toyota had repeatedly gone on record as stating that they had every intention of capturing 15 percent of the world's automotive market – and more. Mr. Cho, who is supposedly a modest man, may have bought into his speech, but I can assure you absolutely no one else did at the time – except the homers in the Japanese media.

Regardless of President Cho's statements, the writing is clearly on the wall for the Motor City and indeed for all of Southeastern Michigan – an area that makes up the support fabric of what used to be referred to as the Big Three. Toyota's inexorable march to the top is bringing about a fundamental change in this region, much of it not good.

The auto industry has been a way of life around here since the early 1900s, and the dynasties forged in that era and the endless generations of families supported by the auto industry are not only being threatened – they're in danger of just fading away. For those of us who grew up here (and for many on the West Coast who are now working for Asian car companies but who grew up here too), it is a very sad thing to contemplate.

But the world has changed forever, and the people in this region, who identified with the hustle and bustle and who prided themselves on the fact that they were from the Motor City, will have to learn to adjust and change with it.

PART FIVE

2006 – THE YEAR OF BEING FUNCTIONALLY DYSFUNCTIONAL IN THE MOTOR CITY

Two thousand six was hands down the most unforgettable year in the history of the Motor City, but then again, we're talking about a place that had been on a relentless roll of unforgettable years of late. Because just when you thought things couldn't get much worse around here, they inevitably did. What used to be a battle of hanging on to market share for the denizens of the Detroit car companies had now turned into an all-out war of survival.

With the Ford Motor Company scrambling for its very existence, Bill Ford brought in Alan Mulally from Boeing to run the show – and just weeks into his new assignment, Mulally had to preside over Ford mortgaging its future in a desperate attempt at avoiding The Abyss of Bankruptcy.

Meanwhile, GM ended up having to justify its existence to Kirk Kerkorian, the casino carpetbagger/hostile investor from L.A., and Jerry York, his bag man/advisor from Detroit – and a guy with a long-festering score to settle with the automotive world.

And finally there was the Chrysler Group, which went from being the darling of the sheep-like auto media to careening completely out of control in its new persona as The Gang from Auburn Hills Who Couldn't Shoot Straight, and which couldn't bring itself to stop churning out cars and trucks – even though dealer lots were bulging with excess inventory, and storage lots all over the city were over-flowing with cars and trucks (as a matter of fact, it became a favorite pastime of frequent flyers coming into and out of Detroit's Metro Airport to spot the various Chrysler storage lots around the city).

Two thousand six was the year when the global realities of the automobile business hit the Detroit car companies like a well-placed two-by-four right across the forehead. Competition ratcheted up as the Asian onslaught on the North American market intensified. The built-in cost advantages that the Asian manufacturers had on Detroit were compounded by the fact that the Japanese government continued to "unofficially" manipulate the yen to suit their home-country automakers – and it did so with impunity (a tactic that continues to this day).

It also became excruciatingly apparent that the bloated contracts that the Detroit car companies and the UAW acquiesced to in the "good old days" (the late '80s and early '90s) were now relics from a wildly short-sighted era. That, combined with the U.S. government's continued failure to deal with the burgeoning crisis in healthcare and pension funds, was propelling Detroit – as an industry *and* a region – head-first to oblivion.

Remarkably, while in the throes of this relentless cloud of negativity that threatened to choke the very life out of the business around here, the Detroit automakers actually started to deliver excellent and even, in some cases, truly outstanding products. Cars and trucks that were appealing from every angle – from design and content to performance and responsiveness, with fuel-economy that even exceeded the foreign competitors more often than not. Yet, in spite of unleashing a slew of these newly-competitive and even class-leading products, long-disaffected consumers *still* wouldn't give Detroit the time of day.

At least not enough to stop the plummeting domestic market share, that is.

In a world where image, like it or not, had become everything, a majority of consumers continued to view cars and trucks from Detroit as second-tier merchandise, commodities that should be tolerated and acquired only by way of some unbelievable "deal"– rather than be aspired to or coveted.

And that, in a nutshell, was what was keeping Detroit up against the ropes and hearing the soundtrack of a standing eight-count in a sound loop that never ended.

Detroit found itself at the end of another tumultuous year in the most intensely competitive market in the world, in a business that veered from the merely chaotic to the uproarious – and did so by the minute.

And there's a reason for that.

The automobile business is a kaleidoscope of people bristling with visionary talent and creativity who unfortunately are, more often than not, offset by barely mediocre, third-team players equipped with the staggering ability to run everything they touch right into the ground. These two forces of Good and Evil in this business are perpetually locked in a swirling maelstrom of absurdity, only intermittently interrupted by the shining light of reason and common sense.

So there would be no let up on the pressure, no rest for the weary in Detroit. That's what it meant to be in the trenches at the front lines of America's industrial war for survival.

Here is a snapshot of The Year from Hell for the Motor City, and how it began to unfold back in the dungeon-like confines of Cobo Hall in downtown Detroit, during an uncharacteristic spell of mild January weather...

Saying that you're "Bold, Innovative and American" doesn't necessarily mean that you're actually Bold, Innovative and American, now, does it? The Ford Motor Company kicked off the media days at the Detroit Auto Show by wrapping itself in the American flag and insisting that it was all about being "Bold, Innovative and American." As a matter of fact, the assembled Ford executives said those three words so often in their prepared speeches that we actually lost track of the number of times they had to interrupt what they were trying to say to remind us what the three words were again. I wouldn't quibble with the basics of Ford's new thematic message – *if* the company appeared to be on the same page, but it wasn't. Then again, it never has been. There always appear to be warring fiefdoms on display when Ford attempts to make a big splash at an auto show – and that January was no different. Ford was all over the map at Cobo Hall, with few peaks and far too many valleys. For every "Super Chief" concept and Shelby Mustang Cobra production car, there was one more glaring example of Lincoln marketers wandering around lost in the desert. This just couldn't' continue. Even though several Ford insiders I talked to at the show insisted that lots of really good things were happening behind the scenes at Ford, even they understood that they were quickly running out of time to convince the non-believers that they had turned the corner.

We're not only going to tell you what play we're going to run – we're going to ram the ball down your throats knowing full well that there's not a damn thing you can do to stop us. What could be said about Toyota that hadn't been said before, other than that they continued in their relentless pursuit of world domination in 2006, and there was apparently no one capable of standing in their way? The Toyota FJ debuted at Cobo, and it was funky, oozing with personality and looked just about perfect. Unlike its domestic competition, Toyota was smart enough to let the consumers find the FJ at the show – and they did in droves. Toyota said that they didn't care about volume (at least initially) on the FJ; they just cared that people were satisfied with its authenticity. Smart move. And their new entry-level car, the Yaris, which was *much* more attractive in two-door form, added one more market opportunity to the Toyota repertoire. They just didn't put a wheel wrong, it seemed.

Best Face-Plant into the Sea of Mediocrity and Biggest Fall from the Top. The media darlings formerly known as the "geniuses" at Chrysler Design imploded at Cobo Hall in an embarrassingly overwrought performance that wouldn't soon be forgotten. It seemed like we had been talking about Chrysler design excellence for a long time up until then – and we had. From the glory days of the product renaissance led by Bob Lutz and Tom Gale to as recently as two years ago, Chrysler could always be counted on to deliver great stuff for the major auto shows – no matter how mediocre and uninspiring their street vehicles were. But as in all great runs, nothing lasts forever

– and the wheels came off Chrysler's golden design era with a thud at the 2006 Detroit Auto Show. Without question, the concept that set Chrysler Design back at least 25 years (and sent the design community as a whole into shock) was the relentlessly hideous Imperial Concept. Imagine if Wal-Mart decided to get in the car business overnight, and the market they were absolutely *convinced* they could succeed in was the $300,000+ Rolls-Royce Phantom/Mercedes-Benz Maybach niche. Being Wal-Mart, of course, they would locate a junior college with a burgeoning wannabe automotive design program (a friend of a friend of a guy over in marketing who's their resident "car guy" said these guys were "good") and commence initial design work. After a month or so and a couple of reviews, they call it "perfect" and then contract an unknown, unnamed manufacturer in China to build the car, so that they can bring it in to the U.S. market for $49,995.

In what will surely go down in recent automotive design history as a gross miscalculation at best and an unmitigated disaster at worst, the Chrysler Imperial was one "blue sky" design notion that should never have gotten past the initial design "idea" meeting. Clumsily rendered and saddled with comical Toon Car proportions, the Imperial was and is simply the most embarrassing concept in my recent memory – and when it comes to design turkeys, I have a lengthy one. There was not one good angle, line, crease or fold on the "thing" – not one. How could this atrocity have been allowed to happen? After all, the men and women at Chrysler Design were plenty talented and capable, but the Imperial was a complete travesty, a design disaster of incalculable proportions. I could go on, but I won't bother. Suffice to say, Chrysler's grand design legacy was virtually destroyed literally overnight by one monumentally bad judgment call – and it will be years before they'll live this down. Not a couple of car show seasons, folks, but *years.*

Ford basically admitted that it is functionally dysfunctional on Monday. And I am shocked at what the Ford executives put out for public consumption – and at the depth and breadth of the utter futility they admitted to.

Everything the Ford executives said about what it would be doing from this day "forward" sounded right and perfectly in line with every basic thought process that should be part and parcel of any contemporary, big-time auto making company – except for the fact that Ford was admitting that it was just now discovering what the hell they were supposed to be doing. And that was simply incomprehensible to me.

If I'm one of the assembled big-time analysts at that press conference, I'm immediately looking at my watch and saying to myself, "Wait a minute – what year is this? And these guys are just now discovering what it takes to turn this enterprise around and compete in the North American market? How long is it gonna take for these guys to become serious players in the market again – and who has that kind of time?" In this, the most hotly contested market in the history of the automotive business, where product hits are now determined in 12-month windows of opportunity rather than in three- to five-year plans, how can Ford expect the market to wait around for them? The quick answer? The market won't wait, and Ford is already behind the eight ball – before they can even get out of their "Way Forward" gate. – Autoextremist Rant #331, 1/25/06

Hey, we're not content to be just *any* car company – no, we're gonna be *America's* car company. Toyota continued on its quest to become "America's car company" by hitching its star to NASCAR. It was a marriage made in marketing heaven if ever there were one. NASCAR had managed to dupe yet another manufacturer into believing that their "spec" racing series was actually worth the exorbitant price of entry, even though NASCAR's peculiar brand of "racertainment" amounts to no more than motorized wrestling on a grand scale. But there was really no surprise in Toyota falling for NASCAR's siren song, because after all, they're falling right in lockstep with the television networks and clueless marketing "experts" in corporate America who also confuse NASCAR's orchestrated popularity with actual marketing impact. The real reason behind Toyota's commitment to the NEXTEL Cup? The company is obsessed with being thought of as an American car company. It's an obsession that dominates its strategic thinking, its marketing, its dealers and every decision it makes in the U.S. market. But Toyota isn't content to be just any American car company, no, indeed – it wants to be *America's* car company. And what better way to continue its marketing push than to seed that notion into the American consumer consciousness while competing in NASCAR's Big Show?"

> *People who flippantly dismiss the fate of the domestic automobile industry in general are simply missing the point. I continue to be amazed by the media intelligentsia on both coasts and by certain members of Congress in Washington (who just happen to have import auto plants in their states) who dance around this issue, insisting that what's going on in Detroit will not negatively affect the entire country in some way, shape or form.*
>
> *And they're flat-out wrong.*
>
> *The core issues facing Detroit – global competitiveness, U.S. trade imbalances, healthcare costs and pension funding – are issues we as a nation must deal with – right now. This is not some isolated bad tiding that will only affect the Rust Belt in the forlorn "flyover" states as the mid-section of the country is often derisively referred to. No, this situation spells trauma for the entire country. Between 1 in 12 and 1 in 14 jobs in this country are still either directly or indirectly related to the domestic automobile business. Think about that statistic for a moment and then insist that it somehow "won't affect me."*
>
> *And you'd be flat-out wrong too.* – Autoextremist Rant #332, 2/1/06

Yeah, but we'll put our gadget-laden techno-wonders up against yours any day. From the "Talk to the Hand" File, it appeared that the old Mercedes-Benz arrogance was back and in full bloom in their latest print ad campaign for the new S-Class. The headline? "At The Top Of The Automobile Industry Is One Company. At The Top Of That Company Is One Car." Then, it goes on to suggest in glowing copy that nothing has changed in the automotive world in the least, that the M-B S-Class has always been the world's premier car and that the latest version is no exception, continuing that tradition. Okay, so let's get this straight, Mercedes-Benz snaps its fingers and presses the "reset" button and everything is okay now? After having squandered the legacy of one of the world's great brands by building gadget-laden techno-wonders with the reliability of a dollar store compass, M-B wanted us all to forget what happened and resume the practice of three-pointed star idolatry? That's notgonnahappen.com. There wasn't a snowball's chance in hell that this was how things were going to work. Mercedes-Benz was once a great brand, but in a world of surprisingly competitive Cadillacs, outstanding BMWs and relentlessly perfect entries from Lexus, Mercedes-Benz was just another car company struggling for the same piece of the luxury-performance pie.

Inventory problem? What inventory problem? Part I. I had predicted late in 2005 that Chrysler's "little" inventory problem would turn into a very big deal indeed. Chrysler offered its dealers $1,000 for every vehicle sold in February and March 2006 with one very big condition – that the participating dealers didn't cut their March vehicle orders and that they continued to take vehicles from Chrysler's overstock lots, which were bursting at the seams with unsold vehicles. This didn't appease some disgruntled dealers, however, because they wanted Chrysler to get real and cut production before the bloated inventory situation dragged down the spring selling season. But Chrysler didn't listen. They were so desperate to hang on to their standing on Wall Street as the perceived "darlings" of the domestic manufacturers that they were willing to throw their dealers under the bus rather than deal with reality and admit that their much-touted momentum had stalled. I had one big question for the folks out in Auburn Hills (which proved to be prophetic) – what good was projecting an image of momentum to Wall Street – when your "Big Mo" was about to take you right off of a cliff?

Maybe we *like* **wallowing in mediocrity, ever think of that? Huh?** In what was no surprise to me, the new Mercedes-Benz R-Class proved to be a *major* disappointment in the retail market. The overblown, overwrought and overweight crossover from Mercedes was so far out of whack price-wise right out of the chute that Mercedes was forced to introduce a heavily incentivized lease on the R-Class in a desperate attempt to jump-start the car in the market, as it was selling at only 60 percent of initial projections. At the end of the day, the R-Class was just the latest disappointment in a long line of disappointments from the stumblebums at Mercedes-Benz. They continued to operate as if the world revolved around them, and incredibly enough, they continued to brandish their classic Mercedes-Benz arrogance – even though the luxury market in the U.S. had blown right by them. Mercedes-Benz seemed to be reliving the bad old days of General Motors – long after even GM realized that business as usual was no longer business as usual. Mercedes now had too many models and too many dealers, and they were trying to chase too many niches in this market while trying to be all things to all people. The pathetic thing is that even when presented with the hard evidence of their errant ways, their arrogance *still* prevented them from having a clue. The brain trust at Mercedes seemed to be hell-bent on squandering every last shred of integrity that the brand once enjoyed in this market – and watching these hacks run what was once one of the most envied automotive names in the world right into the ground was like watching a train wreck that you couldn't take your eyes from.

Washington must get real about the concept of USA, Inc. and start looking out for our own industries. Some people actually think it would be no big deal if this country were to lose most of its manufacturing base, and I feel sorry for them, because they really don't know what they're wishing upon this country when they say that. Once upon a time, there were textbook ideals of a happy economic world that would revel in free and open markets and "fair" trade. That's a nice, idyllic fantasyland to conjure up, but it has nothing to do with what's going on in the world today.

We live in a world where countries will take as much of the economic action as they can possibly get their hands on. And for Washington to continue to embrace the notion of "acquiescing" indefinitely to make the world a happier place for everybody is simply nonsensical and detrimental to this country's welfare at this point.

A few months ago, I said that the looming crisis that the domestic auto industry is facing due to the unfair trade practices and the manipulation of currencies by its foreign competitors' host countries, combined with this country's growing inability to deal with the healthcare and pension issues was the "canary in the coal mine" for the rest of industrial America.

This isn't a Republican issue or a Democratic issue – it's an American issue – and I grow more convinced by the day that Washington's failure to take definitive action to counteract this accelerating crisis will have catastrophic implications for this country's economic well-being for years to come. – Autoextremist Rant #335, 2/22/06

The walking, talking definition of notgonnahappen.com. From the "Flim-Flam" File came word that Malcolm Bricklin, the relentless huckster, was still trying to convince dealers in early March that he really was going to be bringing cars in from China to sell in the U.S. one day. I suggested that any dealer who was seriously considering spending dollar one with this guy should just surrender their franchise and go open a street corner lemonade stand. The announcement would come by November that Bricklin's flirtation with importing automobiles from China was a nonstarter, although he was *still* insisting that it wasn't over yet. Bricklin surfaced again in the spring of 2007 at a dealer management conference that I was speaking at in New York where he touted a new line of hybrid cars that he was looking to import from China. By then, however, his credibility was all but gone, and the members of the audience barely paid attention to what he had to say.

Yeah, we hurled in our cornflakes, too, as a matter of fact. Jeffrey McCracken's excellent piece in *The Wall Street Journal* (3/1/06) about the infamous "Jobs Bank" program that was compounding the domestic automakers' woes on their road to revival made readers choke on their breakfasts after reading it, there's no doubt. McCracken quoted Jerry Mellon, a 34-year GM worker profiled in the piece, who actually said at one point, "I understand the Jobs Bank needs to have an end to it. I mean, they've paid me like $400,000 over six years to do nothing, to learn to deal blackjack. But buy me out. Retire me with something like $2,000 for every year I worked. I need that because you know they're going to keep cutting our healthcare and pensions. You are so vulnerable in retirement."

> *Pontiac has suffered mightily from the bureaucratic gravitational force field that has churned and stirred the traditional GM divisional structure over the years. While GM marketers scrambled to prop up seven other brands, Pontiac always seemed to be left out on the fringe with product initiatives that often fell woefully short of what the brand deserved. After resurrecting Cadillac to the tune of $5 billion, GM marketers launched Hummer. After dumping a boatload of money in a desperate attempt to save Saturn a few years ago, GM finally got around to worrying about Chevrolet. While GM is trying to pump life into Saab and Buick, Pontiac is left to fight*

over crumbs for its product plans. Now, GM's launching the most aggressive new product push in Saturn's history – and Pontiac finds itself left out in the cold again. GM can go two ways with Pontiac at this critical juncture. They can keep starving it to death with brand engineering and clone cars, or they can start over with an all-new mission that adheres to the core essence of what a Pontiac was – and should be.

It shouldn't be hard. All it would take is a total commitment from GM and the right people in place to make it all happen. But then again, those two key ingredients are the two things necessary in bringing focused, desirable products to the street no matter which company we're talking about.

Back in '81, I did a print ad for the Firebird Trans-Am that had the headline, "Soul Survivor." That ad set the tone for the "excitement" era that followed and started Pontiac on its way back. But Pontiac has unfortunately careened in and out of relevance ever since.

The time is now for Pontiac. The division deserves better. Much better. GM needs to get in touch with the essence and soul of Pontiac and put it on a plan not only for survival – but for revival. If done exactly right, Pontiac's marching to a different drummer persona could have tremendous appeal today in this market of vanilla Asian transportation appliances and German techno-wonders. And if GM can't muster the will to do the right thing with one of America's most famous automotive name-plates, then they might as well just take it out back and put it out of its misery.

I'd rather see that than watch it fade away like dust in the wind. – Autoextremist Rant #336, 3/1/06

"Uh, come in Osamu, come in..." With the news that GM was selling all but three percent of its 20 percent stake in Suzuki to raise

$2 billion in cash, Suzuki Chairman Osamu Suzuki came up with a Autoextremist Quote of the Week, when he told reporters in Tokyo, "I wasn't aware that GM was in this much trouble. GM probably had a problem with cash flow." Uh, do ya' think, Osamu? Were you away on vacation on Mars for the last two years, or what?

Hose-O-Rama, Part I. As predicted, Leo Burnett Detroit lost a huge chunk of its Cadillac ad business to Modernista in Boston, in March. Modernista got the CTS, SRX and the coveted V-Series performance line, while Leo Burnett Detroit retained the STS, DTS, Escalade and XLR. On January 18th, I had written the following on Autoextremist. com: "Liz Vanzura, the former head of Hummer marketing, is now moving to Cadillac to assume the same role. Why should this worry Leo Burnett Detroit, which has the Cadillac account? When Vanzura arrived at Hummer fresh from VW, she orchestrated that a newly-formed Boston ad agency (Modernista), stocked with creatives from Arnold with whom she had worked on the VW account, got the Hummer account – even though GM had other agencies spend big time and burn big money on the pitch. Will history repeat itself? We wouldn't bet against it." Rumors had been circulating in recent years that a change was imminent, especially with the tireless and tediously overrated self-promoter Donny Deutsch sniffing around for an assignment, but the move by Vanzura "telegraphed" that a change was finally in the works. Not only was it her MO to put all of her eggs in Modernista's basket, it made it easy for the powers that be down at GM to finally make a change, conveniently directing any flack back to Vanzura. Is this the end of the bleeding for Leo Burnett Detroit? No. The agency will lose the rest of Cadillac by the end of the year. *(Leo Burnett Detroit lost the rest of Cadillac to Modernista over the summer, but then in a stunning reversal, GM consolidated Buick and GMC with Pontiac at the agency in the summer of 2007.)*

He's only the Patron Saint of Corporate Pond Scum, other than that it was a *great* idea. GM once again fell victim to the siren song of "product integration marketing," only this time it wasn't

Pontiac pushing a Solstice long before it was available like it did last year – no, it was Chevrolet hitching its reduced expectations to that Patron Saint of Corporate Pond Scum, Donald Trump, and his tedious NBC sleaze-fest, "The Apprentice." In the latest episode of "Must Miss TV" (from the network that managed to turn the Winter Olympics into a relentless yawn), "Apprentice" candidates were supposed to come up with a three-hour training session for the new Chevy Tahoe for a group of Chevrolet marketing executives and 25 Chevy dealers. Talk about a riveting premise, what could possibly top that idea – a very special episode of "Maury" – ? And just in case the comatose viewers didn't get enough of that tedium, they could go to a Chevy-sponsored Apprentice-themed website and make a Tahoe commercial out of footage provided, espousing the SUV's brand promise of being "more capable, more responsible and more refined." When the car companies started to finally become less enamored of golf sponsorship marketing, we were really encouraged. Little did we know that they would turn their uninspired thinking to this crap. It almost made us long for the days of the Greater Greensboro Open, "brought to you by the fine folks at (your car company name goes here)."

Then again, maybe a very special episode of "Maury" *would* **have been better.** It was bound to happen – and it did. The aforementioned Chevy Tahoe promotion connected to "The Apprentice" gave people a chance to "create" a TV commercial for GM's new full-size SUV online, but instead it turned into a complete fiasco as the Internet Nation seized the opportunity and unleashed a flurry of anti-SUV, anti-Chevrolet and anti-GM spots.

> *As I've said many times before, Ghosn is a proven corporate turnaround artist, but his ability to lead organizations after the turnaround plateau is reached and then take it through the crucial next phase has always been suspect in my book. And by orchestrating the move of Nissan's U.S. headquarters to Nashville, Ghosn is*

demonstrating to me that my gut feelings about him are indeed correct. He is willing to trash the current NNA organization – destroying the culture and the chemistry of the team that did all of the heavy lifting and delivered the goods in the process – as long as it conforms to his "vision" for the company's future. In other words, his "vision" is more important than the reality of the situation – or the welfare of the company itself. Carlos Ghosn may be the King of all he surveys, but this move is pure madness. And it will prove to be the undoing of what once was a pretty damn good car company. – Autoextremist Rant #338, 3/15/06

Inventory problem, what inventory problem? Part II. In the fall of '05 Autoextremist.com nominated the Jeep Commander as one of our leading candidates for the 2006 model year's Answer to the Question that Absolutely No One is Asking for a number of reasons, not the least of which was the apparent delusional thinking by Jeep marketers that had them convinced that what the automotive world was clamoring for more than anything else right that instant was a stretched Jeep Cherokee with obvious Hummer overtones and seven-passenger seating. They were wrong. *Automotive News* reported that the Chrysler group was offering $5,461 per unit in Commander incentives (according to Power Information Network figures) and that there was a 101-day supply of the vehicles as of March 1. Thus began the throes of Chrysler's very public inventory problem that plagued the company all year long. High gas prices played a role in quelling the frenzy that never developed for the vehicle, but the real problem was that the Chrysler Group had so misunderstood and in turn mismanaged the Jeep image in the face of surprisingly strong competition from GM's Hummer that they were throwing everything up on the wall at that point to see what would stick. You only had to take a long hard look at the new Compass to get a grasp of the utter cluelessness at work out in Auburn Hills at the time. But the wrong-headed thinking wasn't confined to the Jeep brand. While other manufacturers were paring their offerings to avoid overlap in the market, the Chrysler Group offered the Jeep Commander, the Jeep Cherokee and the Dodge Durango, which were all priced dangerously close together and sitting in the same showrooms. But it didn't stop there, because the Chrysler Group then proceeded to unveil the leading candidate for *2007's* Answer to the Question that Absolutely No One is Asking – the Chrysler Aspen SUV.

In many respects, now that the imports have gone mainstream, thanks to ill-informed tirades from such automotive "experts" as The New York Times' Thomas L. Friedman, who officially anointed Toyota as "America's Car Company" last summer – Detroit collectively has a shot as the alternative brand for American consumers. As a matter of fact, it's amusing to see some of the import brands veering to the staid and stodgy end of the automotive spectrum, while the Detroit automakers continue to push the envelope, coming up with some of the industry's most expressive designs.

After documenting this industry for the last seven years, it's no secret why this has happened, and I'm not going to rehash it here, but suffice to say Detroit played a large role in the predicament they find themselves in today and have gotten almost everything they've deserved. But some of my lesser colleagues out there have so bought into the imports-are-automatically-better way of looking at the world that they're not only incapable of seeing anything positive come from Detroit – they wouldn't know if it ran over them in the street.

American consumers have followed right along with the program, and they're now so conditioned to the notion that Detroit = Bad, Imports = Good that they're incapable of giving anything with Detroit overtones even a minimal shred of consideration. – Autoextremist Rant #342, 4/12/06

The more you know, the more you just never know. When Rick Wagoner received a "vote of confidence" from the board in mid-April 2006, 30 of GM's top dealers paid for a full-page ad in the *The Wall Street Journal* in support of Wagoner, saying, "Today our CEO Rick Wagoner is leading the best management at GM since Alfred Sloan. He needs and deserves support for the enormous job that he is doing." The ad was signed by 36 heavyweight dealer groups around the country. There was just one small problem with that ad – the majority of those dealers were all heavily invested in import franchises, and in some cases their dealer groups were so dramatically skewed to pushing imports that upwards of 90 percent of their revenue was coming from the sales of imported cars. So their grand gesture was nice and all, but the reality of their businesses is that they started hedging their bets long ago and embraced import franchises by the boatload to cover their asses. A smart business decision, to be sure, but let's just say that it cast their show of gushing support for Rick Wagoner in a much different light. Was it a heartfelt gesture of support? Or were they covering their asses again just in case The Rick pulled off GM's turnaround?

Big Oil, meet Big Jason. Also in April, Jason Vines, vice president of communications for the Chrysler Group, took on Big Oil on the Chrysler Group's company blog. Jason teed-off on the major oil companies, accusing them of greed and indifference to the environment, among other things, and generally just being out of touch with reality. Here are a few of his quotes: "Big Oil would rather fill the pockets of its executives and shareholders, rather than spend sufficient amounts to reduce the price of fuel, letting consumers, during tough economic times, pick up the tab." Jason was just getting warmed up: "Despite a documented history of blowing their exorbitant profits on outlandish executive salaries and stock buybacks, and hoarding their bounty by avoiding technologies, policies and legislation that would protect the population and environment and lower fuel costs, Big Oil insists on transferring all of that responsibility on the auto companies." The tirade by Vines was brought on by a print ad that ExxonMobil ran late the year before that criticized the auto industry's record and infuriated auto executives across the country. In the ad, ExxonMobil said the U.S. economy had become vastly more fuel-efficient since the first oil shock but that Detroit had done exactly zero to help things out in the previous two decades. The news in all of this was that these fights were usually kept behind the scenes, but the new, aggressive, "take-the-gloves-off" fighting mood in Detroit came to the fore – and it was frankly long overdue. One more quote from Jason: "The auto industry is doing its job by building cleaner, leaner, more efficient vehicles and embracing alternatives to gasoline. While we make these important and responsible strides, Big Oil is swimming in profits, content to let the nation's drivers drown in rising prices, every time they fill up."

"Hi, My Name's Dan, and I'm Relentlessly Clueless." Predictably, Daniel Becker, director of the Sierra Club's global warming program, was thrilled to see the dust-up between the Chrysler Group and ExxonMobil. *The Detroit News* reported that Becker said, "I'm happy to watch. Each industry is right – that the other is to blame for a big part of the problem. The auto industry continues to make gas-guzzling vehicles with antiquated technology rather than using modern, fuel-efficient technology. At the same time, the oil industry is perfectly happy to have people addicted to their product." Thanks, Dan, I was glad you weighed in with your two cents (although I had trouble finding anyone who actually cared about what you think). Now, please return to your cave and fire up your pedal-powered computer in preparation for the return of the New Dark Ages – and then have a *super* day.

"I went out with her a few times, but I got tired of the ears, the whiskers, the tail – you know, the usual stuff. I guess we didn't really have much in common." In a real head-scratcher, Volkswagen brought back the Rabbit nameplate for its small car in the United States and Canada. The change went into effect for the fifth generation of the car, which went on sale in the summer of

2006. VW had used the Golf name in the U.S. and Canada since 1984. As some might recall, the original Rabbit was sold in the U.S. from late 1974 through 1984, and built in VW's factory in Westmoreland, Pa., from 1978 to 1988 – when ex-GM executives in charge thought color-coordinated interiors were the sure-fire ticket to American consumers' hearts and damn near destroyed the VW brand in the process. Kerri Martin, formerly VW's "director of brand innovation," said, "Volkswagen customers want a relationship with their cars. Names like The Thing, Beetle, Fox and Rabbit support this." Huh? You have *got* to be kidding. VW customers wanted cars that offered a fun-to-drive Germanic driving experience that was unavailable from the Asians, *without* requiring a "Frequent Guest Pass" to the service department – something that VW had been unable to demonstrate as of yet. This was pure, unadulterated lunacy from a gaggle of people who should have known better. On second thought, they clearly didn't have a clue. These brainiacs just might have successfully accomplished what the ex-GM-ers couldn't do back in the late '70s – and that was destroy the brand in the U.S. once and for all.

Toyota's press conference for the new Lexus LS600hL, which kicked-off media events on Wednesday (at the New York Auto Show), was one of the most embarrassing displays of unbridled arrogance ever unleashed by a car company at a media preview. It even put to shame some of the more outrageous displays by the German manufacturers at auto shows past – and that's saying something. The tone, the language and everything about the presentation confirmed to me that the 'creeping' arrogance that has been brewing at Toyota for years has finally blossomed into full bloom for everyone to see. Toyota not only hinted that the 600hL would be the best car in the world, they came right out and said it – and the tone they used suggested that there was no need for us to attend any other manufacturers' press conferences because we had just witnessed the only newsworthy event at the show.

These people actually now believe that the moon and the stars revolve around their sun – and they're not afraid to lecture everyone about how to act in the presence of true greatness. A few in the media genuflected appropriately in the white-hot light emanating from the greatness of Toyota and dutifully became deputized shills for the Master Manipulators in the Toyota PR machine, generating vacuous stories anointing the 600hL as the new king of the automotive world. But those who did have been transparent Toyota boosters for years, and their stories were treated for what they were – glorified extensions of the Lexus press release package. I detected more than a little skepticism from the majority of the auto media present, however, as Toyota clearly stepped over the line of proud confidence into a dimension of "our excrement smells like a field of spring daisies." These people are headed for a big fall, but predictably, they will be the last to see it coming. – Autoextremist Rant #343, 4/19/06

Who's counting anyway? Nissan gave its final number to the media regarding the percentage of NNA employees moving from its old headquarters in southern California to its new digs south of Nashville, and it left many insiders scratching their heads. Nissan's figure appeared to include just over 200 employees who were temporarily living in California and who had been hired to replace employees who left the company early on in the process. The numbers shook out this way, according to our insider sources: NNA started engineering the move with 1300 employees and then 300 left initially, leaving 1000 of the original employees on staff. Then, factoring those 200 replacement workers back in, the total jumped back up to 1200. Nissan said it retained 42 percent of its employees, which meant that 504 of the 1200 people actually made the move. But subtract the 200 people who were not part of the original NNA roster from that total and you were left with 304. With just 304 of the original 1300 NNA employees making the move from California, the actual percentage came out to around 24 percent of the original NNA staff making the move to Nashville. We knew for a fact that recruiters were frantically scouring Detroit and environs to find people who would consider going to work for NNA in Nashville. Thanks to Carlos Ghosn's so-called "vision," Nissan had decimated its NNA workforce and left the company exposed to horrendous hardships at a critical juncture, as they were in the throes of launching a wave of new products into the market over the next 18 months. I never wavered from my assess-ment of this move from Day One: It would be a major setback for Nissan in the U.S. market at a moment when the company could least afford it. While the remaining Nissan loyalists kept their fin-gers crossed, hoping that the basically all-new NNA staff would "gel" overnight and be able to pick right up where the company was before it started this self-destructive journey, Nissan's competition would be moving forward, confident in the knowledge that one of their fore-most competitors had just shot itself in the head.

I've got news for the auto industry "experts" on Wall Street who believe they have a handle on what will pull GM out of its quagmire. Hint? You don't have a clue. It won't be the Rick Wagoners and the Fritz Hendersons of the world. It won't be some unexpected jolt of common sense received by the UAW, or a sudden infusion of light and clear thinking in Washington, D.C., either. No, GM's future lies with its True Believers, the men and women who actually go to work each and every day with one mission in mind – to design, build and produce the best vehicle they can possibly muster. These are the people who don't concern themselves with the waffling winds blowing in from Wall Street, or the doom and gloom prognosti-cators who seem to be hanging around every corner gas station around town here. No, they let their creativity do the talking, because it's much easier to express themselves that way. And Exhibit No. 1 of their creative efforts?
The sensational Chevrolet Corvette Z06.

I had the pleasure of driving the Z06 last week, and I found it to be an eloquent rebuttal to every half-baked instant expert, every media talking head with a thimbleful of knowledge and a large dollop of "America can't compete" attitude – and every so-called automotive pundit who had Detroit dead and buried long ago.

The Corvette Z06 is simply the most seductive combination of power, speed, drivability, value and overall efficiency that exists in the world today. A high-performance super car for the real world, it is a milestone achievement that deserves recognition as much for its capabilities, as for the people behind it.

"They" basically said that what was accomplished with the Corvette Z06 couldn't be done. You couldn't design and develop a high-performance car that was tractable, relatively affordable and fuel-efficient – yet capable of delivering the kind of performance numbers previously reserved for super cars costing thousands upon thousands more. Well, "they" were wrong. The Z06 demonstrates conclusively that when GM focuses its best and brightest talents on a goal, they can deliver the goods. Period. – Autoextremist Rant #345, 5/3/06

As living, breathing, legacies go, it's pretty damn great. Don Sherman did an excellent tribute piece about the original Corvette Sting Ray in the June 2006 edition of *Automobile.* Sherman weaved the story about the famous Corvette racer and why it was the heart and soul of the corporation's design staff (accompanied by an excellent design analysis sidebar by Robert Cumberford). I had to take my hat off to Ed Welburn, GM's vice president of global design, who, recognizing the significance of the car, had it restored immediately after taking the reins of GM's design staff. Welburn realized that the original Sting Ray deserved to be put back to its proper sheen, so it could be an inspiration to all young GM designers. I had the privilege of riding with Bill Mitchell in the original Sting Ray on several occasions, and it simply was and is one of the most beautiful creations on four wheels ever rendered – and it remains riveting today. If you haven't had the pleasure of seeing it in person, you must make plans to do so whenever you get the chance. It is surprisingly compact in the flesh, and its skin is pulled taut as if it were dipped in molten silver. And no wonder, Mitchell's all-time favorite color for his show cars and concepts was silver – and the original Sting Ray positively glows in it. Whenever I see the original Sting Ray, I'm taken back to those lazy summer days when my neighborhood reverberated with the sound of its open exhausts echoing through the trees, with Mitchell beaming behind the wheel. This car isn't just any Corvette, folks – it is the living, breathing legacy of GM's design leadership handed down from Harley Earl and Bill Mitchell in a chalice of steel, aluminum and fiberglass. I was wild about it when it was new, and I appreciate it even more so today. Ed Welburn deserves the thanks of all enthusiasts for making sure it was treated with the respect it deserves and restored to its proper glory. It is truly one of the great cars of all time.

Only in America, right, boys? Toyota agreed to sponsor Brooks & Dunn's "The Long Haul Tour" for the next two years (2006-7), using the Toyota Tundra as the lead vehicle. I understood Toyota's position on this, as they've made no bones about the fact that they will stop at absolutely nothing in their quest to be perceived as an "All-American" company, which is why they pepper the use of "American Heartland" in every press release and just about every other word uttered to the public. Toyota's intentions are as transparent as their motives – and they fully intend on doing everything and anything in their power to try to pry away the American fabric from Ford, Chevy and Dodge so that they can then become "America's Truck." But Brooks & Dunn? The duo that had hitched their star to countless songs about America and American life was now "hooking up" with a Japanese truck manufacturer? It just proved one thing about their motives, and unfortunately it's an axiom proved almost daily by the less-than-scrupulous performers ensconced in the Nashville scene who have taken whoring for sponsorships to a high art – they'll go where the money is, to hell with principles, integrity or anything else. Whatabunchofhorseshit.com.

Today, I'm happy to comment on a new ad that has been appearing in newspapers and magazines across the country. The ad is simply headlined with the word, "No." – and it's a new image statement from BMW that captures the very essence of the BMW soul – probably even rekindling the company's own internal spirit in the process, reminding them why they actually do the things they do. The copy is simply brilliant – each word resonating with meaning while perfectly setting the cadence for the reader. Here it is:

"The ability to say no to compromise is a rare thing these days. Many companies would like to be able to say it, but so few have the autonomy to actually do it. As an independent company, BMW can say no. No, we will not compromise our ideas. No, we will not do it the way everyone else does it. No, we will not factor designs down to the lowest common denominator. No, we will not sell out to a parent company who will meddle in our affairs and ask us to subject our cars to mass market vanilla-ism.

Because we can say no to compromise, we can say yes to other things – such as building our vehicles with 50/50 weight distribution for superior handling and control, despite the fact that it costs more to build them that way. It's thousands of little things like this that separates BMW from other car companies. By maintaining our autonomy and ability to say no, we can make sure great ideas live on to become ultimate driving machines."

That's it – 175 words that serve as an epic reminder to every other car company in the world of why they will

*never be like BMW. More important, it reminds con-
sumers how one car company can take "marching to a
different drummer" to a high art form.* – Autoextremist
Rant #346, 5/10/06

But we're happy little ferrets at least. Paul Bellew, GM's director
of global market and industry analysis, teed-off on automakers that
constantly change their ad messages at a direct marketing conference
in Dearborn in May 2006. He described the automakers by saying,
"We're like ADD ferrets on amphetamines" according to *Ad Age,*
because of the industry's relentless meddling and tinkering. By his
estimation, consistency of a brand's message should reign supreme
in the auto business. I then pointed out to our readers that clients
meddle, tinker and screw things up – that's their duty, no, make that
their *right,* according to their twisted view of the world. Especially
in the automobile business, the legendary home to the world's most
esteemed short-term thinkers. Left to their own devices, automotive
marketers f--- things up. It's a known fact, and they just can't help
it. Speaking of which, GM had historically been one of the most
egregious meddlers and tinkerers in this business – brand consistency
of any kind has never been GM's thing. As a matter of fact, whole
legions of executives had made careers out of short-term thinking on
behalf of GM. And it shows, doesn't it? But then again, it's not just
GM who has a lock on this particular affliction – it has never been
Detroit's thing for, oh, at least the last 30 years. The dealers, who live
and breathe on their 30-day view of the world, scream bloody murder
at a whiff of trouble in their individual markets and then they in turn
scream at headquarters to "do something!" And inevitably, headquarters does do something – stupid – and then 18 months of strategic
planning, marketing and advertising go right out the window on a
whim and a prayer. Searching for brand consistency in Detroit is like
searching for the local unicorn farm. Actually, we stand corrected –
the local unicorn farm is by the Detroit River – just look for the giant
silos. You just might find unicorns there, but you certainly won't find
brand consistency. At least not yet anyway.

From the "What the Hell is the World Coming To?" File came word that Toyota, the Japanese car company obsessed with becoming "America's car company," had some 'splainin' to do at the end of May. Toyota announced that it was recalling two-thirds of its Prius hybrids sold in the U.S. because of defective parts that could cause a loss of steering control. The recall was a big one – 986,000 Toyotas over ten different models – but it specifically included 170,000 Prius vehicles in the U.S. We didn't know if the company planned on organizing a group hug for all of its Prius owners, or offer free Starbucks and massages for a year, or whatever – but it was clear that Toyota's drive for world domination was causing the company to lose focus, and its vaunted bulletproof quality image was showing signs of being frayed around the edges. This quality issue proved to be more than just a speed bump for Toyota – it was indicative of a trend that could derail the company's efforts on the way to corporate sainthood. Toyota doesn't stand for performance, safety, "built for drivers," design or anything else, for that matter – it stands for quality. And without that, they're just purveyors of bland vanilla transportation devices designed to offend as few people as possible. And that's not going to cut it for long, no matter how much they try to wrap their efforts in the flag.

Just put the air wrench down and move on to the next station – and hurry it up. Dan Neil, the *L.A. Times'* Pulitzer Prize-winning auto critic was at it again with his review of the Kia Sedona minivan entitled, "After a nice stretch, Kia comes up short." Neil opened his review with the following passage: "The Kia Sedona minivan is a huge steaming pile of who cares, and I for one couldn't be more relieved. I was beginning to worry that the Korean carmakers – Kia and its corporate parent Hyundai – could disgorge vast quantities of handsome and precision-engineered vehicles pretty much at will, and sell them for the price of gum. Consider, for example, the absurdly overachieving Hyundai Sonata and Azera sedans, and even Kia's indecently decent Optima. For those considering holy orders, there's even the nifty Kia Rio – if poverty and obedience are giving you trouble, at least you'll have chastity locked up. But the Kia Sedona – a cut-rate riff on Hyundai's 2007 Entourage minivan puts the planets back in their rightful orbits, at least temporarily. Here are the tragic trim pieces, wavering seams and maddening rattles we used to expect from the Koreans. The whole thing feels as if it were assembled at gunpoint."

> *The other thing that has remained dishearteningly the same in the seven years we've been doing Autoextremist. com? There's the classic battle between the bean counters and the True Believers, an epic struggle that continues to define what these car companies stand for and that inevitably determines the rate of their success – or failure. It's horrifying to see how some companies continue to shoot themselves in the head by scrimping on all the wrong things at exactly the wrong times – while wondering why they never seem to be able to catch up to the rest of the competition.*
>
> *Risk-averse managers with little or no feel for the game are impacting crucial product decisions in a dramatically negative way day in and day out in this business. That's how cars and trucks end up being built to the lowest common denominator – safe, homogenized, transportation "appliances" devoid of any point of view that fade into the woodwork almost immediately the moment they're unleashed on the public. When you have the wrong people making the wrong calls you lose market share, lose momentum and just lose, period.* – Autoextremist Rant #349, 5/31/06

Oh no you didn't. Steve Harris, the VP of Global Communications for GM, unleashed a combative response to Thomas L. Friedman's anti-GM diatribe on GM's FYI Blog entitled, "Hyperbole and Defamation in the New York Times." In it, Harris declared, "That a journalist of his caliber and reputation could write such a defamatory, uninformed opinion was shocking to those of us dedicated to this company and proud of what GM builds and contributes to the nation's economy." In another passage, Harris took Friedman to task over the whole gas card issue, writing, "Mr. Friedman sees it as something sinister, an effort to turn hapless Americans into fuel 'addicts.' But let's be intellectually honest here: A gas card is not going to get someone considering a $15,000 economy car to buy a $35,000 Chevy Tahoe." In other words, a cash rebate in a fancy wrapper, is still just a cash rebate. The Harris piece was hard-edged for the staid world of auto company PR, there's no question – especially for the conservative PR troops at GM. It was also measured, tactical and in every way a well-executed, seamless response. It just wasn't enough for the incendiary political battle GM found itself in, where whole sectors of the media were actually *willing* the company (and everything associated with Detroit) to fail, regardless of the consequences to the nation's economy. GM PR was and is quite fond of their blogs, but when you had to search for the GM response – the impact of it became muted at best. GM tip-toed around the fact that they didn't want to come off like the picked-upon bully and react to everybody who has access to a keyboard, but the rope-a-dope tactic was wearing thin at that point. GM (and Detroit) was in the political battle of its life. There were so many blatant lies and half-truths roiling around in the media about what GM was doing and what it was capable of vis-à-vis Toyota that to hope rational people got the message wasn't going to cut it – *especially* when you had irrational blowhards like Thomas L. Friedman running GM into the ground and boosting Toyota's fortunes every chance he got. GM needed to come out swinging. This was a new media era, and all the old "textbook" image and PR management scenarios were about as useful as yesterday's news – and they simply were no longer going to work. If GM continued to allow the anti-car, anti-Detroit factions to spew their relentless GM (Detroit)=Bad, Toyota=Good bullshit unimpeded, then they would continue to suffer the slings and arrows of every misguided hack in the business.

The Toyota Times. **It's gotta nice ring to it, don't you think?**

What with Tom Friedman, the newly self-appointed Supreme Commander of the Anti-Car, Anti-Detroit Intelligentsia, out to convince the nation that GM was the Evil Empire, deserving to be treated like terrorists, and *The New York Times* adding countless articles chronicling Detroit's death spiral and the ascendancy of Toyota to the throne of what's all righteous and good, with little attempt at balance or perspective – it was looking more and more like the newspaper had an agenda to bring Detroit and in particular, GM, down, while boosting Toyota's fortunes on an almost-daily basis. The *Times* and their latte-fueled minions vehemently denied even the suggestion of impropriety, of course, but even the most casual of observers had to notice the barely concealed glee in the tone and tenor of their articles, which castigated GM and Detroit and relentlessly promoted Toyota to corporate sainthood. Although the *Times'* auto section on Sundays and their Internet auto site seemed to be unfettered with the burying-Detroit agenda. with Friedman leading the Detroit=Bad, Toyota=Good charge, I suggested that maybe it was time to rename the paper entirely.

Suspicions confirmed. It turned out that *The New York Times* jerked GM PR around in their attempts at getting a rebuttal published to Tom Friedman's witless attack on GM in the paper. GM PR posted a fascinating, detailed account of the story in GM's "FYI" blog by Brian Akre, a former PR staffer, but the short story was this: After publishing four letters favorable to Friedman's column the day after it ran, the *Times'* editors went back and forth with Akre on the length and the tone of his piece, finally killing it altogether because GM wanted to use the word "rubbish" as a one-word sentence after their opening remarks. The *Times'* Mary Drohan, a letters editor, countered that "rubbish" should be changed to "We beg to differ." GM rightly objected. The *Times* then suggested it be changed to "Not so." GM refused. In the end, the *Times* wouldn't let GM use the word "rubbish," and the column never ran. Why? "It's not the tone we use in Letters," Drohan said. Not the tone they used in letters??? This after Friedman accused GM of supporting terrorists, buying votes in

Congress and being a corporate "crack dealer" that posed a serious threat to America's future? And topping it all off by suggesting that the nation would be better off if Japan's Toyota took over GM? I'd say that's total bullshit. The whole incident *did* serve a very important purpose, however, because it exposed the blatant biases festering in the editorial offices of the nation's most self-absorbed newspaper. There *are* a lot of good people who write about cars and the car business at the *Times* who aren't governed by the anti-Detroit, anti-GM bias that runs rampant throughout the editorial offices of the paper, but unfortunately, their work will now forever be tainted because of the narrow-minded perspectives of a few.

That's good, because if we had to look at another Bland-Tastic disaster like the Ford Five Hundred we'd turn this thing into *LawnOrnamentExtremist.com* **and call it a day.** Our Autoextremist Good Move of the Week for the first week of June, or maybe it should have been the *bold* move of the week, went to Ford's Mark Fields who demanded that his design troops give him, according to *Automotive News*, "a strong dose of in-your-face American styling – even if it means the automaker must delay some key products by several years."

They don't call us the Kings of Self Promotion for nothin'! We survived yet another unveiling of the 2006 J.D. Power Initial Quality Survey, which measures reported problems per 100 vehicles after 90 days of ownership, but afterwards I suggested that it was about time that the automobile manufacturers finally stopped pandering to the Power IQS and start aiming for a higher measure – such as the reliability and dependability performance of their vehicles three and four years down the road, for starters. There's no doubt that the Power IQS is perfectly suited to our instant-gratification-oriented culture and that their relentless promotion of it has been nothing short of marketing genius, but the results tallied in the first 90 days don't mean much when it comes right down to it. Sure, people can tell a lot about their vehicles in the first 90 days, but are there any really earth-shattering discoveries? For instance, is it all that surprising that a majority of German luxury car buyers find that the German manufacturers' out-of-control obsession with electronic applications in the cockpit is infuriating? There's a shocker – did we really need Power's Initial Quality Survey for that revelation? The auto manufacturers have been known to skew their product development and assembly strategies to deliver high marks on the Power IQS, only to let consumers down later in the lifecycle of ownership. This has to change, but as long as the "kings of self promotion" at J.D. Power continue to hold the industry hostage with their IQS, then the short-term thinkers in the industry will continue to aim low.

> *With contemporary society seemingly devolving into a angry sea of entitlement and blissful, soporific mediocrity – consistent excellence is hard to find in this lowest-common-denominator world in which we now live. Consistent excellence simply requires too much for most people. It demands a relentless focus, while at the same time abhorring excuses. It requires a commitment of time and a level of energy that are daunting and all-consuming. It means having a dedication that's unwavering and unrelenting – all fueled by a fiery passion that refuses to recognize any definition of the word "quit." Consistent excellence too often is an elusive goal in this day and age, and that's a tragedy. But I'm happy to report that there's at least one last bastion of it, and it's alive and well in the Motor City – GM's Corvette Racing won the GT1 class at the 24 Hours of Le Mans, the most prestigious sports car race in the world, for the third straight year, after withstanding a withering onslaught from the factory Aston Martin racing team.*
>
> *...It wasn't too long ago that the idea of GM challenging the world with a factory-supported racing effort would have been scoffed at and dismissed as folly internally. Fortunately, those bad old days are long gone. The*

powers that be at General Motors have finally – finally – come to understand that racing can be much more than just a source of company pride or another excuse to fill the France family's over-stuffed NASCAR coffers. They've learned that going up against the world's best in the most intensely competitive environment possible is an ideal way to train and develop engineers – and the engineers involved with the Corvette Racing program are indeed some of the company's best and brightest. They've come to understand that technical lessons learned on the racetrack can be directly transferred into improvements on their production cars – which is why the Corvette Z06 is arguably the best all-around sports car in the world at this very moment. GM has also learned that a winning, world-class racing program is an invaluable image and marketing tool that can transform an organization and translate into a winning image both on and off the track.

It's ironic, but after being a stepchild within the vast and stifling GM bureaucracy for decades, it looks like the Corvette is finally getting its due – in this, its 50th anniversary year in racing. – Autoextremist Rant #352, 6/21/06

I bet we'd be even *happier* little ferrets in Cannes! There is no business on earth more in love with itself and more interested in patting itself on the back than the ad biz. Coveting awards and spending huge amounts of money to gain recognition – no matter how lame the "prize" – is standard operating procedure. Every summer, representatives of ad agencies from all over the world descend on Cannes, France, to participate in an orgy of back-slapping, glad-handing and transparent air kisses of affection – "love your work!" – while burning through agency expense accounts at a prodigious rate. At the end of the day, it's all a monumental beat-off/waste of time, filled with hot air and lofty platitudes signifying absolutely nothing. Message to clients everywhere: Pay less attention to the awards your agencies covet and boast about and more attention to the actual work. And if you find that your agency is spending an inordinate amount of time talking about awards, seeking awards or rearranging their schedule to attend award shows, perhaps it's time to step back and see if this is the agency you really want to be associated with. Either that, or make sure they bring you along to Cannes next year...

No wonder Britney went without panties. Yet another embarrassing recall for Mercedes-Benz happened in the summer of 2006, only this time it was for its SLR McLaren super sports car. It seemed that extremely high temperatures under the hood could damage the alternator and cause a fire on the SLRs from the 2005 and 2006 model years – in other words, every one built – including 433 vehicles in the United States. The problem occurred under "hard operating conditions," according to Mercedes, but there were no reports of any engine fires caused by the problem. Mercedes-Benz dealers were to fix the car by improving engine compartment cooling – although, short of taking a can opener to the hood, how was that going to happen? – and by installing a new alternator and a modified engine control unit. Were we shocked by this development? Hardly. After all, in early development testing of the SLR, the under hood temperatures soared to such dizzying heights that the composite fenders actually started to *buckle*. Not good. Paris Hilton used to drive one to go clubbing in L.A., so we suggested that maybe M-B engineers should study her driving habits – *very* closely.

As a matter of fact, our shit *doesn't* stink. Leaving no environmental cow chip unturned, Toyota codeveloped a cutting-edge composting ingredient and process that drastically reduces nitrous oxide, methane and other greenhouse gases, as well as offensive odors produced by livestock waste. When mixed with cow manure, the ingredient – developed jointly with Menicon Co., Japan's foremost maker of contact lenses – speeds up the time it takes to convert the waste into compost, from anywhere between 90 to 180 days to just 45 days. The resulting compost is also of a higher quality, containing less nitrate-nitrogen, a water pollutant, Toyota said. Toyota Roof Garden Co., a Toyota subsidiary charged with manufacturing the product, Menicon and trading firm Toyota Tsusho Corp. began selling the formula to cattle farmers in limited areas of Japan on July 1, 2006, with a view to spreading it nationwide and to other livestock such as poultry and pigs. The three-way partnership expected annual sales of $17.44 million (2 billion yen) after five years.

Then there was the one about the ad campaign strategy overheard on a Northwest Airlines flight. It happens all the time – executives from the same company seated in First Class, talking about business, conveniently forgetting where they are and who might be listening. Only this time, a high-ranking, high-visibility Ford executive was sitting there, with his laptop opened, minding his own business, when the creative brain trust from Modernista – the Boston ad agency flush with a new Cadillac assignment – began going over their new strategic plans for Cadillac. As the Ford executive realized what was happening, he started taking notes on his laptop. Copious, detailed notes. He then dutifully passed them along to his compatriots at Lincoln for their perusal. Is it any coincidence then that Lincoln launched its new marketing initiative entitled "Advancing the American Dream" last Friday, in which they suggest that "owning a Lincoln is for people pursuing the American Dream?" Which just happened to be eerily similar to the premise that Cadillac's new marketing strategy was to be based on – "Life, Liberty and the Pursuit?" For the record, Al Giombetti, president of Ford and Lincoln Mercury marketing and sales at the time said, "The 'Dreams' marketing platform is about the vision that motivates successful people and the rewards for achieving success. It's an idea that fits perfectly with our brand because we are turning Lincoln into a new American success story on the strength of innovative products. In fact, eighty percent of our showroom is all-new for 2007." No mention was made of the Northwest incident, for obvious reasons, but the word was all over the street about what really had happened. Ah, Dee-troit, there ain't nothin like it. Jim Cain of Ford PR called to explain later that though our story about the incident on the Northwest flight was 100% accurate, the strategy and plans for the new Lincoln campaign were already in place from Ford's "Way Forward" directive at the end of last year. The overheard conversation on the plane *did* cause them to accelerate the rollout of the new strategy and ad theme for Lincoln, however.

Anyone who actually believed that Kirk Kerkorian and his designated spear-carrier, Jerry York, had benevolent intentions with their "investment" in General Motors had their attitude adjusted Friday afternoon (June 30) when the two roving quick-buck aficionados revealed their "Plan" to GM (and of course, the media) – which amounts to demanding that GM consider a linkage with Renault SA and Nissan. And it was also revealed that the two had even gone so far as to have secret meetings with Carlos Ghosn – the diminutive megalomaniac and dual CEO of Nissan and Renault, who was looking for another ego boost, apparently – to float their proposal and get his buy-in.

Make no mistake – this isn't about creating a new global automotive powerhouse well equipped to do battle deep into this century, one that will keep Toyota from taking over the world. And this certainly isn't about doing what's best for General Motors and the people who have so much invested in the fortunes of the company. And this in no way, shape or form has anything to do with solidifying America's manufacturing base or shoring up the economy.

No, this is about flat-out greed, pure and simple.

It's about spiking the stock, roiling the markets and getting the media worked up. Forget the noble intentions espoused by York early on – that he and Kerkorian were just trying to get GM reshaped and on-track for survival so that it could thrive in the future. Forget about all the genuine concern that York spoke about in his speech to the investment community in Detroit last January – that he knew what GM needed to do to become a healthy industry player for years to come, if they'd only listen. No, this is about getting Kerkorian's investment going in the right direction as soon as possible – and if they have to set up a logistical nightmare of an "alignment" to get their financial return jacked-up ASAP, then they're going to do what they have to do.

The three "players" involved here are the Three Amigos of Greed, Unfulfilled Aspirations – and Ego. – Autoextremist Rant #353, 6/28/06

The Rick, aka Mr. Cool? The GM CEO proved to be far cagier and much more formidable than Kirk Kerkorian and Jerry York bargained for. Positively glowing with optimism with the media, Wagoner went out of his way at the height of the "alliance" frenzy to bless the idea of a proposed alliance with Renault and Nissan on CNBC: "It's an interesting idea," Wagoner said. "We look forward to sitting down with Carlos Ghosn soon. When this idea was presented, we said we'll take a good look at it. We are looking forward to sitting down. Our minds are completely open." Kerkorian and York expected a stone-walling obstacle in Wagoner. Instead, they got a guy who was going out of his way to engage the media, while reiterating that he has an open mind. As I predicted, Wagoner and Co. would take their sweet time to cherry-pick/consider any obvious synergies available to them at Nissan and Renault. But that's as far as it would go. Short of a boardroom coup – which didn't happen – the Kirk and Jerry show would go nowhere. It was a brilliant strategy by Wagoner and crew.

The first recipient of our brand-new Autoextremist "Alfred E. Neuman – What, Me Worry?" award was none other than Jim Morton, Vice Chairman, Nissan North America. His Smarmy-ness turned up everywhere in the Detroit media during July 2006, extolling the virtues of Nissan North America while claiming that everything was just swell with the re-lo to Nashville, thank you very much. And how happy everyone was, and how "We'll be up to speed in a couple of weeks." A couple of weeks? Nissan was *still* trying to desperately fill some key slots in Nashville in the summer of 2007. For his blatant cluelessness in the face of the mounting chaos down in Nashville, Jim Morton was our hands-down winner. Way to go, Jimbo – you deserved it.

And then we'll get David Lynch to direct the movie. From the "Hell Freezes Over" File came word that a Chinese company, the Nanjing Automobile Group, which purchased the assets of the bankrupt MG Rover Group in 2005, announced that they would be the first Chinese carmaker to open a factory in the United States. If that weren't enough, the company announced plans to build a newly designed MG TF Coupe in Ardmore, Oklahoma, starting in 2008. According to the company, the coupe would compete with cars like the Mazda Miata and Pontiac Solstice. American and European operations for the new MG Motors would be based in Oklahoma City, 90 miles north of their new factory in Ardmore. The company said it would also build a convertible TF Roadster version at MG's factory in Longbridge, England (currently closed), and three sedan models in China. As of this writing, there were no firm plans for the Oklahoma sight.

You're not worthy. And we're not worried. On the one hand, Steve Wilhite, the ex-Nissan senior VP of global marketing left Nissan (and an assignment in Tokyo) while the leaving was good, what with Chairman Ghosn's Little Red Book coming apart at the seams and the future of Nissan looking a bit iffy – and headed back to California to become the COO of Hyundai Motor America. On the other hand, it wasn't not the top job in Hyundai's operation in America – that job belongs to Ok Suk Koh, who is the CEO – and therein lies the rub. In fact, the Koreans are such control freaks that it will take everything that Wilhite has *not* to become a mere figurehead, which some observers think is fundamentally impossible anyway. Hyundai seems hell-bent on doing things their way and ignoring reasonable judgment at all costs. They want to be players in the luxury market, and they refuse to listen to anyone or anybody who has even a modicum of common sense. It wasn't too long ago that observers were racing to anoint Hyundai as "the next Toyota" – but with a seemingly never-ending series of problems back in Korea and a creeping arrogance that's preventing management from listening to anyone, let's just say Toyota needn't be worried.

They're good, but they're not *that* good. U.S. automakers teed off on the Japanese government in the first week of August 2006, accusing it of funneling more than $2 billion in windfall profits for Japanese automakers in the past quarter by artificially depressing the value of the yen, according to a Reuters report. "It's not us making this up. It's the balance sheets of the Japanese automakers that show the companies are earning big profits from the low value of the yen," said Stephen Collins, president of the Automotive Trade Policy Council, which represents GM, Ford and DaimlerChrysler. "These are windfall profits that we say translate into subsidized exports" to the United States, Collins said. Collins insisted that even though the Japanese government has not directly intervened in currency markets since March 2004, Japanese government officials have kept the currency artificially low by "jawboning" it down. "Every time the yen starts to move in a substantial way, 'Japan Inc.' and the Japanese finance minister roll out thundering noises," discouraging currency traders from betting on a stronger yen, Collins added. The latest quarterly reports from Toyota, Nissan, Honda and other Japanese automakers showed that they earned more than $2 billion in windfall profits due to an artificially weak yen, Collins said. The Automotive Trade Policy Council said in a statement that Tokyo's exchange rate policies could easily give Japanese automakers an $8 billion subsidy this year.

Amen, Robert. Amen. In his intro to *Automobile* magazine's design feature in the September issue entitled, "The Importance Of Good

Design," Robert Cumberford had this to say: "It's always amusing to see the solemn list of criteria people claim to use when they are choosing a car. Sometimes they give fuel economy as their principal consideration, and sometimes reliability, safety, or another responsible, practical and respectable value such as overall cost of ownership. Never 0-to-60 times, and certainly not something as frivolous as styling or design. What total nonsense. We choose cars because we like the way they look and because of how we think they make us look. Appearance and appearances. Everything else is subsidiary."

Raucous, irreverent and unsanitized, it's the way we roll around here. For one week at least, this town is up for grabs in a good way – lost in a sea of horsepower, fat tires, candy-colored paint and drop-dead gorgeous sheet metal. The Dream Cruise is simply a singular event that must be experienced by any car enthusiast worth his or her gearhead credentials at least once. It's the singular car happening that sits at the complete opposite end of the spectrum from the events in Pebble Beach and Monterey – but it's every bit as great in its own way.

> *My advice to the suitors who will line up to pursue the possibility of acquiring Jaguar? Immerse yourselves in the tradition of the brand – and if you don't know where to look, it can be found in the magnificent C-Types, D-Types, XKSSs and E-Types from the '50s and '60s. And if after studying those fantastic automobiles, you still don't get it, please move on, because you're not worthy.*
>
> *Whoever ends up with Jaguar needs to understand one fundamental, High-Octane Truth about what Jaguar needs to survive and hopefully thrive from this point forward – an iconic Jaguar "statement" car must be created for the future. No, I'm not suggesting yet another retro-mobile, but I am suggesting a design for a lightweight, two-seat sports car that embodies everything that Jaguar stands for, with sensual, if not outright sinful styling, cat-*

quick agility and riveting performance. It must look like it is a continuation of the greatness of Jaguar's heyday – and it must exude the very essence of Jaguar.

Anything less – and it will ensure the death-knell for one of the great automotive brands of all time.
— Autoextremist Rant #359, 8/9/06

Ever wonder what the real numbers are behind our statement that "GM is virtually out of business in California"? Well, the *Los Angeles Times* brought those numbers into focus with a report on the retail car market in California that was the first published look at new-vehicle registrations in the state. The report by the California Motor Car Dealers Association found that in the second quarter of 2006, Toyota-brand cars and trucks accounted for 23.4 percent of all sales, followed by Honda at 12.4 percent. Ford was third with a 9.6 percent share, and GM's Chevrolet weighed-in with 8.2 percent. When Lexus was added into the equation, Toyota April-to-June share of the California market rose to a whopping 27 percent. Bert Boeck-mann, chairman of Galpin Automotive Group and president of its Ford dealership in North Hills, the brand's highest-volume outlet in the country, had this to say to the *L.A. Times:* "I live with it every day. When manufacturers in the U.S. were making big money on their trucks and SUVs in the 1990s, they were losing $1,500 on every car they sold and they allowed the car market to drift over to Toyota and Honda." And that, ladies and gentlemen, is what has happened to the Detroit Two in a nutshell – and why they've been hovering on the brink of disaster ever since.

To say the Sierra Club is misguided and humorless is an understatement. But their agenda is veering into a territory that goes beyond improving the planet, because now the Sierra Club fancies itself as being at the forefront of a burgeoning movement in this country that expands upon the anti-car rhetoric (that they seem to be able to spew at the drop of a pine cone) to include an "anti-conspicuous consumption" message. It's not only about what you drive and how you drive it; it's how you conduct your daily life, how you act in public and what you think too. No one has appointed the Sierra Club as Final Arbiters of our Existence that I know of, but given the opportunity, I have no doubt that they would jump at the assignment.

Fortunately, car enthusiasts across the country are able to put the Sierra Club's misguided bleating in perspective. Car enthusiasts are not anti-environment, anti-children, anti-trees or any other wild-ass scenario that the Sierra Club can conjure up. And even though the Sierra Club wants to shove their agenda down our throats every chance they get, car enthusiasts aren't interested in shoving fried Big Macs (or anything else) down anyone's throats.

Car enthusiasts have one thing that the Sierra Club will never be accused of having – and that is perspective. They understand the role that the automobile has played in the growth of our nation and the personal impact that the automobile has had on all of our lives. And they also realize that many of life's most memorable moments were brought to them in one way or another by the cars and trucks that now frame the memories of a lifetime – the very cars and trucks evident on Woodward Avenue and the Monterey Peninsula this week, and at car shows around the country.

So, do yourself a favor and go out and celebrate the High Holy Days of America's car culture this week any way you choose, before the card-carrying members of the No Fun League do their best to eradicate it from the American landscape.

Because after all, the memories you're protecting just may be your own. – Autoextremist Rant #360, 8/16/06

No discussion about German automakers would be

complete without mentioning Porsche, the certifiable Dr. Jekyll & Mr. Hyde of the auto business. On the one hand, their rich legacy is filled with light, efficient sports and racing cars with a pedigreed lineage as decorated as any in all of motordom. How can a car company responsible for the 911, the Boxster, the new Cayman and the Carrera GT be anything but great? On the other hand, how can a car company with those credentials stoop to build the lowest-common-denominator vehicle on the planet – a bloated, overblown SUV with all of the redeeming qualities of a motorized anvil – while having the temerity to suggest that it's every inch a Porsche? The legendary German sports car maker used to bandy about ad slogans like "Excellence was expected" and "There is no substitute." Now, the company uses the phrase, "The most profitable car company in the world" in all of their media releases. What does that tell you? I'm happy to report that after the initial euphoria derived from the early success of the Cayenne, the Porsche truck is now deader than a doornail in the U.S. market. And there's no telling the extent of the damage those short-term profits generated by the 5,500-lb. SUV did to Porsche's long-term reputation and brand image. The greed merchants at Porsche seem to be undaunted, however. Next up from the Wizards of Zuffenhausen? A 4500-lb. four-door Porsche "coupe." At least that's what they'll call it. I'll call it like I see it, however. The company whose founder came up with such mechanical artwork as the 550 Spyder will now be producing a four-door sedan. Not good. – Autoextremist Rant #361, 8/23/06

And another thing. One of our AE Quotes of the Week came from Anne Stevens, who retired from her post as Ford's chief operating officer for the Americas on October 1, 2006, because she found that she couldn't accomplish anything in Ford's layer-burdened organization that was 103 years in the making. "The company has too many layers, the company is too bureaucratic, and it takes too long to get things done," she told the *Detroit Free Press* in an interview. Ford's poisonous, bureaucratic, nightmare of a culture is the single most glaring reason that the company had dissolved into a punch-drunk boxer slumped against the ropes. The talented people at Ford – and there are still many there who qualify as such – have repeatedly run up against a slumbering cesspool of a bureaucracy that moves in slow motion (if it moves at all), one that rewards non-decisions and ritual inactivity over risk-taking and flat-out creativity. The clock is ticking for Alan Mulally – if he can't break through Ford's embalmed organizational structure, the company simply will not survive.

> *Carlos Ghosn is trying to goad GM into taking some sort of deal by using every tactic at his disposal. Talking in vague generalities to the media about these momentous synergies just ripe for the picking, Ghosn has been sounding like a traveling medicine man imploring the locals to buy his potent brew – promising it will cure everything from unfavorable union contracts, to non-competitiveness, to bad product decisions in one big gulp. 'If you (GM) would only dig deep enough, my surefire formula will help you feel good again! Drink this, and you will be smart enough to see the world just as I see it! It's your only hope to stave off the Toyota hordes! What are you all afraid of? Don't you want to be part of a new Global Auto Empire that will dominate the world? Don't you want to save $10 billion? Are you afraid of prosperity? Are you afraid of winning? Drink this! You will think with my brilliance and see with my vision! And you will taste victory!'*
>
> *Or something like that.*
>
> *As I said months ago when this alliance idea was proposed and have said repeatedly since, I'm not buying any of Ghosn's pronouncements for a minute. Yes, of course,*

there could be some synergies gleaned from the three car companies getting together, but any realistic, cohesive, effective partnership would take years to develop – if ever. And when I say years, I'm not talking Dieter Zetsche's concept of time – when everything magically works itself out in just a couple of quarters – but years, as in more than a decade.

None of the car companies involved in this discussion has that kind of time. – Autoextremist Rant #365, 9/27/06

Well, *that* was special. GM's CEO Rick Wagoner and Carlos Ghosn, CEO of Nissan and Renault, decided in a phone call in the beginning of October 2006 that the two sides were too far apart on the value of a potential tie-up and decided to stop the high-stakes talks, which had been under way for two months. As I had insisted all along, the deal was doomed from the start because the "alliance" talk was nothing but a smokescreen masking a blatant attempt by Kirk Kerkorian to throw Rick Wagoner out and hand over the keys to General Motors to Carlos Ghosn. It didn't work. Wagoner rallied his troops, GM's product offensive showed signs of real life, and the benefit of an alliance to Renault-Nissan was much greater than it was to General Motors. The bad thing is that GM spent a lot of time dealing with this instead of focusing as much as possible on the job at hand.

Thanks, Ben. One Sunday in *The New York Times*, Ben Stein penned a beautiful column entitled, "Suddenly, California Hates the Car" – which lambasted Bill Lockyer, the attorney general of the State of California, who had distinguished himself as a bonehead of monumental proportions with his lawsuit against all of the major manufacturers, including GM, Ford, DaimlerChrysler, Toyota, Nissan and Honda, alleging that these automobile manufacturers had been building cars and trucks for years that burn gasoline and cause emissions – which add to global warming, harm people's health, damage the welfare of the state, lessen the snowpack on California's mountains, pollute rivers and generally create a "nuisance" for which his office was seeking tens of millions of dollars. I'm not even going to try to top Stein's comments, so here are a few of them: *"Now, for all of you who were not law students, Mr. Lockyer's suit is a tort suit, such as you might file if you were parked at a stoplight and a car behind you failed to stop and slammed into your car, crushing it and injuring you. The reason it's called a tort suit is that the French word "tort" means a wrong or a wrongdoing, and failing to stop at a stoplight is wrong. The same would apply if a restaurant negligently poisoned you or if your neighbor crashed his car into your mailbox. The point is that a wrong has to have been done in order for there to be a lawsuit. This is the problem, or one of the problems, with the attorney general's lawsuit. The car companies have done nothing wrong. It's that simple. They manufacture a perfectly legal product, a car or truck. They manufacture it in accordance with strict regulations about every single aspect of its building and use...The car is not only a legal product, but also a totally necessary product. There could basically be no life in California – or in the United States generally – without cars and trucks. So, for making a lawful product that complies with regulations and is necessary and bought by millions of Californians each year, all knowing that their cars produce emissions, G.M., Ford and the others are being sued. Where is the wrong here? What have the car companies done that is a wrongful act, except in the imagination of an attorney general?...Businesses are big, powerful entities. That does not mean they are without legal rights. That does not mean they are automatically wrong. That does not mean they deserve to be sued without any good reason. The only 'tort' here is what Mr. Lockyer is trying to do."* We could think of all kinds of other lawsuits for the reality challenged Mr. Lockyer. How about calling Hollywood on the carpet for every bad movie or TV show that has ever been produced – which might have polluted our minds and consequently ruined our lives? That's flat-out stupid, right? May we submit "Jackass Number Two" for state's evidence? Or was Lockyer just another in a long line of attorney generals in this country whose sum-total contribution to their profession and our quality of life amounts to manufacturing attention-grabbing crusades in the pursuit of higher office? We think the latter, in which case he was a prime candidate to star in "Jackass Number Three."

The Short Story? Detroit is Screwed. It came to light in the fall of 2006 that the Detroit automobile companies were operating at a competitive disadvantage to their Japanese competitors, making $2,400 less per car, according to a study by Harbour-Felax Group, a Michigan-based consulting firm. Co-authored by Laurie Harbour-Felax and Jim Harbour, the study pointed out that the domestic auto manufacturers were operating at a competitive disadvantage in several areas, including their reliance on heavy discounting and rental fleets, while spending $1,400 *more* for health care costs per vehicle, for instance. Though various figures have been bandied about for years as to the Detroit manufacturers' financial disadvantage to the Japanese, this was the first extensive study that attempted to come up with a solid number (even though it doesn't take into account the ongoing currency manipulation practiced by the Japanese government, which contributes a considerable additional amount to the Japanese automakers' profitability). Though the Detroit car companies are making huge strides, they're running out of time. It may have taken 25 years to put themselves in this hole, but they certainly don't have 25 years to pull themselves out of it. They might have 7 to 10 years to do it – if that.

But we can still organize in Oblivion, right? In interviews with the media in October 2006, Ron Gettelfinger, the UAW President said that that controversial Jobs Bank program – which requires auto companies to provide workers laid-off for a year or more with full pay – must stay intact in the 2007 contract with the domestic automakers. Whether it was meaningless posturing before the negotiations to make him look good to the union membership or just a momentary bout of insanity, Gettelfinger was quoted as saying, "We don't have any reason to be convinced to do away with it." Don't see any reason, huh? Here were a few: 1. The domestic automakers' share of the North American market is in freefall, with no real end to the downward spiral in sight. 2. The emergence of global competition from the Far East is threatening the very existence of the domestic automakers – and the jobs they supported. And 3. The future of the UAW is hanging in the balance. Gettelfinger's ham-handed, head-in-the-sand approach to these 2007 contract negotiations with the domestic automakers reaffirmed the obvious – he's out of touch, and his union is out of time. If Gettelfinger doesn't back off his stance, he will "jobs bank" the UAW to oblivion.

The Washington political establishment continues to believe that the precarious fortunes of an industry that still either directly or indirectly is responsible for between 1 in 12 and 1 in 14 jobs in this country will not affect the rest of the country – and that's sheer lunacy.

And the media establishment centers on both coasts continue to beat the drum suggesting that this country would be much better off if one of our iconic American industries simply faded away or better yet, was absorbed by Toyota. You can practically set your watch to the now-almost-weekly article in The New York Times extolling some heretofore unrevealed secret of Toyota's success, while concluding yet again that the only formula that should resonate with anyone is Toyota = Good, Detroit = Bad. That's fine too. The New York Times anti-Detroit bias is blatant, calculated and plain to see to all who bother to actually read between the lines.

So, it's time for Detroit to get real about their lot in American life. No one cares whether or not Detroit automakers survive or not – not in Washington, not in the anti-Detroit media establishment and certainly not with the legions of consumers who continue to make pur-chase decisions based on past horror stories with Detroit products – the people who now won't consider giving the new-wave vehicles coming out of the Motor City even a cursory glance.

For Detroit, it's now a flat-out, 'Us vs. Them' situation. And it will not magically get better by cajoling clueless Washington bureaucrats or courting the stone-faced automatons in the media who regurgitate the Toyota company line at every opportunity. – Autoextremist Rant #370, 11/1/06

From the "Hell Really *Is* Freezing Over" File came word that Siemens, one of the world's largest electronic companies was now the brand spanking new headquarters of the No Fun League, apparently. The company developed a system that prevents a motorist from going over the posted speed limit (gulp). Using an on-board camera placed near the rearview mirror that "reads" speed limit signs, the system then feeds the information to a computer, which then restricts your speed to that exact posted limit – no exceptions. It can even read a speed limit sign that has been altered by spray paint vandalism. In order to activate the system, you have to have the cruise control engaged, but still, Siemens says a European manufacturer (who will remain nameless, probably for good reason) is planning on adding the system as an option in a couple of years. Wait a minute, No Fun League (check), electronic overkill (check), technology for technology's sake (check) – we thought we had a real good idea who that manufacturer was...see below.

We are Mercedes, and we are clueless. Finally abandoning all pretense of portraying itself as a "hip" automaker, Mercedes-Benz shifted its marketing focus in Europe from chasing the sporty crowd (BMW) to going after the real money, which lies with the Well-Off Older People, or "Woopies" as marketers call them, according to *Automotive News*. The industry trade journal quoted Klaus Maier, the head of sales and marketing for Mercedes, as saying, "If you drive a Mercedes and you are more than 55, we want to say, 'You have made it.'" Wait a minute, wasn't this the same advertising premise that had ruled American luxury car advertising since Theodore Mac-Manus wrote the famous "Penalty of Leadership" ad for Cadillac back in 1915 that appeared in the *Saturday Evening Post?* You have made it, you have arrived, you 'da man, etc., etc. Hell, even Lincoln was using that approach. But then again, how could we forget, when *Mercedes* arrived at this strategy it's suddenly The Answer, and no one has done it quite like them, right? *Right.* Is it any wonder that these "geniuses" have floundered for years since they walked away from arguably the greatest auto advertising theme in history – "Engineered like no other car in the World" – ? How about, no? We long for those simpler days of yesteryear when Mercedes let their overengineered cars do the talking, because every time these guys deign to think or open their mouths, things inevitably get screwed up.

Our Autoextremist "Quote of the Week" (November 8, 2006) went to Bill Ford, who, in commenting to *The Wall Street Journal* about the emerging sophistication and capabilities of the Chinese automobile industry and its effect on the fortunes of the U.S. auto industry, said, "Americans don't get it. They don't understand what's going to happen."

Just when Detroit was starting to get a handle on this idea that The Product is King... While the Detroit automakers were desperately trying to build great cars and trucks that people actually want to buy on their own volition instead of with a cash rebate or some sort of incentive, Toyota threw them a big fat changeup. Toyota announced that it would consciously *curtail* the number of Scion cars it builds, according to *The Wall Street Journal*, in order to keep the brand special, desirable – and cool. They could easily exceed the 150,000 unit sales goal they have for the brand, but they're not going to. Toyota is eerily operating in another dimension of space and time – building and selling automobiles in a way that the other auto manufacturers around the world simply aren't familiar with. Toyota, that champion of precision-crafted blandness, is changing the game yet again – trying new things, taking chances, never standing still and always, *always* thinking of their next move. It's pretty damn remarkable when you really sit back and think about it.

We are Mercedes-Benz and we are clueless, Part II. *Fortune* reported that Mercedes-Benz publicly bristled at the *Consumer Reports* New Car Preview for 2007, which basically stated that Mercedes-Benz vehicles were among the least reliable in their classes across the board. Of the eleven Mercedes models reviewed by *Consumer Reports*, *none* were recommended, with seven left off of the list entirely for poor reliability (four were left off because they were too new to the market). In short, Mercedes-Benz delivered a disastrous performance. According to *Fortune*, a spokesman for Mercedes said that the data in the *Consumer Reports* rankings "is totally out of sync with what we're seeing in the mainstream research as well as our own customer satisfaction and warranty data." The problem is this: For people who know nothing about cars, *Consumer Reports* is the bible, like it or not. So for Mercedes to complain or squawk about it was just silly. This company has been in a downward spiral for going on seven years now. It doesn't matter how cool their AMG specials are or how good the new S-Class is when things are going wrong with their vehicles on a consistent basis. In the attention-deficit-dominated world we live in today, if people have just *one* bad experience with a vehicle then they walk away – for good. Brand loyalty, or at least the old quaint notion of it, is gone forever. And that's it. Mercedes-Benz might be more "approachable" in the market and they might be selling at greater volumes, but the fact remains that M-B is selling to a lot of first- and *last*-time buyers these days. Mercedes vehicles are overpriced, over-complicated, and when it comes to delivering real value – they consistently don't measure up. We have an excellent suggestion for the geniuses at Mercedes-Benz: Stop trying to be all things to all people and stop trying to cover every lame-ass niche in the market, because you absolutely suck at it. Two glaringly obvious examples? The R-Class and the GL-Class. Build fewer, flawless cars, and take the long view patented by the Japanese car companies, which means nothing really good happens overnight. That's what it will take to build your brand's equity back up. And then we'll see what *Consumer Reports* has to say about M-B three years from now. If you're still out to lunch by then, no one will care anymore anyway.

First, some background. Written-off and given up for dead long ago, Buick – as it exists in the new General Motors, the car company that is counting on its global reach and the promise of its reenergized product future (not the one that is staring at the abyss and threatening to fall in at any moment) – is not only alive and well, it has become a serious player in GM's future product plans. Buick's role in GM's future is fortified by its prestigious presence and winning image in China. Driving in from the airport in Shanghai, a huge billboard for Buick – with Tiger Woods looming large – only gives a hint as to the brand's impact on that burgeoning nation. A brand that won favor with the Chinese long ago – the first Buick sales office opened in Shanghai in 1929 – Buick is now considered one of the high-image automobile brands in a market that has an almost limitless future. With potential sales figures approaching staggering levels in the huge Chinese market, GM is making more money in its China operations than anywhere else in the world. And more Buicks are now sold in China than in the U.S. Something that is a little difficult to fathom for those who still believe that the North American market is the be-all and end-all of the car business. Buick's successful position in the Chinese market has given it a rejuvenated relevance in the U.S. No longer considered one of GM's disposable brands, Buick is now making a strong comeback both within the corporation and where it counts the most – out on the road, with new, desirable products.
– Autoextremist Rant #374, 11/29/06

From the "NASCAR Bubble" File. It's not often that the first family of NASCAR gets rebuffed in its ongoing efforts to take over the world, but that's exactly what happened when the Daytona Beach-based marketing juggernaut threw in the towel and ended its campaign to build a new NASCAR track in Staten Island, New York, after local political factions convinced everyone that it would be a disruptive undertaking and a bad idea. In a stinging and extremely costly defeat, International Speedway Corporation was forced to pursue "alternative strategies" for the 676-acre parcel of land it currently owned in the borough – the largest undeveloped acreage of land in the five boroughs of New York City. Even if ISC were to sell it off for $100 million (according to their estimates but considered highly optimistic), the decision to discontinue the speedway development efforts on Staten Island will result in a non-cash, pre-tax charge in the company's fiscal 2006 fourth quarter results of approximately $75 to $85 million, or $0.90 to $1.02 per diluted share after tax. ISC had spent $150 million in pursuit of the deal through November 30, 2006. Let's see, declining attendance, declining TV ratings, disgruntled sponsors and now this embarrassment? NASCAR insisted that 2006 was a mere "bump in the road" and that things would return to normal for them in 2007. I, on the other hand, preferred to revisit my physics textbook and read up on gravity, because what goes up must certainly come down – and NASCAR could not and would not stay hot forever.

Your actual mileage may really suck. Those famous words "Your actual mileage may vary" will soon become even more critical after the Environmental Protection Agency finally gets around to changing their woefully inaccurate testing procedure for their miles-per-gallon ratings. Beginning with the 2008 models arriving over the next year, the E.P.A. will begin to factor real-world driving habits into their evaluations such as using the heat and air conditioning systems and accounting for hard acceleration and higher speeds – and the result will be a reduction of around 8 percent in the highway ratings and as much as 25 percent in the city numbers. Anyone who drives knows that the city and highway fuel economy numbers from the E.P.A. have been gulp fiction for a long, long time – no car or truck delivered what was on the sticker. But the real impact of this new testing procedure could be dramatic, especially for hybrids (which could see an overall reduction of as much as 30 percent), and for the full-size truck and SUV markets.

That brought us to the end of another year. The auto industry circa 2006 had become a teeming cauldron of global competitors, all jockeying for position in the North American market, while the giant Chinese market loomed ever larger in the future. And more often than not, these manufacturers were vying for the same piece of pricing real estate – the magical $30,000.00 to $50,000.00 window of opportunity. That meant that there were too many car companies with too many models aiming their considerable resources at the same target – and something had to give.

So far, the Detroit-centric automakers had borne the brunt of this market shakeout. Detroit's share of the North American market plummeted precipitously yet again in 2006, and even with wave after wave of new products coming online, their market slide continued. Why? It came down to the fact that for many American consumers the domestic-branded cars and trucks were simply missing from their radar screens, for any number of reasons.

Getting these consumers to even *look* at domestic products continued to be the marketing challenge of the new century. Because even when presented with impeccable evidence that a particular domestic vehicle was equal to or even better than a foreign competitor in terms of design, engineering, quality, safety, performance, fuel economy *and* value, these consumers shrugged their shoulders and said, "Whatever."

On that somber note, 2007 was shaping up to be even more unpredictable and uproarious.

Which we found out soon enough to be true.

PART SIX

CAN DETROIT SELL THE *IDEA* OF AN AMERICAN CAR?

THE EVE OF DESTRUCTION – OR
THE DAWN OF A NEW ERA?

The start of 2007 brought a new sense of foreboding to Detroit. It was clear that a fundamental shift was taking place in the automobile market in the U.S. that could not be slowed, let alone reversed. Toyota's inexorable march forward continued unabated, and their campaign for the hearts and minds of the American consumer public was progressing swimmingly well. With gas prices suddenly accelerating into the stratosphere and the price of oil in the world market regularly climbing to more than $70.00 per barrel, Toyota's momentum threatened to gain even more steam.

Despite a flurry of extremely competitive products reaching the street from GM and Ford, Detroit overall was saddled with product lineups overly dependent on full-size trucks and massive SUVs. The Detroit automakers were clearly out of position in a market that left no room for error even on a good day.

Detroit's dire straits were compounded by the fact that there was a growing green movement in the U.S. being fed by a political lynching posse led by Nancy Pelosi, the newly-minted speaker of the house and firebrand from California who was clearly out for Detroit's head, even if it meant the destruction of one of this country's most vital manufacturing centers.

Detroit was the new Whipping Boy for all of America's problems, and according to the vitriol aimed at the domestic auto industry by political operatives on both coasts and by such clueless soothsayers like Thomas Friedman of *The New York Times*, Detroit was almost single-handedly responsible for global warming and needed to be eradicated – and the sooner the better.

The Ultimate Bad News for Detroit was that America's car-buying consumers' apathy toward Detroit and Detroit-sourced cars and trucks was growing by the month. To say that things were looking gloomy for the Motor City was a gross understatement.

Yet in the midst of this rancor, the Detroit-based car companies – Chrysler, Ford and GM – were attempting a radical restructuring and a new product push that was unprecedented in the industry's history.

Would it be enough? Or was it just a prelude to disaster?

Two thousand seven was shaping up to be the year that would determine Detroit's fate.

TROUBLE IN THE GLASS HOUSE

By January 2007, Ford was floundering, trying to rectify a woefully inadequate product lineup while in the throes of an organizational upheaval led by the ex-Boeing leader, Alan Mulally, a forceful presence the likes of which the entrenched bureaucracy at Ford hadn't seen before – or at least since Henry Ford II's reign anyway. Mulally combined a disarming, "aw shucks" native-Kansan enthusiasm with a laser-like focus, a quick grasp of the facts and an unwavering lock on the goal that was on his front burner 24 hours a day – to save the Ford Motor Company from implosion.

Bill Ford Jr. brought Mulally in because he couldn't get the company turned around – his unfailingly "nice guy" persona kept getting in the way. Ford is the nicest billionaire you'll ever meet, a genuine and decent man who just so happens to have the weight of the Ford family's legacy hanging over his every breath. The Ford bureaucracy exploited Bill Ford's niceness by ignoring direct orders from him when those orders didn't suit the myriad divisive agendas festering in the place.

And it was killing the company

It didn't help that Bill didn't instill fear in his employees like his Uncle – "Hank the Deuce" – did. Everyone knew that if they didn't agree with an order from Bill, they'd just sit on it until the urgency faded. This contrasts sharply with life at Ford in Henry Ford II's day, when people regularly got fired for incompetence or for just being in the wrong place at the wrong time – just ask Lee Iacocca. "Lido" was fired for a number of reasons, both real and imagined, but ultimately it came down to the fact that Henry just didn't like Iacocca's insatiable desire for being a media hog and his penchant for taking credit for any success that the Ford Motor Company enjoyed. (Iacocca took sole credit for the Mustang, for instance, even though several key people were involved in its gestation.) And that never sat well with Henry, so he fired Iacocca, just like that – when he had had enough.

Bill Ford Jr. is 180 degrees different from Henry, and there was no amount of schooling or toughening that could change or alter his "nice guy" persona. Bill finally understood that the future of the Ford Motor Company hinged on his ability to bring in someone who could break through the congestive clutter in the Ford "system." And if he couldn't accomplish that, then there was a real good chance that the company would be lost.

I wrote a column directed at Mulally when he was given the reins at Ford that not only outlined Bill Ford's predicament but also clearly stated what I saw as his agenda to fix the Ford Motor Company...

Dear Alan,

Judging by the tone of Bill Ford's most recent memo to Ford employees, he's had it up to "here" with the pundits, the critics and the instant experts who seem to have drawn a bead on the Ford Motor Company – and it's easy to see why. It's much tougher to attack the challenges facing Ford with a horde of critics second guessing your every move, even though the cumulative knowledge of the inner workings of your company harbored by said critics can at times amount to somewhere between slim – and none. Be that as it may, as you well know, Alan – it comes with the territory. After all, Bill Ford's name is not only on the building, he had the unenviable dual role of representing his family's interests, while at the same time trying to right the fortunes of one of America's industrial icons – a company that has been so inexorably linked to the very fabric of this nation that the idea of it now being up against the ropes and gasping for air is almost unfathomable.

But saying all of that, I feel compelled to offer some pointed recommendations of my own, because now it's your turn, Alan.

And although I risk the danger of being lumped in with the negative cacophony that is hovering like a black cloud of doubt over the Glass House, I believe you need to hear the High-Octane Truth, minus the spin from your would-be "handlers" and others of their ilk over in Dearborn who seem to offer more obstructions on the road to reality than clarity. And with you just being given the reins of an American industrial icon, this is as good a time as any.

Please dispatch any remnants of the touchy-feely, "I'm-the-world's-most-understanding-and-benevolent-boss" regime. *Great leaders have to be hard-asses sometimes; I hope you know that, because Bill certainly didn't. That doesn't mean anyone will think less of you, and even if they do, maybe their usefulness to you and the Ford Motor Company borders on the inconsequential anyway. I really think that at times Bill overcompensated by wallowing in those tedious textbook consensus management techniques just so that people would think he's a nice, regular guy despite his considerable personal financial standing. Well, as you know, Alan, at the end of the day it doesn't buy you a damn thing. Instead, it allows a bureaucracy of agreeable "yes people" to multiply and grow fiefdoms all around you – the very people who have conspired to keep the truth from Bill Ford at all costs over the years and the very people who have gone out of their way to make sure direct orders don't get carried out, should it not suit their particular agenda that week. These are also the very people who have played a key role in pushing the Ford Motor Company to the brink. I'm not suggesting you recreate the opening of "Patton" on video (with you playing the George C. Scott role) and play it over the company broadcast feed every morning, but you must assert yourself as The Boss. Not the "huggable" boss. Not the "nicest guy in the world" boss. And not the "most regular-guy billionaire I know" boss, which is what Bill's MO was. But The Boss. And if you do, I guarantee you'll find the tough decisions will be easier, the tempo around the shop will be much livelier – and the account-*

ability quotient will increase exponentially. Think George Steinbrenner. Better yet, channel Bill's uncle – Hank the Deuce. He pounded on the table. He kicked Ferrari's ass. And he fired Lee Iacocca. It would be a good thing for you if your underlings were a little afraid of you – that in and of itself would be seismic cultural shift for the Ford Motor Company.

Stop putting the Ford Motor Company in the position of being America's Corporate Whipping Boy. *The fact that every group in this country with a two-bit cause and a politically-polarizing agenda can garner a cup of coffee and a hug either from Bill Ford or his PR minions is simply unacceptable. Bill started it when he decided to hug the green movement and declare to the world that the Ford Motor Company would be the environmental leader. Then, he had to backtrack when the realities of the business prevented him from delivering on that promise. Yes, Bill's environmental sensibility is admirable, and I know it's consistent with his personal view of the world, but you have a company to run, and you can't be held hostage by the Dan Beckers of the world just because Bill made a pronouncement that couldn't be backed up. You just have to remind yourself of one remarkably simple thing: The Ford Motor Company is in the business of selling cars and trucks to anyone who wants and can afford them – and that means everything from little green pea shooters and fire-breathing Mustangs, all the way up to Super Duty trucks. To occupy your time with anything else at this point is a complete waste of it. There will always be groups coming out of the woodwork looking for a handout and a pat on the head from Ford – that doesn't mean that you have to put out the welcome mat for them to the detriment of the overall goals and the fundamental well-being of the company.*

Save Lincoln, before it fades into oblivion. *Under Bill's watch, the Lincoln brand has fallen into almost total disrepair. And seeing as it's one of America's iconic automotive brands, you have got to put a stop to it, or at least slow the carnage. Suffice to say, the people who have been in charge of Lincoln have* *fumbled every last opportunity to restore what once was one of America's most prestigious luxury brands. I could devote the rest of this letter to the egregious sins, missteps and flat-out bungling that have gone on over the last seven years in the name of "marketing" the Lincoln brand and nurturing its product portfolio, but I will sum it up briefly instead: You need to develop a proper rear-wheel-drive Lincoln – a "flagship" – immediately. I don't care how you spin the new Lincoln MKZ – it's a "me-too" car with a "me-too" shape that is totally devoid of character, distinctiveness or even a whiff of Lincoln heritage. In an automotive world populated with bland appliances boasting manufactured pedigrees, the fact that Ford has continued to squander the Lincoln legacy borders on the criminal. And on top of that, the previous regime has blown an opportunity to generate a considerable chunk of revenue too. I know there are many pressing product issues facing you and your troops, but if you don't assign a crack team tasked with the resurrection of Lincoln, you won't have it around to worry about anymore – and Lincoln will have died on your watch. Not good.*

Unleash your talent and swing for the fences. *I just had the opportunity to sample two exemplary Fords, the Ford GT and the new Shelby Cobra GT500 Mustang, and to say I was impressed is an understatement. Critics will suggest that it's "easy" for the American companies to do performance cars, that the real test is in creating mainstream vehicles with real appeal. I disagree. There's nothing "easy" about doing great high-performance cars. It requires discipline, focus, creativity – and talent. And make no mistake – the Ford GT and the Shelby Mustang are indeed great high-performance cars. But the creativity and talent bristling in the Ford GT and Shelby Mustang are easily translatable to your mainstream offerings, if you let it happen. Ford has demonstrated time and again that when it is focused as a company, it can deliver great products. You have tremendously talented and creative individuals at work at the Ford Motor Company. And now is not the time* to play it safe. Your new advertising campaign – "Bold Moves" – is the perfect description of what Ford needs to be all about right now. Don't waste your time "benchmarking." Instead, go beyond the expected and reach for the unexpected. Redefine a segment or better yet, invent a new segment. This business holds no future for traditional lockstep thinking and the typical formulaic Detroit attitude. You have nothing to lose – and you have the talent to pull it off. As they say, Go Big – or Go Home.

Put a stake in the ground – and give your company something to shoot for. In line with unleashing Ford's talent, it's time to reenergize the company from top to bottom. You need to put a stake in the ground and get your company's juices flowing again – while giving your organization something to shoot for. There's no more dramatic way to do that than to very publicly announce that you're committed to reaching a difficult but attainable goal. One that requires sacrifice, dedication, talent and most important – the will to win. Imagine if you got up in front of the assembled media at the Los Angeles Auto Show media days this coming November and declared that Ford was not only going to go back to compete in the Indianapolis 500 and the 24 Hours of Le Mans – but that you would win. Ford's glorious history is embellished by its long record of success at racetracks around the world, and it is uniquely positioned as one of only two automobile manufacturers in the world that has won at the Indianapolis Motor Speedway and achieved overall victory in the world's most prestigious endurance race. This is consistent with Bill's stated goal of Ford being a leading, innovative company too. As a matter of fact, winning the two most famous races in the world not only demands innovation – it requires technical know-how, creative thinking on the fly, efficient use of fuel and energy, and an unwavering commitment to excellence. As an added incentive, the organizers of the 24 Hours of Le Mans are making a concerted effort to convert to running E85 in all of their cars, and the Indianapolis Motor Speedway will run 100 percent ethanol beginning in 2007. So, Ford could *not only win – but win while being consistent with Bill's overall position on the environment too. This would underscore the fact that Ford is not just an American automobile company hanging on for its very existence, but a fully engaged, technologically capable entity not only willing to compete on the world's biggest stages – but daring enough to go out and win against the best in the world.*

It's time to go on the offensive, Alan. Great leaders lead when times are toughest. I think the Ford Motor Company has spent more than enough time wallowing on the Planet Doom and Gloom – as a matter of fact, it's in danger of establishing permanent residence there. You must change that immediately. Bill's rope-a-dope tactics were wearing thin months ago – after all, how many more body blows can a company withstand before you finally say, "Enough?" It's time to turn up the wick and get on with it, Alan. This is no time for the "hugs and a smile" school of management. Kick your organization in the butt and demand brilliance, because needless to say, only the very best will do.

Anything less at this point would be a disservice to you – and to the Ford family's legacy.

Mulally looked promising by January 2007, and he looked even better that summer. The Ford bureaucracy was finding out – at times the hard way – that you do not mess with Alan Mulally. You better be prepared, and you better be ready to answer the tough questions – or else. Mulally was exactly what the Ford Motor Company needed. Now, if they can only get the new products online that they so desperately need, they just might have a shot.

CHRYSLER'S WAY BACKWARD

By the fall of 2006, Chrysler's festering problems had finally caught up to them. The inventory "situation" had turned into a full-blown crisis – after they kept repeatedly insisting that things were under control and that there was only a need for minor "adjustments" before things would be in order.

Chrysler had been living on borrowed time ever since Dieter Zetsche's departure to run the whole DaimlerChrysler shebang back at headquarters in Germany. Up until that point, Chrysler was the "darling" of the media, the Detroit-based automaker that loved to tout that it was smarter than its crosstown rivals – too smart to get caught up in the downward spiral that was paralyzing the fortunes of Ford and GM. They loved to flaunt their smug swagger every chance they got, too, reveling in the fact that their "That thing gotta Hemi?" campaign had become part of the country's lexicon and that their 300C was the poster child of why they were better than GM and Ford.

My, how things had changed.

After shouting from the rooftops that their Hemi was the performance engine to have, Chrysler had been caught out by two rapidly escalating developments: 1. The 300/300C was yesterday's news (which is anathema in our faddish "of the moment" culture), and 2. The sustained high price of gasoline was counter to the image of the Hemi's muscle + power persona. Chrysler aimed to counteract that with an ad new campaign that touted the mileage of the Hemi, but who was kidding whom? After spending millions upon millions of dollars burnishing the image of the Hemi in the American consumer consciousness as a high-performance icon, that dog wouldn't hunt – even with a T-Bone.

High gas prices had also decimated sales of the Dodge Ram trucks, which crippled the company's effort to stay above water. And on top of everything else, product mistakes and missteps were just killing Chrysler. The Jeep Commander – which was the winner of AE's 2006 "Answer to the Question that Absolutely No One was Asking" award – was a massive disappointment and contributed mightily to Chrysler's inventory woes. And the Chrysler Sebring was a major miscalculation, boasting a design "language" consisting of its "Let's throw every recent Chrysler styling gimmick we can think of on it and call it good" school of design culminating in a rolling monument to mediocrity that had knowledgeable Chrysler insiders wincing with embarrassment. And how about the Dodge Durango-based Chrysler Aspen "luxury" SUV? Talk about the wrong vehicle, at the wrong time, from the wrong company. Then, there were the Jeep Compass and Jeep Patriot, an unwise proliferation of the brand that had a negative impact on Jeep's reputation. On top of every-thing else, Chrysler was now spending more on incentives per vehicle on average than their crosstown rivals, and they were loading up on fleet sales to boot. Funny, but we didn't hear much "we're smarter than the average car company" talk coming out of Auburn Hills by the end of 2006, because the shit had well and truly hit the fan.

Chrysler had one bright spot to be sure – the new four-door Jeep Wrangler was looking to be a runaway success – but the company couldn't survive on that standout vehicle alone.

The Dieter Zetsche/Wolfgang Bernhard era was now officially ancient history out in Auburn Hills. The replacement regime had been living off past laurels and its "smoke-and-mirrors" marketing strategy for too long. The car company formerly known as "hot" was now in the dumper – a territory that Dieter Zetsche all but guaran-teed to the media on numerous occasions that the Chrysler Group would *never* visit again. And now that they had adopted the classic Detroit mantra of "the really good stuff is just around the corner" and "it won't be long now" – the skeptics came out of the woodwork.

And they proved to be dead right, too, because the rumblings coming from Auburn Hills were unmistakable.

The Chrysler Group was in deep trouble – again.

DaimlerChrysler AG *very* quietly announced that it would be reducing its 2006 operating profit forecast due to the fact that its Chrysler Group division expected a $1.52 billion loss in the third quarter, which was more than *two times* the original amount that had been bandied about the previous summer. In a prepared statement, the German automaker said, "The Chrysler Group is facing a difficult market environment in the United States with excess inventory, non-competitive legacy costs for employees and retirees, continuing high fuel prices and a stronger shift in demand toward smaller vehicles."

What was significant about that official announcement wasn't just the fact that the company was losing big money, but that Chrysler had finally gone on the record and admitted that its "little" inventory problem was a major, crisis-inducing event. Was it classic German-driven blind arrogance that wouldn't allow the Chrysler Group to admit they had an inventory/manufacturing capacity/sales problem in the first place? Or was it the fact that the post-Dieter Zetsche/Wolfgang Bernhard management team put in place out in Auburn Hills had now been exposed for what they most assuredly were – lost.

How about all of the above?

The Germans at DaimlerChrysler absolutely loathed admitting mistakes, even though they had been staring them in the face like a storage lot full of Jeep Commanders. That was painfully consistent with the unbridled arrogance that permeated the old Daimler-Benz culture, a smug air of superiority that was rearing its ugly head during this latest Chrysler slide – in the form of executives insisting that they had a "handle" on things – in order to make target numbers that made zero sense in the face of a North American market in complete turmoil.

The lingering stench of the old Daimler-Benz culture – where executives were trained in the life or death struggle to "make" the numbers at all costs, no matter how nonsensical or completely unrealistic they were – is the reason why production schedules were not cut back, inventory grew, and Chrysler Group executives like Tom LaSorda (President & CEO), Eric Ridenour (COO) and Joe Eberhardt (Executive VP-Sales and Marketing) couldn't come up with an honest appraisal of just how screwed-up things were, and beyond that, why they were unbelievably late in attempting to execute a serious plan of attack to right their now severely listing ship.

Let's just say the LaSorda/Ridenour regime didn't exactly light up the board, given the fact that the company's one legitimate market hit – the Chrysler 300 – was brought to life under the direct, hands-on tutelage of Wolfgang Bernhard. Instead, they seemed to have spent most of their time spinning their wheels, feting Dieter Zetsche, letting GM's Hummer swipe Jeep's marketing position right out from under them, and putting all of their marketing muscle behind the Hemi engine and Ram pickup trucks – while apparently ignoring the mounting evidence that the U.S. market was undergoing a fundamental shift to fuel-efficient cars.

Though Tom LaSorda's good guy, salt-of-the-earth persona was eminently likable, the ex-GM manufacturing guru seemed to be a bit out of his league in wrestling with Chrysler's deep-rooted problems. After all, it had been under his watch that Chrysler's over-capacity and subsequent inventory problems went out of control (even though Dieter Zetsche was still there when those production schedules were determined).

Then, there was the ire being directed at Joe Eberhardt, Chrysler's Executive VP-Sales and Marketing, by the dealers. According to Jean Halliday in *Advertising Age*, by the end of Eberhardt's tenure dealers were calling him out as the leading culprit responsible for most of their problems. The ex-Mercedes-Benz marketing guru, who was one of the architects of M-B's disastrous "more approachable" marketing strategy in the U.S. market before his assignment in Auburn Hills, deserved particularly harsh scrutiny as he was the most classically-trained German executive in the Daimler-Benz school of numbers making – and one of former CEO Juergen Schrempp's chosen "boys" to boot. His answer to Chrysler's inventory problems all along had been to put the onus on Chrysler's dealers, shoving inventory down dealers' throats, while using financial incentives for leverage, instead of pushing to deal with the problem at the manufacturing level – where it should have been addressed from the beginning. To say it didn't work out was not only the understatement of the year – it hastened the Chrysler Group being put up for sale.

Eberhardt was also one of the chief boosters (along with the Chrysler Group's PR chief, Jason Vines) of the "Ask Dr. Z" advertising campaign – a high-profile image campaign that spent all of its time trying to tell us why the German-American connection at DaimlerChrysler was a good thing (American consumers didn't care), used Dieter Zetsche as pitchman (to his detriment) and failed to move the sales needle one iota (Chrysler Group sales slid even further during the costly marketing effort).

Eberhardt had been a Teflon Man during his career, deftly shedding all of the bad things that happened under his watch with remarkable aplomb, while taking credit for any positives – whether they were his doing or not. But he wasn't so lucky this time around. Eberhardt ended up being forced to leave the company to stave off a dealer mutiny, with large, high-profile dealers demanding that he go – or else. And what did Eberhardt get for running the Chrysler Group into the ground and alienating everyone he came in contact with? He was gifted a Mercedes-Benz franchise in California for his years of loyal service by his German cronies. Who says relentless mediocrity doesn't pay in the end?

After all of the boasting, all of the "we're-smarter-than-thou" pronouncements and the smack-talking, the Chrysler Group's "can't miss" ticket to greatness had now become their very own Way Backward Plan.

DIETER ZETSCHE'S TARNISHED STAR

The continued missteps and flat-out screw-ups by the management team handpicked by Dieter Zetsche were now killing the profitability of the parent company.

The Chrysler Group, which had careened from the depths of despair to the glory days – and back – time and time again, was headed for one of its classic face-plants into The Land of No Profitability (which abuts The Sea of Mediocrity, by the way). And no matter how the DCX corporate spin-meisters attempted to deflect this bad news, the spin had now officially been spun.

It wasn't supposed to happen this way, of course. While running the Chrysler Group, Dieter Zetsche never missed an opportunity to hammer the assembled media over and over again, insisting that the roller-coaster ride emblematic of the bad old Chrysler days were officially over – thanks to the brilliance of him and his team.

But the reality was that Chrysler got caught in a classic Twilight Zone of "Our new stuff coming is kick-ass, and it won't be long now!" boastful bluster and the crushing reality of a mounting inventory that just wasn't selling – even with massive incentives. In truth, the Chrysler Group had been barely treading water for more than eighteen months. In the past, you could almost forgive (almost) the painfully amateurish marketing initiatives and lame-brained ad campaigns that emanated from Auburn Hills, because the product story used to be the one thing you could count on from the Chrysler Group.

Not anymore.

And all eyes were now focused on Dieter Zetsche. After engineering the Chrysler Group's latest "miracle," Zetsche was tapped to lead DaimlerChrysler out of the wilderness, replacing the imperious

Jürgen Schrempp, who had damn near run the parent company into the ground. Schrempp was the "genius" leader of Daimler-Benz who engineered the "Merger of Equals" with the Chrysler Corporation for $36 billion. Although a thinly-disguised takeover of Chrysler, the two companies never meshed in eight years of trying, and by the end, DaimlerChrysler would have to actually *pay* to get out of the deal and hand the Chrysler Group to Cerberus Capital Management. (Schrempp eventually retired early, having establishing himself as one of the most incompetent, misguided and destructive executives in automotive history.)

There was no doubt that Zetsche's task was compounded by the mess that his disgraced predecessor left, but he took it upon himself to personally guide the once-vaunted Mercedes-Benz brand out of its precipitous decline. And though Zetsche made a few noteworthy initial moves (like relocating the executive offices back to the main manufacturing center in Stuttgart, where they had been in the firm's heyday, in order to reinvigorate the musty executive ranks in the company, as is his style), his victories were modest, at best.

On the one hand, the new Mercedes-Benz advertising campaign (and products like the new S-Class) clearly tried to wake up the echoes of the company's "Engineered like no other car in the world" glory days, even though too many of its products failed to even approach that lofty perch (see the R-Class and the dreadful GL-Class as exhibits A & B). But on the other hand, the homogenization and gradual decline of the Mercedes image and *raison d'etre* continued, with word that an upcoming DCX "Phoenix" V-6 corporate engine program would see identical engines shared in Chrysler and Mercedes-Benz products not helping the situation.

Mercedes' problems were just one set of challenges for Zetsche, because the Chrysler Group's grim prospects were conspiring to wreck Zetsche's once-solid-gold reputation. To make matters even worse, Zetsche had allowed himself to be dragged into one of the most ill-advised ad campaigns ever foisted-off on the American consumer public – the painfully dreadful "Dr. Z" embarrassment – which had managed to single-handedly turn one of the titans of the automotive world into a mewling, preening dolt overnight.

The sad thing to contemplate about this campaign in retrospect was that the assembled brainpower in Chrysler Group marketing and at their agency, BBDO Detroit, actually thought the stuff was good and that it did wonders for the public's perception of the Chrysler Group, which, when you really stopped and thought about it, was simply beyond comprehension – not to mention just flat-out scary.

Never have so few done such inexorable damage to so many under the guise of doing "advertising."

Needless to say, the curious derailment of Dieter Zetsche's much-ballyhooed image got my vote as one of the auto industry stories of the year. Here was a guy who was well on his way to auto industry "legend" status, only stopping by briefly to grace us with his brilliance on his way to full-blown corporate executive sainthood, when all of a sudden he found himself presiding over a mountain of excuses and a "legacy" in Auburn Hills that was disintegrating at an alarming rate.

But then again, it lends itself perfectly to one of my other auto industry stories of the year – and that was that the Chrysler Group found itself back in the tank – yet again.

And the buck clearly stopped with "Dr. Z."

The table was set for Zetsche to do what he had to do – and that was to jettison the "Chrysler" part of DaimlerChrysler – to Cerberus Capital Management, the private equity firm. Interestingly enough, one of the hired guns leading and advising the Cerberus play for Chrysler? None other than Dieter Zetsche's longtime crony, Wolfgang Bernhard.

Zetsche couldn't do the deal, however, without first publicly admitting that the Chrysler Group's latest swoon, though the result of a number of contributing factors, was directly the result of Zetsche taking his eye off of the ball and letting his handpicked successors run amuck.

In short, Zetsche blew it, and his "can't miss" ascendancy to legendary automotive industry stardom was derailed. Now? He was just another auto company CEO trying to keep his company afloat – and keep his head above water.

THE IMPENDING DISASTER
CALLED THE "NEW" CHRYSLER

On Friday, August 3, 2007, Cerberus Capital Management closed on their purchase of the Chrysler corporation from Daimler AG, a move that signaled a new era for Chrysler as well as Detroit, because for the first time in decades one of the Detroit Three would be in private hands. Cerberus, the company filled with ex-General Electric disciples of Jack Welch, and which had also rounded up an impressive posse of auto industry executive advisors to assist them in their quest for Chrysler, looked to be charting a course to right the severely listing Chrysler ship, with the mercurial but extremely talented executive, Wolfgang Bernhard, slated to become non-executive chairman of the new enterprise. But in a stunning move that unfolded the following Sunday night, Cerberus shifted gears completely.

In what could only be described as a desperation, "Hail Mary" move, the GE-addled brain trust at Cerberus Capital Management – fresh with the news that Wolfgang Bernhard had unexpectedly turned down their offer to become non-executive chairman of the "New" Chrysler – named the ex-CEO of Home Depot, Bob Nardelli (another GE alumnus), to the post instead. Tom LaSorda would now become Nardelli's No. 2 (although no one expected him to stick around long), and Eric Ridenour, the alleged former COO of Chrysler – who was simply overmatched for the job from the get-go – left the company. My inbox on that Monday morning had ten emails in it, all with "WTF?" in the subject line.

WTF? Indeed.

First of all, let me debunk the ludicrous speculation about Wolf-gang Bernhard, that he somehow wasn't a "good fit" to run Chrysler because of his recent track record. That notion was simply absurd. There was simply no one in this business better equipped to run Chrysler. There was simply no one else even close, for that matter. Bernhard had the deep knowledge, the incomparably diverse skill set and the relentless drive necessary to do justice to that job – in his sleep. But in the last six months of his involvement with Cerberus, Bernhard learned two things: 1. He got an up-close and personal view of how Cerberus went about its business, and he could see the writing on the wall in that a potential for conflict to his authority loomed, whenever Cerberus managers decided to question it. He wasn't in the mood to have people who didn't know the business start telling him what to do. And that was clearly more than a distinct possibility with the disciples of Jack Welch on the loose. And 2. Bernhard clearly came to understanding that the potential for a Chrysler recovery was *much* less than the reality of the situation indicated. There were just too many "ifs" roiling around for Bernhard to think anything else. *If* Chrysler managed to negotiate a favorable contract with the UAW, *if* they could get their product roster turned around in time, *if* they could favorably repair the relationship with the dealers while they tried to winnow their ranks, *if* the U.S. automakers got a favorable break in Congress with the timetable of the new CAFE standards coming up for review that fall. That was one too many "ifs" in Bernhard's book, so he declined the Cerberus offer to become chairman.

But that being said, the hiring of Nardelli was a jaw-dropper. I succinctly summed-up my feelings on the matter in my column that week with the following question: What part of hiring Bob Nardelli to become the new CEO of Chrysler seemed like a good idea? This impending disaster was such a disastrous fit at The Home Depot by the end that paying his ridiculously exorbitant severance package of $210 million was more palatable option than having him around for one more day. Nardelli's blunderbuss reputation for being a ball-busting cost-cutter lost in a GE-tinged Six Sigma fog and blessed with the people skills of a drill sergeant caught up with him at The Home Depot, and I predicted it would catch-up with him at Chrysler too.

Even the hard-bitten "old-school" managers operating at the Detroit Three had finally learned that you can't cut your way to prosperity – and that's a lesson that Nardelli hadn't even *begun* to come close to understanding.

There was much hand-wringing in the media that Nardelli's abrasive demeanor wouldn't be a factor because of the fact that Cerberus was a private company and it would free him from having to deal with cranky shareholders. That perspective was simply unmitigated bullshit, because running a Detroit car company had become as much a political job as it was anything else – if not more so, in fact. If you're the head of a Detroit car company, you are its most visible spokesperson, period. And to pretend otherwise was simply futile. Alan Mulally got it, and even Rick Wagoner sort of gets it (at least when he feels like it). But Nardelli? You have to be kidding.

The other myth being propagated in the media that fateful Monday was that Nardelli, like Alan Mulally at Ford, was part of the new wave of "outsiders" who would finally cure Detroit of what ails it once and for all. That perspective was blatantly wrong-headed too. The difference between Mulally and Nardelli was that Mulally came from a company that actually *manufactured* things and sold them to real live customers. There were and are distinct similarities between the car business and the airplane business, which had served Mulally well so far. Nardelli? Nothing in his track record suggested that he was equipped to succeed at the "new" Chrysler, because he flat-out knew nothin' about nothin' when it came to the car business.

What does this business come down to every single time? Great product. You can't "process" your way to product desirability. Period. Chrysler desperately needed great product, first and foremost – and the sooner the better. Of the Detroit Three, Chrysler was clearly out of position for the market – embarrassingly so, I might add - and the clock was ticking. The last time I checked, great products are not a by-product of a system like Six Sigma, because it becomes all about the process itself and the cold, hard numbers. Usable to a degree, but that's all it is, because Six Sigma is a system that leaves out the essence of this business and conveniently neuters what really matters. Great products flow from the guts of people who know and love cars and have the fire and the will to succeed at all costs in bringing those great products to the street. You can't quantify that, and it's not a "process" that can be learned.

So here was Chrysler on the Edge of Oblivion once again. By choosing Bob Nardelli to run Chrysler, Cerberus had charted a course for disaster – yet another in the long line of disasters for this star-crossed car company. Nardelli was simply the wrong man, in the wrong business, at the wrong time – a perfect storm of negatives that would prove to be the very definition of Not Good.

The Cerberus-owned Chrysler debuted the new ad campaign, "The New Chrysler: Get Read for the Next Hundred Years" as a signal that this whole enterprise would be a long and fruitful one. I'm not as optimistic. As a matter of fact, I predict that the "new" Chrysler will be lucky if it survives the decade. I fully expect Carlos Ghosn, the CEO of the Renault-Nissan conglomerate, to come calling on Detroit once again – only this time, he will get his hands on one of the Detroit Three – after Cerberus finishes running Chrysler into the ground, that is.

Note: On September 6, 2007, Robert Nardelli named Jim Press – the first non-Japanese President of Toyota Motor North America and a 37-year Toyota veteran – Vice Chairman and President of Chrysler LLC. Press will be Nardelli's clear No. 2, but there are no guarantees – far from it, in fact – that this will be a panacea for all of Chrysler's ills. It will be interesting to see how Press – a notoriously prickly and self-righteous executive totally immersed in the "Toyota Way" and one who never hesitated to lecture the media (and anyone else within earshot) about how great Toyota was and how lacking the "Detroit Three" were – will dance his way around his recent pronouncements and make the transition to saving an American car company like Chrysler. With or without Press, I'm still not optimistic about Chrysler's fortunes.

TOYOTA GETS "OUT-GREENED" BY A RESURGENT GM

GM opened 2007 determined to take the fight directly to Toyota. After years of rumbling, stumbling and bumbling through a relentless state of mediocrity brought on by the tyranny of the Brand Management era, the Bob Lutz-led product renaissance at GM was starting to bear fruit with a flurry of new models across a wide range of segments slated to hit the market throughout the year. New cars and trucks that bristled with arresting design execution inside and out, vehicles that were capable of generating the kind of word-of-mouth street "buzz" that no amount of advertising spending could generate.

It looked like GM's long trek through the wilderness to get back to a product-focused car company was finally happening, and even GM's harshest critics started to take notice.

But there was also a none-too-subtle shift in GM's attitude too. No longer content to sit back and have the market dictated to them by Toyota, GM executives were out to make a statement – and they had something in store for their Asian rivals at the 2007 North American International Auto Show in Detroit.

In a surprise to most everyone in attendance, GM dominated the show from start to finish. Getting things rolling with the "GM Style" event on the Saturday night before the first media day, where it used a fashion show format to unveil a flashy new convertible version of its upcoming Camaro, GM followed up by capturing the North American Car and Truck of the Year (voted on by a panel of 49 journalists) for the Saturn Aura and the Chevrolet Silverado pickup truck on Sunday morning. From there, GM introduced two future product hits and one giant technical breakthrough that left its competition reeling.

The next-generation Cadillac CTS – with a front-end design heavily influenced by the magnificent Cadillac Sixteen concept from a few years ago, and an interior design and execution that needed no explanation or apologies – would be a formidable competitor in looks, feel *and* dynamic ability. The original CTS was GM's first foray into "reimagining" Cadillac, and it was a pretty good effort with a few nagging flaws. The 2008 version of the CTS promised to be a completely different animal, however – one that will establish Cadillac as a serious player in one of the most hotly-contested segments in the U.S. market.

GM also unveiled a new Chevrolet Malibu that takes aim squarely at the perennial leading lights in the market, the Toyota Camry and Honda Accord, with a handsome exterior and most important, a first-rate interior. When the new Malibu arrives in late fall of 2007, it will be the first time in *years* that Chevrolet has a passenger car to seriously compete with in the heart of the U.S. mid-sized car market.

But the big news by far at Cobo Hall was the Chevrolet Volt, the car that signified GM's renewed commitment not only to the electric car, but also to the *electrification of the automobile* as the singular technology of our transportation future. Unlike traditional hybrids, which are first and foremost automobiles run on internal combustion engines (ICE) with electric assist, GM created a new vehicle architecture that is first and foremost an electric car, with only an assist from an ICE – in this case a 1-liter, 3-cylinder turbo engine.

Clearly dependent on needed advancements in lithium-ion batteries, the Volt concept was nonetheless designed to run on its batteries alone for 40-45 miles. Once that plateau is reached, the ICE is engaged to recharge the batteries. For people who drive fewer than 40 miles a day, it's conceivable that you'd never use the ICE, and thus never use gasoline, or much of it, for the life of the car, because it can be plugged in at night. The cruising range of the Volt was projected to be more than 600 miles with the ICE and the batteries.

The Volt also perfectly positioned GM's vehicle architecture of the future to accept hydrogen fuel cells down the road.

The Volt had the potential to be a game changer.

It is a rare occurrence when Toyota gets "out-greened" at a major auto show, or anywhere, for that matter. But GM had done exactly that with its Volt. As a matter of fact, GM not only "out-greened" Toyota, it established the next playing field for the industry by pointing the business toward a future dominated by electric vehicles and ultimately – toward an industry dominated by electric vehicles powered by hydrogen fuel cells.

The Chevrolet Volt wasn't just another concept – it signaled the fundamental transformation of the automobile and transportation as we know it.

And it was a gutty show of confidence by GM.

THE BOB LUTZ LEGACY

The Volt would not only perfectly position GM for a competitive future, it would solidify Bob Lutz's legacy as the most significant automotive product guru of the last 35 years and one of the most influential industry executives of all time.

Lutz is the 76-year-old dynamo of a man with a relentless drive and seemingly boundless energy who literally picked-up GM's beleaguered design and engineering troops by the lapels and *willed* them to greatness. When GM's CEO, Rick Wagoner, brought Lutz on board seven years ago at the post-retirement age of 69, he wanted to break the company free of the dismally repetitive and debilitating "three-steps-forward/five-steps-back" product dance that GM had been locked into for the last 25 years.

Anyone with even a casual interest in cars and the automobile business knows about Bob Lutz, so I will not bore you with the same rehash of his CV. The only thing I would like to add is that in my previous life in advertising I worked with him up close enough to know what he's like on a day-to-day basis – and that everything you've ever read about him is true. He gets to the point, he knows what he's talking about, and his gut instincts are second to none in this crazy business.

I accompanied Lutz on a two-day trip to southern California in the fall of 2006 to preview and drive the fourth-generation GM Sequel hydrogen fuel cell vehicle, and I was amazed all over again at his focus, his drive, and his command of anything and everything going on in the auto business. It struck me that he is simply a one-of-a-kind individual at the very top of his game.

What "Maximum Bob" Lutz has accomplished at GM is nothing short of extraordinary. He took a moribund company filled with disheartened designers and rudderless engineers and literally gave them a reason to come to work and actually enjoy what they do again.

How did he do it? Well, the easiest explanation is that he did it by "just being Bob," which, anyone who has worked closely with him knows, is a full time job in and of itself.

To be in a meeting with Bob Lutz is to know that there's no time for the typical bullshit. You get in, you get it on the table, you discuss it, a decision is made, and you get out. You have to be prepared, you have to have the answers, and you better know the "whys" and the "hows" *with* those answers. There's no time for the usual territorial posturing or the typical out-loud hand-wringing that plagues corporate America right now. Lutz doesn't give a damn about corporate "culture" or all the usual touchy-feely bullshit that goes with it. The way he does things makes it obsolete simply because he just blows right past it.

Before Lutz got to GM, the company had been at the mercy of an endless succession of so-called marketing "gurus" whose sum total qualifications for making decisions about GM's product lineup were that they were successes in other types of businesses. But in most cases, those success stories didn't translate worth a damn when applied to the car business – especially with the scope of GM's monumental problems. As previously stated, these people contributed immeasurably to GM's product and market share *slide* in that same period.

But Bob Lutz changed all of that.

The moment Lutz walked through the door, The Product was the focus again at General Motors. For the first time since Ed Cole retired, there was an executive at the very top of GM who not only really understood the business, he knew what needed to be done and how to go about doing it too. And it was clear to the GM faithful that Lutz would not rest until the company was going in the right direction again.

Lutz instantly connected with the True Believers at GM. The kind of people who fought for every last inch of product integrity despite GM's previous forays into abject product stupidity. The people who had to wince and watch in recent years while the good ideas got sidetracked or killed and the mediocre or just plain bad ideas got into production. These were the same people who had to stand by and watch as non-car people basically did everything in their power to run the once-proud corporation right into the ground. Yet these same people were the ones who still brought the fight with them every single day. The same ones who did stunning design concepts and who managed to get some pretty respectable cars and trucks to the street – against some unbelievable odds – before Lutz arrived.

These were the people Bob Lutz jump-started, and these were the people who delivered for him – in spades. These people could now look at the top of their company and see someone who "got it," someone who had fought the battles and won the wars, someone who understood what they'd been up against and someone whom they could finally believe in – *because he was one of them*.

When Bob Lutz got to GM he hit the ground running, and the True Believers responded to his drive and his energy. They burned the midnight oil and did everything in double and triple time, but they relished every moment of it because for the first time in a very, very long time they had someone at the top whom they could respect.

And nowhere was that more evident than at GM Design.

Of all the problems facing GM, resurrecting the integrity, the vision, the spirit and, most important, the *swagger* of the Design Staff was Priority Number One for Lutz. After all, more so than any other design house among the domestic car companies, GM Design could trace its lineage directly to the very beginnings of the "idea" of design in the automobile business.

But over the past 35 years, the glory days of GM Design faded. The once-proud GM Design Staff had become nothing but a neutered creative force that, though still incredibly deep in talent, had given up and was just going through the motions.

Lutz set out to resuscitate GM Design's attitude right off of the bat. One measure of how important Lutz viewed the situation was that he initially had his office right in GM Design, down the hall from Ed Welburn, the new GM Design chief. This was not only a hugely symbolic move, it was also a genuine indication of where Bob Lutz felt he needed to be on a daily basis. He knew that GM's short-term and long-term success and/or survivability hinged on cars and trucks that had that built-in "drool factor" to the nth degree. Vehicles that make people crazy with desire and excitement. Vehicles that people react to with statements like "what the hell is *that* and where can I get one?" Lutz unleashed Welburn and his troops and spurred them on to reach higher and go further – and they delivered spectacular concepts and production vehicles at a dizzying rate. GM Design was back in business.

Lutz had transformed the once-downtrodden organization back into the kind of free-wheeling artistic haven it once was, bristling with creativity, excitement and yes, *swagger*. After all, who would know more about putting some "swagger" back into GM Design than Detroit's current King of Swagger himself?

No, Bob Lutz isn't flawless by any stretch of the imagination, but he's the best product guy in the business – bar none. And at 76 years of age, he still has the gasoline in his veins, the fire in his soul, the will to do things right and the drive to get things done.

After decades of fumbling and floundering, after dealing with various "Messiahs" of The Week who turned out to be the Bums of the Year, after countless bad decisions on top of non-decisions, after suffering from years upon years of non-car mercenaries running rampant over the corporation for their own personal gain, GM finally got one very big thing right by bringing Bob Lutz on board.

Because with Lutz there is only one mantra that matters: The Product *was, is* and *always will be* King.

GM'S NEWFOUND PRODUCT SWAGGER RUNS UP AGAINST ITS BUILT-IN ACHILLES' HEEL

There was no doubt about the impact that Bob Lutz had on GM's product fortunes, because for all intents and purposes it was now a different company product-wise. GM's product offensive was delivering impressive vehicles across all segments – from small cars and small crossovers, to competently competitive mainstream sedans, luxury performance sedans, sports cars, and all-new trucks and SUVS. GM's product transformation was for real, and in most cases consumers had no idea just how many good new cars and trucks could be found at GM dealerships. The transformation was shocking in some respects, especially to observers who had grown used to GM's plodding bouts with product mediocrity in recent times.

But there was one aspect of GM that Bob Lutz couldn't get his arms around – and that was GM's Achilles' heel – its obsolete divisional structure. And nowhere was that more evident than at GM's reinvigorated Saturn division.

Bristling with such new, eye-catching products as the Sky roadster, the Aura sedan, the Vue crossover, the Outlook large crossover and a new small premium entry from its German Opel affiliate called the Astra, it would seem that GM's "focused attention" strategy first employed to great effect to turn the Cadillac division around had worked exceedingly well for Saturn.

The transformation of Saturn was so dramatic and complete that the oldest vehicle in the Saturn lineup is the Sky, which debuted in early 2006. But all was not well in Saturn land, and the reason goes back to GM's perennial product conundrum of "too many models, too many divisions and too many dealers," which I had been writing about since Day One of Autoextremist.com.

For instance, for all of its North American Car of the Year luster, it seemed that the excellent Aura sedan was languishing in Saturn dealerships across the country, according to *Automotive News* in the first quarter of 2007. Why was that, exactly? For one thing, GM decided to change its ad agency for Saturn midstream, moving the account from Goodby Silverstein & Partners in San Francisco to Deutsch/LA, GM's current agency darling of record. Any time you do that, the marketers involved can't help but take their eyes off of the ball, and things inevitably fall through the cracks – it's just human nature.

Then, hard on the heels of the Aura launch and in the midst of an agency change, Saturn marketers shifted their attention to the launch of the Outlook, the first-ever large crossover from the touchy-feely brand and an excellent product in its own right. And from the moment the advertising/marketing push began on the Outlook, the Aura got lost in the shuffle. In the summer of 2007, Saturn and its dealers were scrambling to jump-start the Aura all over again, confident they could do so through a newly energized marketing blitz.

But could they, really?

This market is all about "windows of opportunity," and auto marketers have a very limited chance to make a first impression. That first impression has to make a big-time, enduring impact – before it gets swallowed up by the next car company's "window" of marketing opportunity.

And therein lies the fundamental issue with the Aura. Imagine if Toyota had the Aura and launched it into the market with a $100 million dollar Camry-like marketing offensive. I guarantee you that there would have been no articles appearing in industry publications talking about languishing Aura sales – I would bet it would be just the opposite, in fact.

GM's product offensive is indeed stunning, but who would have thought that *too many* hit products could ever be a problem after the automaker struggled for so long with a series of mind-numbing, mediocre products?

Well, it is, and here's why: GM's antiquated divisional structure is the company's built-in Achilles' heel, and it will directly impact their ultimate success in this, the most competitive retail market in automotive history.

The Saturn Aura is an excellent effort in its segment, there's no question, but when GM marketing wakes up every day trying to appease all of its constituencies at the various divisions and dealers, the train wreck is inevitable.

And the Aura came up on the short end because of it.

Let's go back to those new GM crossovers for a moment. I spent three weeks driving the GMC Acadia, the Saturn Outlook and the Buick Enclave last spring and summer. Designed to attract people coming out of larger SUVs, these vehicles are exceptionally executed and bristle with smart details. But the most impressive thing about them is the way they drive, with the kind of "feel" not associated with vehicles approaching 4,900 pounds. I rate these new entries from GM as being superb in every respect. But does GM really need the Outlook, the Acadia, the Buick Enclave, an upcoming version from Chevrolet and even a rumored version from Cadillac in the works? Can GM properly launch all of these nameplates into a market already jam-packed with vehicles? Do they have the marketing muscle to do each vehicle justice?

Using the Aura as an example, by all indications they don't. Something always has to give within the GM divisional structure, and new product is going to come out on the short end of the stick and not get the attention it deserves.

What's next in this scenario? Which car gets more marketing money, the new Buick Enclave or the Saturn Astra? And if you're launching the ultra-crucial new Chevrolet Malibu, what other new GM model will have to play second fiddle while it gets its big push? The new Cadillac CTS? It never ends with GM, and that's exactly my point.

I look at the excellent new products GM has either on the ground or in the pipeline, and I think *great,* a domestic manufacturer is finally fighting back with some excellent, seriously competitive stuff. But then I look at what has happened with the Aura, and I shudder to think which new GM nameplate is going to be next to fall through the cracks.

GM can't keep "hoping" that dealer attrition will pare down its bloated dealer count. And they can't keep thinking that they can properly support the number of excellent products they have coming just by winging it, because it's clear that they can't.

As outrageous as it may seem given GM's recent history, the excellent new products the company is bringing to market are now becoming an embarrassment of riches, exposing GM's hoary divisional/dealer structure for the anachronism that it is – and that it has been for at least the last 25 years.

The Saturn Aura was more than just an excellent new mainstream passenger car entry for GM in the U.S. market, because its role within the corporation was much more important than that. The Aura situation was a warning to GM that they must make fundamental changes in the way they do business.

GM needs to be reminded of one thing when it comes to their new found product swagger: Having all the great products in the world counts for nothing if you can't afford to properly support them in the market.

GM seems to be determined to learn that lesson the hard way.

ORGANIZED LABOR IS PATHOLOGICALLY OUT OF TOUCH – AND OUT OF TIME

Of all the things affecting the domestic automobile industry in 2007 – the lingering problems associated with high healthcare costs, the pension woes, the artificial competitive advantage that the Asian manufacturers received due to their governments official and unofficial manipulation of currencies, the plummeting market share, etc., etc., etc. – nothing compared with the impact that the contract negotiations with the United Auto Workers would have on the fortunes of Detroit. Without a realistic contract that takes into account the new global economic realities of the automobile industry and the shrinking size of the Detroit-based auto companies, the future of the Detroit auto companies will be in serious jeopardy.

Canadian Auto Workers union leader Buzz Hargrove is an interesting character. He's quick with media-friendly quips that garner a lot of attention, he's a fierce defender of his union membership, and he fancies himself as the only bright light of rational thinking in the whole union versus management dance. But he's also a loose-cannon firebrand who is firmly entrenched in organized labor's "entitlement" past, and he loomed as an impediment to any substantive progress in the contract bargaining talks with the Detroit-based automakers. He proved that convincingly with his idiotic statements during a union rally in Windsor, Ontario, in May 2007.

The purpose of the Sunday meeting, according to the *Windsor Star*, was to rally the 1200 members of Local 1973, who were upset with the fact that GM had decided to build a new six-speed transmission at their St. Catharines (Ontario) plant instead of in their Windsor (Ontario) transmission facility. Hargrove, in classic management-bashing rhetoric, told the assembled workers, "They made the decision to put the transmission in St. Catharines, and they say publicly if they don't get the right deal in St. Catharines it will not come to Canada, therefore eliminating Windsor. I say to them, you better find a goddamn product for Windsor or we'll take all of the General Motors Corporation down in September 2008. General Motors workers have earned the commitment, especially in Windsor." Hargrove went on to say that a strike action would be used as a weapon to destroy GM when his union's contract negotiations begin in 2008 (the UAW contract negotiations began in the summer of 2007).

In effect, Hargrove was saying, let's take an entire industry that's literally and figuratively hanging by a thread and destroy it with a strike – and destroy our own jobs in the process. Makes a lot of sense, doesn't it? To the highly corrosive mindset at the helm of the CAW, apparently it did, unfortunately.

Hargrove's comments were not all that dissimilar from Ron Gettelfinger's before the upcoming talks. Gettelfinger, the UAW president, had been spouting off like it was 1972 – hammering home organized labor's classic refrain revolving around the concept of "more" – more money, more healthcare, more pension increases and of course, more entitlement. Remember, this was the same guy who firmly believed that the infamous "Jobs Bank" – where workers get paid to do nothing – is perfectly rational in this day and age, and should remain in effect indefinitely.

Whether these guys live in a weird Twilight Zone of Denial or they're just pathologically out of touch – or both – it was clear to everyone within a hammer's throw of their senses that there wasn't a snowball's chance in hell that the Detroit-based automakers could survive in the newly-limned global automotive market if the existing union contracts were left essentially untouched in the negotiations – as these union leaders were making noises suggesting that they should be.

All of the eye-popping concessions and agreed-upon perks that seemed so "fair" in the late '80s and early '90s were now so outrageously out of sync with reality that you would have thought that these union leaders would be embarrassed to even mention them in public, but *nooo,* they not only mentioned them, they were under the impression that they were *entitled* to them – as if the domestic-based automakers would always be there and would always be able to foot the bill.

Gettelfinger and Hargrove's powers of selective rationalization must be truly awe-inspiring. Either that, or they actually believed that the plummeting market share of what was left of the car companies quaintly known as the "Big Three" was but a temporary hiccup and that there was a virulent plot of some sort at work here – part of a vast conspiracy to deprive them of their benefits packages.

If the Detroit-based car companies had the *cojones* to do it, they could, in fact, function just fine in a world in which the UAW simply didn't exist. I am absolutely convinced that if Chrysler, GM and Ford got together and presented their package of reduced wages and benefits to the UAW and said that this is the deal, take it or leave it – and then locked the union out if it balked – there would be a lineup 20 people deep applying for every single job available at the reduced package price all around the country.

The union leaders don't believe that could ever happen, but perhaps they should pay attention to what happened to the 1,500 members of the Aircraft Mechanics Fraternal Association when they went on strike against Northwest Airlines three years ago. Northwest stuck to their guns, and the entire workforce ended up getting replaced.

The current management of the UAW and CAW not only doesn't get it, they're frighteningly *incapable* of getting it. They are unable to function in a world that has changed around them to such a degree that their views on the issues are simply irrelevant in a global automobile industry that has been turned upside down and sideways.

As of this writing, Hargrove and Gettelfinger had yet to come to terms with the fact that they faced a clear-cut choice in these upcoming contract negotiations. And that choice comes down to this: They either accept a reduced number of jobs at a reduced pay scale and with reduced benefits, or they will be left with no jobs at all.

If the UAW deigned to think that they were going into those

negotiations from a position of strength and power, then we're talking Eve of Destruction-type scenarios here. In this global economy, the classic UAW position of entitlement and "getting what we deserve" is so obsolete and out of touch that it's excruciatingly painful to even contemplate. Simply put, the UAW has to get their arms around the idea of reduced jobs, reduced pay and reduced benefits, or face the ugly alternative, which is no jobs at all. I have not seen one shred of evidence that the UAW actually "gets" this idea, however, as dealing with reality has never been its strong suit.

The American automobile industry is in crisis. And with plants and jobs teetering on the brink of disaster in the U.S. and in Canada, these times demand serious people willing to seriously contemplate the issues at hand in a rational and realistic manner. We need deep thinkers capable of seeing the Big Picture, people who are willing to reconfigure the status quo, leaving the hoary old rhetoric right where it belongs – in the past – while working on molding a future filled with hope and promise. One that's fueled by a boldly competitive mindset in tune with the rest of the automotive world.

Buzz Hargrove and Ron Gettelfinger had given every indication through their inflammatory statements and juvenile grandstanding that they are shockingly ill qualified for the task.

The end of the UAW?

Let's just say that at this juncture, in August 2007, the fate of the union is hanging by a thread.

DETROIT'S INFATUATION WITH NASCAR BEGINS TO UNRAVEL

I have long been the most outspoken national critic of NASCAR, using the term "NASCAR Bubble" to forecast the inevitable decline of the stock car series more than three years ago. It is now clear that the automobile companies, television networks and corporate America will not only have a front-row seat for NASCAR's slide – they're all going to be dragged down with it.

With NASCAR's sudden decline in popularity catching corporate America off-guard in the beginning of 2007, marketing types around the country were choking on their cornflakes with the realization that their "can't miss" investment in NASCAR was starting to look more than a little shaky. When even *The New York Times*, a publication that has been notoriously slow on the uptake when it comes to its motorsports coverage, finally noticed that NASCAR's seemingly unstoppable upward trajectory in popularity had not only flattened out – it was starting to head downward in a hurry – then you knew things were heading for trouble in NASCAR-ville.

By late spring, *The Times* ran a headline at the top of the Sports section, which blared the ugly reality: "NASCAR's Days of Thunder Are Giving Way to a Period of Uncertainty." The article outlined the fact that the NASCAR money machine was running out of gas, reeling from a merry-go-round of empty seats, declining TV ratings and a growing resistance across the U.S. to roll over for NASCAR's push into new markets. Funny, but you could almost hear the corporate marketing honchos across America wincing and groaning from here, because after all, they'd bet the farm on the idea that the sun would never set on the France family empire – and a lot of people who should have known better were going to get caught up in the wreckage when the NASCAR marketing juggernaut finally imploded.

How bad was it? *The Times* reported that from 2004 through last season (2006), television ratings – NASCAR's bread and butter as far as corporate America is concerned – plummeted. Down 28 percent in Philadelphia, 22.2 percent in Los Angeles, 12.5 percent in Chicago and stagnant in New York. NASCAR apologists quickly pointed out that the cities mentioned weren't exactly hotbeds for stock car racing "fans," and they would be correct. Fair enough, but how do you account for the fact that NASCAR's ratings in Atlanta dropped *18.2 percent* in that same period?

Much to corporate America's consternation, the pendulum had begun its inevitable swing back the other way for NASCAR – and this in just the *first year* of an eight-year deal with ABC/ESPN, Fox, TNT and the Speed networks valued at $4.5 billion, or a hefty $560 million a year. Not good would be an understatement, but it would get even uglier than that for the France family's "racertainment" series.

The fact that the wheels were coming off the NASCAR money train shouldn't have been a surprise to anyone, because you could see it coming a mile away. Sky-high ticket prices, empty seats, market oversaturation, too many sponsors creating a paralyzing amount of message clutter, the abandonment of traditional dates and race tracks, cookie-cutter cars that bear no resemblance to recognizable production car versions, too many races, etc., etc., etc. – the France family had provided a working model of how *not* to keep momentum going.

I should point out that everyone saw NASCAR's inevitable slow-down coming *except* for the so-called marketing experts in corporate America who fueled the runaway frenzy to begin with – and they're being caught flat-footed. After all, the denizens of The Land of Synergistic Brand Extensions, Co-Promotional Partnerships, Targeted Media "Buckets," Marketing Myopia and Flat-out Stupidity had distinguished themselves time and time again over the years by their innate ability to flog a marketing "sure thing" right into the ground.

There wasn't a chief marketing officer in corporate America

worth his or her bonus over the last five years who didn't blindly "green light" some sort of NASCAR marketing, advertising or sponsorship program. And the beauty of it is that they didn't actually have to *sell* a damn thing or conduct their due diligence when considering it, either. Instead, they were greeted by a conference room full of blithering yes-heads chanting in unison – NASCAR! NASCAR! NASCAR!

It's no wonder, then, that this inevitable plateau reached by NASCAR had caused anguished cries of "What the f---?" from people who should have seen it coming a long time ago, because the herd mentality that is so pervasive in corporate America is driven by one fundamental guiding principle day in and day out – and that is that there's never *too* much of a good thing – until that good thing bites you in the ass.

But what were we to make of the all-knowing and all-powerful seers at the television networks? What part of paying a cumulative $4.5 billion to broadcast NASCAR programming seemed like a good idea at the time? After the 2007 season, you can rest assured that you will hear reports filtering through the media that the networks and NASCAR are in talks to "adjust" the contract payouts. There's no way this TV deal will remain untouched in the face of the declining ratings numbers.

And how smart does NBC look right now, by the way? They had the *cojones* to actually walk away from NASCAR in favor of going after the new Sunday night football package with the NFL. Now, *that's* genius. But *except* for NBC, everyone else involved in the NASCAR circus is looking like the corporate equivalent of the Village Idiot.

With corporate America and the TV networks guilty as charged, what about the automobile companies involved in NASCAR? Let's review, shall we?

Remember the meteoric rise of NASCAR that everyone was talking about just a few years ago? Remember the eye-popping TV ratings numbers, the big-time sponsorship deals, the business magazine cover stories and the network news coverage of NASCAR that went on and on?

Well, in the same period that NASCAR was front and center in the nation's media, the three domestic auto manufacturers involved (Chevrolet, Ford and Dodge) saw their market share in the U.S. sink. Not just fade a little bit, but drop right off a cliff. So, for continuing to support the France family circus, what were the Detroit-based manufacturers actually getting for their cumulative $400 million-plus per year, exactly?

In the giant scheme of things, not much.

The brand-name recognition that the manufacturers boasted about that came with their involvement in NASCAR? It's a stretch, at best. If the popularity of NASCAR actually counted for something, wouldn't it make sense that Detroit's fortunes in the showrooms across America would have trended upward instead of down? Or at least held steady instead of falling off the map?

Mention this to a room full of marketing people at your typical Detroit car company, and you get blank stares and a bunch of blurted, "buts..." in protest. As in, "But we have research showing that what we're doing is really beneficial to our cause!" Or, "But the dealers swear by it!" Or, "But we've *always* been in NASCAR!"

In other words, a lot of hot air that fails to answer the question.

As for Toyota, they've made no bones about the fact that they're hell-bent on becoming part of the American fabric, and they're sinking a ton of money into the France family circus to stake their claim. In September 2007, Toyota signed Joe Gibbs Racing, a team that had been with GM/Chevrolet for 16 years, to be its No. 1 NASCAR team in 2008, after offering a rumored 50 percent *more* than GM was offering to renew. Wouldn't it be ironic if after spending all that money that Toyota's first major marketing mistake in recent memory was the direct result of their involvement in NASCAR's plummeting fortunes?

So, here we are. The nation's obsession with NASCAR is on the wane. It was good while it lasted, but now corporate America, the automakers and the TV networks have some *'splainin'* to do. As in what the hell were they thinking by assuming that the good times would never end?

As I've said time and time again when writing about NASCAR – nothing stays that hot forever. NASCAR was due for a tumble, and now they're in the throes of one, big time. Oh, sure, the NASCAR apologists will come out of the woodwork and say that nothing's really broken, that with a few tweaks here and there they'll resume their upward trajectory, but that's just unmitigated bullshit.

No, NASCAR has serious, fundamental issues to deal with that go to the core of its very reason for being. Namely, the idea of fewer races, relevant cars and technology, refocusing on their roots *and* their hard-core fans goes against the grain of the modern France family doctrine, which revolves around *more* races, *more* money, *more* stars and *more* of everything that pushes them away from the "old" NASCAR.

Humpy Wheeler, the incomparable president of Lowe's Motor Speedway – whom I consider to be the smartest guy involved in NASCAR – summed it up perfectly when he posed these rhetorical questions in *The Times* article, "Are we moonshiners, country music, banjos and Route 66? Or are we merlot and Rodeo Drive?"

Amen, Humpy, amen.

THE WHIP COMES DOWN ON DETROIT

The doomsday scenario that everyone in this business around the Motor City feared would happen happened in the summer of 2007. A bill that emerged from the U.S. Senate in June (approved by a 65-27 vote) requires cars and light trucks to meet a CAFE (Corporate Average Fuel Economy) standard of 35 mpg by 2020 – an increase of about 40 percent. Though the measure still had some distance to go in the House, the anti-car, anti-Detroit politicians in Washington, D.C., finally let the dogs out on the automakers for past sins committed – both real and imagined – and are poised to impose strict new fuel economy rules on the industry, which will fundamentally alter the business – if not force the elimination of one of what was once quaintly known as the "Big Three" altogether.

The U.S. auto industry faces the most daunting challenge in its history and will now bear the brunt of this sea change in Washington (even though Toyota was dead-set against these proposed tougher fuel economy standards too), armed with balance sheets that come up short when it comes to the kind of investment needed to deliver *marketable* vehicles – a key distinction here – to the American driving public under these proposed regulations. After all, it's one thing to meet these new fuel economy standards head-on – it's quite another to deliver vehicles to the streets that people actually want to *buy*.

The biggest loser in all of this, at least initially? Cerberus.

Washington's broadside into Detroit immediately made the Cerberus play for Chrysler look shaky, because all of a sudden the cost of doing business in the New Age of Fuel Economy just went up – way up. Ironically, the day the whip came down on Detroit's future in

June, Chrysler staged a media dog-and-pony show at their Chelsea proving grounds, where they were hoping to convince the assembled media that they were very much technically "with it" when it came to advanced environmental and fuel-saving technologies. It was sort of a "we've got the bit in our mouths and we're headed for Greenville!" revival meeting, but instead of wowing anyone with new stuff, they managed to prove convincingly that the "new" Chrysler was just barely in the game.

The $3 billion figure that Chrysler bandied about at the press conference for investments in cylinder deactivation technology, two-mode hybrid systems developed for larger SUVs, trucks and large sedans (in conjunction with GM and BMW), new dual-clutch transmissions, a Grand Cherokee Bluetech diesel in 2009, mild hybrids and a new "Phoenix" V6 engine family coming in 2010 – *2010!* – is all well and good and sounds like a lot to spend on new technologies, but it is just a drop in the bucket compared to what Chrysler is going to need to meet the upcoming fuel economy standards.

On top of that, other than the jointly-developed two-mode hybrid system, the rest of the technology Chrysler talked about qualified as simply meeting the price of admission in this business – the minimal requirements going forward to play this new fuel economy game. There was no "there" there for Chrysler – no breakthroughs and no gee-whiz glimpses at their *real* future technology-think – and that said to me that Cerberus will immediately be behind the eight ball from here on out, chasing the technology and the funding in order to compete. And there were no guarantees that they're going to pull it off, either, let alone come up with the kind of breakthrough technology they're going to need to succeed.

No matter what their glowing pronouncements may suggest, the clock was ticking on the viability of this whole enterprise, and I predicted that Chrysler would get smaller by closing plants, reducing their product offerings (a very good idea anyway given their lackluster product lineup), and doing everything they could to conserve cash in order to keep up in this new fuel-economy technology race that had well and truly begun.

I remained unconvinced that the Cerberus-owned Chrysler – even with its star-studded executive/advisor lineup – had the kind of financial firepower and technical wherewithal to survive in this new order.

DETROIT'S REAL CHALLENGE? SELLING THE *IDEA* OF AN AMERICAN CAR

Do the following statements, or something like them, sound familiar? "When I get out of school, I'm going to trade my Chevy in and get a 'real' car." Or, "This is just my airport car – I've got a BMW back at home." Or how about something like this, "That Cadillac was an okay rental car for our summer trip, but I'd never buy one." We've all heard these statements, or something similar, before. There is still a very definite perception "out there" in consumer land that domestic-branded automobiles are, for the most part, the equivalent of cut-rate merchandise – that they're definitely not to be considered seriously when it comes time to get a "real" car.

Yes, there are several recent stellar exceptions to that generalization from Detroit, but the perception held by a lot of consumers is that Detroit cars in general are second-rate and decidedly lacking in cachet of any kind. And it's easy to understand why this perception remains so strong.

Bob Lutz's broadside at the American Magazine Conference in Rancho Mirage, California, in 2002, when he took on the media over their apparent biased coverage against the Detroit automakers – as opposed to the glowing coverage given the Japanese and European automakers – begged the question, what *can* Detroit do to convince the American consumer (and the media) that its cars are worth owning again?

We're not talking about something that can be easily overcome or "fixed" with a slick marketing campaign, because the mind-numbingly depressing formula of Toyota (and all Imports) = Good, Detroit = Bad has the domestic automakers literally by the throat.

The enduring belief in this formula is due in large measure to Detroit launching an endless series of mediocre products into the market while seemingly ignoring what was taking place in the automotive world around them. While the import manufacturers kept building better and better cars and growing the integrity of their brands, the American car companies were spinning their wheels by generating one largely forgettable car after another, interrupting this constant din of market mediocrity with an occasional hit that would generate staggering profits (the minivan phenomenon, the light truck/SUV explosion, etc.). But every time Detroit stopped to revel in those profits and celebrate their success, a different corner of the market that they took their eye off of would fall under the spell of the import brands – and then Detroit would find themselves knocked right back on their tails again.

It's no wonder that Detroit has to deal with overwhelmingly negative perceptions "out there" in the real world. Every time Detroit has either invented a segment or redefined a segment, an import manufacturer has eventually come along and done it better – and delivered almost bulletproof quality to boot in the process.

And now Detroit – which has finally seen the light (for the most part) and is launching a string of all-new vehicles into the market in virtually every possible segment you can think of – is running up against a fog of negative perceptions that seems to hang over every product launch and every media conference that Ford, Chrysler and General Motors conducts.

So what can Detroit do? And how can they make driving American cars cool again?

The most obvious thing is to build outstanding products. Quality and reliability used to be the basic price of admission for a reputable entry into the car business. But that's no longer good enough. Now, the market demands *great* product to even get noticed – let alone be successful.

So, building great, "gotta have" products is all Detroit needs – and then the problem is solved, right?

That seems simple enough, but in Detroit's case, the answer is never simple.

And therein lies the crux of the problem. After 35 years of mediocrity and losing a generation of buyers to the imported brands – consumers who have never even *driven* a Detroit car or truck in their lives – Detroit won't be able to snap their fingers and say "Forget the past, we're better now" to an entire country of skeptics and naysayers.

In fact, there is a large group of consumers in the U.S. who now consider Detroit-made cars to be, in a manner of speaking, *import* brands – in that they're such a foreign concept to so many buyers that they're actually becoming a rarity in certain parts of the country.

Detroit will have to take their fight to the trenches and return to a time-honored cliché in this business – and that is to go after each new customer, one person at a time. It won't be good enough to have great cars and trucks – because Detroit is saddled with an additional burden of proof and a legacy of negative perceptions that will require it to dig deeper and sway a disbelieving bunch of consumers who have "show me" written all over them. That means getting people behind the wheel – there's no other way of getting around it. Do you wonder why so many manufacturers are staging "experiential" consumer events all over the country? It's because they have found that the best way to generate positive word-of-mouth about their products (still the best form of advertising, by the way) is to get people to drive them by providing meaningful seat time. And in this era of constant media clutter bombarding us 24 hours a day – word-of-mouth advertising has become even *more* crucial.

Detroit manufacturers will have to fight tooth and nail to convince people to even put them on their shopping lists – let alone get them into the showrooms. So-so reviews in the car magazines, or in newspapers, or on television or on the Internet won't cut it. If an American car is up against its import competition in a test, it either has to win outright or finish in a tie for first place to be noticed.

Detroit not only has to meet or beat its competition in straight, head-to-head shootouts, it needs to take chances by striking out in product directions they can call their own.

Detroit can also do well by reestablishing the *American-ness* in its products – with distinctive designs that boast real attitude and genuine passion – and it needs to do so unapologetically and proudly.

Detroit either needs to come out with guns blazing by offering class-leading products, or they need to walk away from the particular segment they're coming up short in entirely. There's absolutely no room or tolerance for just being in the game in this market – and no one will make a dime in this business by just showing up.

Despite all of the overwhelmingly negative bleating that seems to be in vogue in the media these days about Detroit's chances, however, Detroit has more than a shot. As a matter of fact, it has a *strong* shot to get right back in the thick of the fight.

But it won't be easy.

For Detroit to make its cars become cool again, they will have to build outstanding products that bristle with passion – cars and trucks that exude grittiness, attitude and real presence.

But even more important, consumers "out there" in the real world will have to become enamored with the *idea* of an American car again.

That's the real challenge facing Detroit, and it's a lot more difficult than coming up with "gotta have" products.

SAVING THE MOTOR CITY – FIVE THINGS DETROIT MUST DO TO SURVIVE

You know you aren't in the Motor City anymore when you drive around on the streets and freeways out in Southern California. The biggest thing you notice right away? Very few daytime running lamps. Oh, sure, there are a few, but nothing like back in Detroit where GM vehicles are seemingly the choice of almost half of the population – at least the ones with access to employee discounts, accompanying family discounts or the "just showing up" discounts available to anyone who walks into a domestic showroom these days. The streets and byways of sunny Southern California are refreshingly free of the glare from those borderline-annoying "DRLs" – except for on motorcycles, where they belong – and it's an indicator of how far out of touch GM is with the California market.

But it's not just GM cars that you don't see out there. There's a shocking lack of passenger cars evident from all of the Detroit manu- facturers. Yes, there are more sightings than there were as recently as three years ago, with Cadillacs, Corvettes, Chrysler 300Cs, Mus- tangs, Saturns and the usual assortment of blingified domestic SUVs making the scene, but for the most part, any bread-and-butter-type domestic cars you see are usually rental cars – with their DRLs announcing their arrival (and terminal un-hipness) long before they get there.

California is exhibit "A" of just how precarious the situation is for what's left of the Not-So-Big Three.

I have already detailed how Detroit got to this point – a per- fect storm of astonishing complacency, rampant mediocrity and a level of serial incompetence that is simply staggering in its scope

– and its now-dire consequences. As hard as it is to believe, however, Detroit *has* gotten the message. The only problem is that the car-buying public is having trouble getting, or worse, *believing* the message. That "lost generation" I referred to is – big surprise – less-than-eager to sign up for the latest offerings from the Motor City. Oh, sure, they might be mildly interested in the select brand "hits" running around right now, but actually going in and trading their Toyota/Lexus, Honda/Acura, BMW, Subaru, Mazda, Mercedes-Benz (you can fill in the rest) on a Detroit brand?

As I like to say – it's just notgonnahappen.com.

Certainly not at the rate or in the numbers that Detroit needs it to happen, that's for sure – and certainly not without a massive discount or cash incentive. That's not pouring salt on the wound, that's just the ugly reality.

So, what can Detroit do? How can the denizens of the Motor City car companies close this hugely negative perception gap? How can Detroit convince America's car-buying consumers that Detroit brands are not only worth buying, but actually cool to buy again?

Here are five things Detroit must do to survive.

1. Stop Following and Start Leading. Detroit needs to stop waiting around for other manufacturers to do things first. They need to dig deep from within for inspiration, instead of always looking somewhere else for ideas. In Detroit's "glory days" innovation was a way of life. The operative word was "new," and risks were taken in the pursuit of doing a better job. Today's Detroit is too often a seething cauldron of paranoia, where opportunities are wasted and advantages missed because decisions are based on not losing – instead of going for the win.

2. "Good Enough" is Definitely *Not* Good Enough. The common misperception out there is that Detroit doesn't have the talent to compete with the Asians and the Germans. That is flat-out untrue. Detroit has just as much talent, if not more, as any other auto manufacturing center in the world. Detroit just doesn't know how to use it. Detroit needs to purge the "engineering to the lowest common denominator" mentality that permeates its bureaucracies – the one that states that something is "good enough." Because I would be willing to bet that as soon as those words are uttered in the midst of a product development cycle in Detroit – it's most assuredly *not* good enough. Example? Look at the new Chevrolet Corvette. From every angle, the sixth-generation Corvette is a sensational piece. Taut, tasteful and extremely quick – it's a handsome, competent design with great road presence. But get inside of it, and it's clear that someone yelled "good enough" somewhere along the way, and the development stopped. The interior is okay, but that just doesn't cut it in today's market. Defenders within GM and Chevrolet mentioned the Corvette's price point and the fact that it was the best high-performance value in the world, but Corvette customers were clamoring for something more. Chevrolet finally responded with the 2008 Corvette – and offered a substantially nicer optional interior. The 2008 Corvette is a perfect example of how Detroit needs to stop saying "good enough" and take their game to the next level. Detroit needs to unleash their talent and create an environment where creativity, innovation and vision are the operative words – and make sure it translates to the products that get to the showroom, not just reserve it for their cool concept cars at the auto shows.

3. Get Smaller to Get Better. This point applies to GM more than the other Detroit manufacturers, but all of them could learn from it. Detroit controls less than 50 percent of the U.S. market, yet they act like they still have 80 percent of it. GM in particular still conducts itself as if it's the early '70s when it comes to their product offerings. GM has products stepping all over each other up and down the spectrum of the market. GM needs to get real with their place in the automotive world and start cutting the number of models they offer, not adding to them. GM (and Detroit) needs to get smaller to get better.

Instead of blanketing the market with a bunch of "good enough" nameplates that they can't properly support in terms of marketing and advertising dollars, they need to do fewer cars that are class leading. And that doesn't mean "sort of close" to the class-leading vehicles but class *leading*. Period. Would a typical GM dealer prefer a "full line" of vehicles to sell when only a quarter of them actually have street "buzz" and generate consumer interest? Or would that dealer be happy with two or three models that sell like gangbusters? Trust me on this one – most dealers I know would gladly broom the mediocre crap they have to sell all day long in favor of a couple of vehicles that consumers actually *want* for a change.

4. Stop Losing the PR War. If you listen to the constant Public Relations-driven drumbeats emanating from the Asian and German manufacturers, you'd think that they're the only automakers operating in the U.S. Toyota PR is so masterful, for example, that they have card-carrying members of the anti-car, anti-Detroit intelligentsia absolutely convinced that the only answer to our transportation needs in the future is a hybrid, and the only hybrid vehicle worth owning is made by Toyota. But it's not just Toyota – the other import manufacturers have fared tremendously well in the PR wars too. Ever notice how the national media makes a bigger deal about "yet another recall" from a Detroit automaker, when they gloss over equally serious recalls from a German or Asian automaker? Don't believe it? Watch the next time a series of auto recalls is announced – then see how long the Detroit angle to the story stays alive and how quickly the import angle fades.

After 35 years of stinking up the joint, Detroit has been written off by the national media and by people on both coasts as a Rust Belt anachronism that wouldn't be missed if it went down for the count. But the reality of the situation is that this country can't afford for that to happen. Detroit doesn't need a "handout," however. What they need to do is roll up their sleeves and tell their story. Their new vehicles are equal to or better than a lot of "prestige" import nameplates when it comes to quality. Why aren't we hearing it? If some in the national media and in Washington, D.C., are biased against Detroit – then get off your asses and take the message of the "reinvigorated Detroit" to those people. Detroit keeps waiting for people to come around to the idea that they're back in the game and that their products are worth considering again. Well, that's fine, but the "people" aren't going to come around to Detroit on their own. Rather, they need a compelling reason to do so. And the PR mavens at what's left of the Big Three haven't given them one yet.

5. As a matter of fact, it *is* the Product, Stupid. You can take the previous four points and throw them out the window if you don't get this last point. One bright spot in the national media for Detroit right now is the latest GM crossovers from Buick, Saturn and GMC. Why? Because they're excellent vehicles that have that elusive street buzz. They're cool American cars that exude a passionate point of view, and they have genuine on-the-road presence too. GM was smart enough with these products, at least, to go with their gut and demonstrate real conviction for a change. In other words, they gathered the wherewithal from within to execute vehicles that *they* liked and that *they* wanted to build. They didn't dumb them down by "benchmarking" them to oblivion, and they weren't interested in making the cars "me-too" clones. They didn't get cold feet, either – and the words "good enough" were refreshingly left out of the development process. The reward for GM's risk taking? Their new crossovers are among this year's product "hits."

After 35 years of rampant mediocrity, Detroit has the opportunity to convince America's car-buying consumers that their products are definitely worth considering again. But they have to do it with one great, class-leading product at a time – and in every segment too.

It will only be then that Detroit can get away from the "furniture store" sales mentality that has virtually paralyzed the Motor City of late and get back to the *real* automobile business – the business of building great cars and trucks.

Detroit may not be down for the count, but it's fourth and ten with no time-outs and three seconds left on the clock.

It's the ballgame, folks.

HELL FREEZES OVER – GM
FADES TO NUMBER TWO

What was unthinkable not too many years ago has finally happened – Toyota is now the number one automobile company in the world, surpassing General Motors in sales in the first quarter of 2007 and never looking back. Toyota announced in late April that it had sold 2.348 million vehicles worldwide in the January through March quarter, surpassing the 2.26 million vehicles GM sold during the same period. Yes, it was only one quarter, and GM mounted a challenge in the second quarter of 2007, but the momentum has been building for years now. Don't expect Toyota to lose their lead any time soon.

This was a milestone event for several reasons. General Motors hadn't been just the largest U.S. automaker, it was the largest business enterprise in the world, a glittering showcase of American industrial might that mirrored the upward trajectory of this country in the blue sky '50s and go-go '60s. GM was a source of pride for Detroiters of all stripes, because along with Ford and Chrysler, the center of the automotive universe was in the Motor City – and we liked it that way. But due to a series of dramatic product missteps, strategic blunders, managerial incompetence and flat-out arrogance confined to a crucial period over the last 30 years, GM was now – for the first time in, oh, let's just say history for all practical purposes (since 1930, to be exact) – the number two automaker in the world.

Ironically, despite this historic upheaval to its place in the automotive pecking order, GM has a lot to tout right now. It is the number one automaker in China – the fastest growing automotive market in the world – and its inroads in the Pan-Asian markets are gaining momentum.

And GM's product renaissance – led by the legendary Bob Lutz, whose gut-level instincts and sheer will to succeed have literally pulled the company up by its bootstraps – is showing signs of coming to fruition, big time. There's no question in my mind that GM has some of the most distinctive and forward-thinking products either in-market or due to arrive shortly – competitive entries in terms of quality, content, design, engineering and detail.

But four crucial problems remain for GM that will continue to vex the company going forward:

First, a favorable labor contract with the UAW is absolutely essential. (At the time of this writing, the 2007 contract negotiations had just begun. So, as you read this, either a new agreement has been hammered out, or a crippling strike is under way.) Without major concessions from the union, all bets are off. And judging by the statements emanating from Ron Gettelfinger, the UAW president, the UAW is hell-bent on clinging to their founding principle of "entitlement" – even if it means bringing the entire domestic auto industry down with them. Not good.

Second – GM's divisional structure here in the U.S. is still constructed around an era when they controlled almost half the market. It's a no-win dance that is simply untenable with the current and future realities of their situation. With too many models, too many dealers and too many divisions, GM is flailing away trying to prop up a system that was obsolete 25 years ago at least. And it's killing the company. Not good, Part II.

Unless the previous point is rectified, I predict that General Motors will *never* see their North American operation return to being a real live profit-making endeavor for the company. Yes, I know never is a long time, but this constant flailing about trying to wring profit out of North America is a fool's errand. GM's mind-numbingly unfavorable structural costs here, combined with the recalcitrant labor situation, will not allow them to see a profit in North America. Rick Wagoner admitted as much last summer in statements when he said GM was going to be focusing on its global expansion, because that's where the profits will be coming from for the foreseeable future.

But the most difficult challenge facing GM? Trying to convince the American consumer just how good the new products they're offering are. It does absolutely no good for GM's new products to be excellent in every respect if the American consumer public doesn't believe it or buy into it. The negativity in the market aimed at GM (and Ford and Chrysler) continues to hang over the company like a black cloud. GM is finding it exceedingly difficult to make inroads with these import-oriented American buyers. And if GM can't connect with these consumers – and can't change their negative perceptions – then its market share threatens to erode even further.

This historic moment for GM will stick in its craw and linger over everything they do going forward – as well it should, because after all, GM has squandered one of the great industrial legacies of all time. In 30 short years, a phalanx of GM managers has presided over the biggest swoon in the history of corporate America. They took their eyes off of the ball and assumed that everything would be as it always was, only to wake up and find that they're number two.

Could it have been avoided? Absolutely. But it's all over but the hand-wringing now. GM better get used to its new world ranking, because unless Toyota abandons its "way" and just slacks off, GM will never see the top spot again.

Today, we find ourselves living in The United States of Toyota, a state of mind more than anything else but a fundamental shift in our nation's psyche nonetheless.

After years of calculated mediocrity and engineering to the lowest common denominator, Detroit finds itself literally and figuratively on the ropes. A once-shining beacon of American innovation and corporate manufacturing might has been reduced to a national punch line. And Detroit has no one to blame but itself.

Yes, the Japanese government manipulates the yen to the Japanese car companies' advantage. Yes, Detroit is saddled with a crushing competitive disadvantage with it its built-in legacy and healthcare costs. And yes, this country's trade practices leave its own domestic auto industry hanging out to dry on a regular basis. But in the end, none of that matters, because Detroit, as we know it, has become expendable – and to a large degree the rest of the country just doesn't care, because now Toyota *is* America's car company.

Is there any room for hope? I believe there is, but Detroit needs to lead again and not follow. Detroit needs to seize the technological and environmental leadership role, which it is still very capable of doing, and not look back.

But if Detroit fails to seize this opportunity, we will continue to witness the slow, dizzying spiral downward of a once-great American industry.

AFTERWORD

In what has become as inevitable as the changing of the seasons, 2007 meant another year of losing overall market share to the imports for the Detroit-based car companies. And even though some could point to individual success stories, Detroit's fortunes are definitely trending downward. Detroit's share of the U.S. market officially dipped below the 50 percent level (49.4 percent) when the July 2007 sales figures were tallied. And it could be just a matter of time before Detroit's share of the North American market ultimately finds a permanent home at 40 percent.

As Detroit races to unleash a series of dramatically improved products on the American landscape, they're not only fighting their formidable Asian and European competitors, they're fighting public perception that the domestic brands (except in a few notable instances) just aren't worth considering. And if that isn't enough, Detroit is saddled with a bloated dealer structure, a proliferation of models and nameplates that begin to defy rhyme or reason at times, and crushing legacy costs that are just absolutely killing profitability.

Then, there's Toyota. What's left to be said? The Japanese Juggernaut is on a forced march to take 15 percent of the world's automotive market by 2010, if not sooner. That is, not coincidentally, equal to the share owned by GM, soon to be *formerly* the world's largest automobile company – and there is no doubt that Toyota will get it done. Toyota delivered a jaw-dropping profit report in the April-June 2007 time frame – a staggering 491.54 billion yen ($4.1 billion), up 32.3 percent, yet another all-time record for the company. And its quarterly sales increased 15.7 percent over the year before, to a record 6.523 trillion yen, or $54.7 billion. A performance that, factoring the exchange rates, was more than GM's record quarterly sales of $54.5 billion in the second quarter of 2006. So it's clear Toyota has the financial war chest to keep up its relentless campaign to win the hearts and minds of the American car-buying public too. Storm clouds? Hardly. Anytime Toyota gets a less-than-stellar quality report they go back and not only fix things, but make them better than they were to begin with. They are relentless, and they have the will to succeed. In short, Toyota is the most formidable car company in the world, and they will keep pouring it on. Not exactly comforting news to Detroit and the rest of the industry.

But even as I write this, Toyota finds itself having to get used to looking over its own shoulder, because it is clear that the emergence of the Korean and Chinese automobile manufacturers and the burgeoning auto markets in China and India will influence the essence of this business far into the future. The furious competitiveness in the highly sought after U.S. market has created a sea change in this industry – forcing automobile companies to scour the world for new sources of low-cost, high-quality automobiles and the parts that go in them, while at the same time looking at new markets for long-term sustenance and profitability.

The drastically changing complexion of the North American market is reflective of the fact that the global automotive landscape is on the precipice of a new world order, with the emerging markets of China and India poised to transform the future of the industry for the next 50 years.

As if we needed more evidence of the turbulent times we live in today, and as much as journalists and analysts are reveling in doomsday scenarios for Detroit and its automakers, we're also witnessing a new phenomenon, too, as Asian and European manufacturers and suppliers are turning to, of all places, Detroit and southeastern Michigan to locate design centers, engineering and manufacturing facilities and other key organizational components. It seems they have identified Detroit and the surrounding areas as being deep in talent and capability – so ironically, it appears that this region may remain, if not the center of the automobile universe, certainly viable for the foreseeable future after all.

But that's not the same as this region being a manufacturing center for American cars and trucks, however. And it doesn't conceal the fact that the Detroit-based domestic auto industry is in danger of imploding.

Detroit simply cannot cut their way to profitability for survival. And they're not going to do it by offering even *more* models and nameplates, either, although there are some in this town who believe that The Answer to Detroit's problems lies in the blanketing of the market with even more choices. Glorified badge engineering will never be the answer, and the Detroit manufacturers have to get it through their thick, collective heads that they have too many models and too many divisions – and that they must get smarter – and smaller – to get better.

The Detroit car companies are killing themselves by fighting over a dwindling slice of the market share pie and cannibalizing their own brands while doing it. They must focus on *fewer* offerings and then make those products the best they can possibly be. But that is anathema to the Detroit mentality and frankly, to their dealers.

I once believed that whichever Detroit-based car company demonstrated the genuine vision needed to confront this dire situation, and make these difficult decisions, would have a head start on survival down the road. But now, that clearly won't be enough.

Even if they *do* deliver best-in-class vehicles wrapped in industry-leading designs, with interiors second to none, there are no guarantees of Detroit's long-term survival, because now the new proposed CAFE standards brought forth by the U.S. Senate present an added threat to Detroit's fortunes. With much of their product planning already locked-in as far as 2012 in some cases, Detroit will have just eight years to plan and, more important, *fund* the technological development required to meet these new standards.

No one would argue the point that aggressive new fuel economy standards are needed at this juncture, but *how* and *when* they're enacted will directly affect Detroit's long-term future.

In order for the domestic automobile industry to survive, it's going to require one of the Detroit CEOs to step-up and say that this business model – as we know it – is obsolete. And unless fundamental changes are made, Detroit's downward spiral of market share erosion will continue unabated.

Confronting this dire situation will require drastic changes in the union agreements, a total rethink of the healthcare system, and an intelligent reappraisal of all legacy costs. It will require a painful upheaval and ultimately a drastic contraction in this business on a scale never seen before – but unless and until these issues are confronted and dealt with, Detroit, as we know it, is living on borrowed time.

Lightning Source UK Ltd.
Milton Keynes UK
UKHW021844141220
375092UK00009B/559/J